Gavin Bolton:
Selected Writings

Gavin Bolton:
Selected Writings

Edited by
David Davis and Chris Lawrence

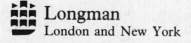 Longman
London and New York

Longman Group Limited
Longman House
Burnt Mill, Harlow, Essex CM20 2JE, England
and associated companies throughout the world

Published in the United States of America
by Longman Inc., New York
© *Longman Group Limited 1986*

First published 1986

ISBN 0 582 36206 7

Set in 10/12 pt Plantin, Linotron 202

Produced by Longman Group (F.E.) Ltd
Printed in Hong Kong

Contents

Contents

General introduction

It is the intention of this selection of Gavin Bolton's writings to make available to the reader some of the rich contributions which he has made to drama in education theory over the years. The fact that we have had to make a selection from his writings testifies to the prolific nature of his work. Some are published in journals not readily available and others are published abroad. It is our hope that this selection will provide a rich source of stimuli for teachers and others interested in drama in education and will serve as a *starting point* for their thinking about the use of drama for learning. Gavin Bolton's own perspective has always been that his writing is based on his own developing experience of drama teaching and should never be regarded as prescriptions hewn on tablets of stone. This selection is offered in that same spirit.

Since writing *Towards a theory of drama in education*,[1] Gavin Bolton has characteristically made significant developments in his approach to drama teaching. These are most usefully encapsulated in his second book *Drama as education*,[2] but in order to put these present writings into some sort of perspective, it may be useful to attempt to summarise the major features of this development in Gavin Bolton's theory and practice of drama in education.

The essential feature of the teaching that he has developed relates to the nature of the experience the learner has in the drama. The major movement here has been away from direct experiencing to a shifting dialectic* between experiencing and demonstrating. In other words the dialectical unity of the experience is made up of a submission to the experience and a reflection upon it. In his previous work he was more concerned with total submission to the dramatic experience which involved at its highest level experiencing a moment of awe in a situation of heightened significance brought about by the child's involvement in a symbolisation process in the art form. Reflection was a process separate from this significant experience although this did not necessarily mean it came after the drama was finished. It may have come within the drama or at a later period.

But, along with Dorothy Heathcote, Gavin Bolton has come to the conclusion that the same criticisms apply to 'gut-level drama' that are made of Stanislavskian theatre by Brecht i.e. that if the audience just

---

* For a discussion of Gavin Bolton's use of the term 'dialectic' see Introduction to Section One.

submit themselves in a feeling way to a piece of theatre they miss the chance to participate *actively* in the theatre experience in a thinking/feeling way. Both Dorothy Heathcote and Gavin Bolton have been keen to ensure that the children do not hang up their brains with their hats on the way into the drama lesson.

Gavin Bolton has, therefore, become more concerned with the structure(s) within the drama lesson that will most readily promote learning for the participants. This structure will need to allow for conscious reflection at any stage of the drama process.

This greater concern with shifting the experience of the participant up and down a sliding continuum from direct experiencing to representing has led Gavin Bolton to move away from make-believe play as his fundamental model and building block in educational drama. Make-believe play has too strong an emphasis on direct experiencing. Rather Gavin Bolton has taken game as the model for the structure of the drama experience.

Brian Watkins[3] has long advocated game as an analogy for drama as a whole. Gavin Bolton takes the game element and relates it to the structure of the drama. This fosters a conscious self-projection into the rule-governed interaction, and, as with game, it allows for maximum self-release without ever losing sight of the need for strategy and tactics. Moreover, it *demands* of the participant a constant analysing of the state of play. This leads Gavin Bolton to underline that the learner's focal awareness must be on the activity itself and not on the 'things' to be learned: the learner is only subsidiarily aware of the learning area. If the child is focally aware of aesthetic dimensions, as Ross would have it, s/he cannot have a primary learning experience in another area.

This whole notion of the way a child is exposed to a learning area in creative drama as an art form has led Gavin Bolton to conclude that in his earlier work he was asking the teacher to be too precise in detailing in advance the particular learning the child will catch as he is trawled through the net cast by the teacher. If the analogy of the net is amplified it would be as though the net were the learning area and the children might be caught fast at different points on the net (i.e. different refractions of the learning area), without any one's learning being necessarily weaker than any of the others'.

It may, therefore, be impossible or unwise for the drama teacher to specify that the children will learn X or Y.

Gavin Bolton has also accelerated his movement away from any notion of knowledge as propositional knowledge in a Hirstian sense, to an openly admitted phenomenological position. Here the knowledge that is developed in a drama lesson is brought about by subjective engagement with the object which more importantly results in an inter-subjective negotiation to reach a *common understanding*. This would seem to echo clearly the inter-subjective negotiation of meanings, which structures reality for sociologists like Berger and Luckmann.[4]

The developments in Gavin Bolton's theory and practice identified thus far, are then in summary form: moving away from 'living-through' drama; replacing make-believe play with game; being less precise about learning outcomes; being clearer that the participant must not be focally aware of the learning taking place and adopting more clearly a phenomenological position in relation to claims for knowledge and learning in drama.

These developments, and others, identified in the course of the writings, form the 'back-drop' against which we have written, attempting to draw attention to the movement in Gavin Bolton's thinking, rather than simply elucidating what may have already changed gear.

References

1 Bolton G M 1979 *Towards a theory of drama in education*. Longman.
2 Bolton G M 1984 *Drama as education*. Longman.
3 Watkins B 1981 *Drama and education*. Batsford Academic and Educational.
4 Berger P L, Luckmann J 1931 *The social construction of reality*. Penguin.

Introductory papers

Introduction

These three essays are collected here as introductory papers to the rest of this volume: in the style of the first essay, the *hors d'oeuvre* to the other meat courses. Here however, unlike at the Bristol conference in 1970, the other meat courses are *his own*, nearly all of them written since that time. All three papers are included here for their quality of generality, and of 'taking stock'.

The historical perspective of the first, and, to some degree, the second, essay provides an indication of features of great importance in considering Bolton's writings:

1 it indicates a sense of *development* of practice and reflection upon practice;
2 it helps to place his writings in *time*;
3 it indicates *influence* upon his practice by other authors and practitioners.

The latter is a very important point: in a recent interview Bolton indicated his current interests:

> I am enjoying re-evaluating work of early people in drama. We keep going round in circles refining things, re-evaluating them, finding new significance in them and I find this very exciting.

One important influence upon Gavin Bolton, who receives a rather wry battering from him in this first essay, is Peter Slade. The re-evaluation of Slade finds expression in Bolton's second book (*Drama as education*[1]).

The second essay takes stock of the world of drama up to and contemporary to 1981, providing a simplified summary of some important features of his thinking expressed in his first book, *Towards a theory of drama in education.*[2]

The third essay looks forward. It indicates current concerns, particularly the question of autonomy within the art form.

To return to the first paper. As 'an early attempt to take on the career of being a theorist', in its central questions it contains the seeds of all the other essays in the volume:

> 'What is drama? When is drama, drama? When does educational drama go to the heart of drama? We should be able to ask this question: what is the nature and function of drama when it operates at its highest level of achievement?'

References

1 Bolton G M 1984 *Drama as education*. Longman.
2 Bolton G M 1979 *Towards a theory of drama in education*. Longman.

Drama and theatre in education: a survey

This paper delivered in 1970 to the Bristol conference (the first attempt to bring together drama in education and theatre in education personnel) was presented in the form of an extempore performance. It included a number of self-deprecating imitations of earlier Bolton teaching-styles which regretfully cannot appear in the text which is but a condensed summary written immediately after the event for the purposes of publication. It was Gavin Bolton's intention in the introductory session to get members of this 200-strong audience to laugh together – and they did!

The prospect of preparing a survey of educational drama and theatre in this country has alarmed me. Although by the nature of my job I am in a privileged position that allows me to see a great deal of drama teaching in many parts of the country, anything I do by way of formal assessment would fall far short of the admirable document published by the Department of Education and Science two years ago.

So I discounted the idea of a survey and decided that what I ought to do was perhaps to present a very seriously-minded paper on some aspect of drama in education, but when I looked at the programme for this conference I realised that those attending were already getting that kind of meat – in fact five meat courses. I wondered if I might miss out the soup and just treat this essay as the *hors d'oeuvre*.

One admirable quality of the DES report was that it was objective, utterly reasonable in tone and fair-minded in its comments. I should like to be utterly subjective, unreasonable in tone and quite biased in comment.

In the blurb that was sent out to us about this conference, it says

3

quite firmly, 'it is appreciated that no final answers should be given to questions that this conference will be considering'. One appreciates that if there is to be any advance at all in any area – philosophy and science or the arts – the advance takes place when somebody asks a new question, but it is an unfortunate feature of our profession that the practitioner in the classroom is never in a position to ask questions because, faced with thirty expectant faces, he must know (or think he knows) the answer; and because he is usually desperately short of time and generally wrung dry by the end of a week, he depends on the answers other people have cooked up for him.

Such has been my career. My thirteen years of teaching in schools seems to have been measured out by whatever educational theories (sometimes half-digested) I happened to have bumped into at any one stage. I suppose it can be divided nicely into three phases. The first phase is called 'The Play's the Thing'; the second phase is called 'The Play is certainly not the Thing' and the third phase (which is now) is called 'The Play's the Thing'. All I seem to have done is to get back to where I started – with a significant difference.

I propose, therefore, to be somewhat autobiographical, not because there has been something special about my career, but rather the reverse; I suspect that many teachers will find their own experience outlined in mine so that although I am avoiding doing the kind of survey implied in the title my personal account may indeed reflect the many kinds of activities that function under the name of drama in this country today.

A testimonial on leaving college suggested that my talents for acting and play production would prove to be very useful skills in the promotion of drama work in school. This view concurred with my own. Teaching in a primary school, I applied these skills at every opportunity, in spite of the obvious handicap of not having a hall with a stage. However, a local hall could be hired for the bi-annual occasion of the school concert so that children would have the full-blooded experience of footlights, stage-sets (box and/or pantomime varieties) and a packed house.

By comparison, the classroom drama done inbetween productions fell a long way short of the ideal. However, we did our best by giving the children (the best readers I'm talking about of course) a fairly wide range of characters to act from various publications of nice little plays for nice little people and then training them to understand that as the front of the classroom represented 'on-stage' anyone standing by the windows or by the door was off-stage right and left respectively and my role as producer was to sit at the back of the classroom (a dual function here of keeping an eye on the fidgety spectators) giving constructive advice like, 'I can't hear you' or 'You're slow on your cue' or 'No, say it this way, dear.'

Pleasant as this was for me and for the actors, drama lessons were marred by the growing lack of attention of the audience, so I changed tactics. I had for some time been concerned that in our school productions many children failed to project their voices to the back row of the parish hall. This was allied to the other problem of having a number of children who, although fluent readers, could not be cast in decent parts because of their inexpressive speech.

So drama lessons became speech lessons. (In the meantime I gained for myself a certain Speech and Drama Diploma qualification that had very little to do with the teaching of drama but a great deal to do with professional promotion to drama posts.) All the class, relishing every carefully graded consonant and vowel, participated in the hilarious chorus of jingles and tongue-twisters with admirable uniformity. Until I read a book on mime.

It seemed so obvious, once I had read the book, that precision in speech should be matched by precision in bodily movement. And this book was so helpful. It told me how to divide a lesson up so that all the senses were imaginatively activated ('All smell an orange') and every main section of the body duly exercised ('You're great tall trees'). But it also guided me on which exercises were appropriate to different age-groups. Not that I kept rigidly to the set text – threading needles for example seemed popular with all ages. And it was all so peaceful.

Thus for me a pattern for the teaching of drama to primary school children had emerged – speech and mime practice culminating in the climactic experience of presenting plays to an adult audience. Life seemed well ordered. Until I attended a course of lectures.

It was supposed to be about how to teach drama – but the speakers kept talking about the child. Apparently the child had his own kind of drama, if only teachers would give him a chance. This was a revelation and pretty unpalatable. The advocates of this child-centred philosophy talked of drama in terms of developmental growth, or natural rhythms and of spontaneous expression, and of the teacher as an observer, as a follower. But in fact they were asking me as a trained teacher of some three or four years' experience to unlearn the very skills that had made me a good teacher. I had seen myself as an interpreter of texts, as a manipulator of children towards artistic standards, as a trainer in speech and mime. Now I was being asked to abdicate from all this in favour

5

of freedom of expression. Theatre and scripts were now dirty words.

It was during my post in a secondary modern school as teacher of English, Drama and Maths that I first tried the new drama. I made the mistake, committed by many impressionable young teachers who are anxious to absorb the latest methods, of abandoning all I knew from my own experience and allowing myself to be taken over by what I understood of the new principles. In practice, therefore, I conveyed to my classes that the drama session was theirs and that they should get on with it. They did.

As the volume of sound rose above permissible metal-work class noise-level the headmaster's distressed eyebrows would appear over the pane of glass in the door. It was some time before he challenged me openly about my creative drama work. He appeared to be more than satisfied with the successful rigidity of my school play production and the silent formality of my maths teaching (it did not occur to me at that time that the philosophy I was attempting to acquire was not just applicable to drama but should form the basis of all teaching situations) but what did I think I was doing in drama lessons? My reply was a masterpiece of self-righteous arrogance. I pointed out to him, using my recently acquired tone of spiritual dedication, that form 3A whom we had always regarded as a bright set, co-operative enough under firm treatment, were really misunderstood, emotionally disturbed, deprived adolescents for whom this kind of drama was therapeutic release.

My answer to the headmaster sounded confident enough, but my faith in child-centred drama failed me as I bit my finger-nails through endless sessions of robbing banks, and cowboys and Indians without any apparent change taking place. But when I went on some more courses I discovered that other people who were interested in the 'free' drama hadn't taken it as literally as I had. It didn't simply mean, 'Let them get on with it'. They had all kinds of controls. There are four which I think are most common.

One is called 'take one record' control. With this one you have a record and you work out a sequence of actions to the music and they are controlled by it. Marvellous! The piece that I kept using was from the *Peer Gynt Suite*, 'In the Hall of the Mountain King'. You tell them what the situation is, you tell them what to do to it and then away they go. You have them all as trolls – fast asleep of course; they awaken slowly moving (for some reason no one ever challenges) just one small part of the body, gradually building up to a frenzy of twisting and twirling and reeling and writhing. But you don't worry because you have told them that the three crashes in the movement at the end are three cracks in the roof of the cavern and they are all going to fall down, when the right moment comes, and they all dutifully collapse on the floor . . . dead. Splendid! Then they say, 'Can we do it again, sir?' and you say, 'Yes,' secure in the knowledge that it will be a pattern repeated.

Another form of control is to send them into their drama groups. I was sold on this idea for a long time, where you begin the lesson 'Right, into your drama groups! Make up a play,' and the teacher either sits down and lets them get on with it or chases round from group to group giving encouragement to almost anything. Even when I was Drama Adviser I used to recommend this to teachers until I realised one day on visiting a school that I was seeing a group of children who were in their same drama corners making up the same kinds of plays they had made up two years earlier.

Another kind of control is to have your list and a tambour. Now with this kind of control you have a sequence of events that you put them through. As the narrator you say 'When I shake this tambour' (you've got to have the right kind of voice for this) 'you slowly will wake up and before you there will be a great mountain' tap the tambour and they all blithely wake up and go up a mountain. 'When you get to the top there is a castle with great gates and I want you to push those gates, P–U–S–H   H–A–R–D. Good!' And so it goes on and on and then you might give them a little imaginative touch by saying they go through a door, and may risk something by 'I don't know what there is on the other side . . .'

And then the fourth kind of control is possibly the easiest way of doing drama altogether; let the BBC do it. A kind voice comes over the radio and tells you to find a space. This is called 'drama by remote control'.

Having half-absorbed all these methods of doing drama, I was obviously qualified to become a drama adviser. I don't know whether my advice to teachers was of any value, but I always had to preface it with an admission that I needed to learn from them as much as they from me. It was about this time that I learnt of a different approach from anything I had known so far. I went on a Ministry Course. They told me that the way into drama was not through speech, was not through mime, was not through the child, but through movement.

In all my course attending, nothing has brought me as much personal satisfaction and pleasure as this experience in movement. I was very thrilled though I discovered it rather late in my career. I have never been very happy, however, about the theory that movement leads to drama. It seems to me that it leads to everything. I think it is the most

7

basic form of education and will have its effect on maths and science and art and PE and dance, writing and drama. It certainly has its effect on drama. But it doesn't naturally lead to it because, as I see it, it tends to work on an abstract plane that moves in an opposite direction from drama.

Now in thinking about all these possible methods (and if you do think about them, surely the aims behind them are contradictory), the emphasis has been on the script, the emphasis has been on speech, on mime, on the child and on movement. But it was never on the thing that is created (unless, of course, scripted work may be said to put the emphasis there but scripted work was not the children's creation, and tended to mean more to me than to the children I taught). And this seems to me to be the problem. What is drama? When is drama, drama? When does educational drama go to the heart of drama? We should be able to ask this question: what is the nature and function of drama when it operates at its highest level of achievement?

It seems to me that possibly an answer to this is, when it is composed of those elements that are common to both children's play and to theatre, when the aims are to help children to learn about those feelings, attitudes and preconceptions that, before the drama was experienced, were too implicit for them to be aware of. This means going to the dramatic situation, to the created play, for drama is concerned, as I see it, with the refining of those concepts to do with inter-personal relationships. There is no escaping from this. It may be that there are times when, for valid educational reasons, we put the emphasis on speech and movement and so on, but I feel we must aim at using the heart of drama, which is the dramatic situation. And our aims are not concerned with developing confidence, developing poise or even, primarily developing a tool of expression. Our aims are helping children to understand, so that (if I may use some phrases from the Farmington-Trust Research in another context), they are helped to face facts and to interpret them without prejudice; so that they develop a range and degree of identification with other people; so that they develop a set of principles, a set of consistent principles, by which they are going to live.

I believe that when drama is a group-sharing of a dramatic situation it is more powerful than any other medium in education for achieving the kind of aims that I have listed. But this kind of drama puts tremendous strain, tremendous responsibility on the teacher. He has a very positive role because children left to themselves can only work horizontally at a 'what should happen next' level. It is the teacher's judicious questioning and the timing of that questioning that is going to translate a play about robbing a bank to a play that has 'robbing the bank' as a framework for a challenging theme. It can be about a group of men who are struggling for leadership in a gang. It can be an examination of the quality of a man who is a gang member and a family man and a citizen. It can be about each individual's claim to a share of the loot. It can be about the women who are left behind when there is a job on. It can be about what it's like to do a job for which you have got to get 10 out of 10 because 9½ out of 10 is a failure. And it is the teacher and only the teacher, who can dig deep and make a frivolous or a trivial (in the eyes of the adults) suggestion something worth pursuing, something worth getting to grips with, so that there is a deeper understanding of a fundamental human issue. Things that the children have always understood implicitly will come to the surface. It may be that they don't come to the surface as they do it as much as when the teacher asks the question after it is done. They suddenly know that they have learned because they have been allowed to verbalise it, and the verbalisation is rooted in the concrete sensory/motor experience of the dramatic action.

Of course, all this, where the teacher is helping to make the drama about something, where cowboys and Indians finishes up with a theme, is very close to what theatre is about. But curiously, young children, and here I am meaning particularly mid-juniors and above, who are quite capable of being intellectually stretched by their drama because they are identifying with it so completely and because the identification takes place when they are on their feet, are not able to derive the same benefits from seeing adult theatre do its equivalent of cops and robbers. The form of identification required is too sophisticated for young children. The physical element is taken out and there is no teacher there prodding, asking the right questions at the right time as the theatre experience takes place. The children in their own drama are experiencing a growth and a process. Theatre is the end product of someone else's process, and drama in schools doesn't concern itself primarily with end-products.

So it seems, therefore, that it doesn't really matter if junior school children never go to the theatre and even secondary children find this process of identification very difficult indeed. But they can be trained. The question is 'who should do the training?' I believe that the right people for training secondary children to appreciate theatre are professional theatre people themselves. I have seen some brilliant lessons to small groups of children given by some young directors in this country. They have the know-how, they have the equipment and they have the actors to demonstrate. So they, I am sure, are potentially more capable than most of us who are teachers. What I do object to very strongly as far as the professional theatre is concerned, are those companies that claim that they know how to train teachers for their classroom work. Indeed one company runs a course for teachers called 'Drama in Schools'. It is very important that we respect each other's professionalism and expertise more. Opportunities need to be created for actors, directors and teachers to meet to learn from each other.

Now there is an interesting aspect of theatre in education, handled over a great number of years by one leading professional company and employed occasionally by a number of experienced amateur/teacher groups, where the educational value is clearly defined and the form of presentation is dictated by an attempt to understand the developmental needs of children. I call this work 'theatre in the classroom'. A number of professional companies are now springing up who offer many different variations of this work where the teacher skill needs to equal the acting skill. It is exciting to note the growing number of professional theatre-in-education people who have teaching qualifications as well as actor training. Critics may be justified in some cases in labelling this zeal for children's theatre as educational band-wagon jumping, and I have seen some pretty dismal, tongue-in-the cheek 'we are acting down to children' presentations by one or two professional companies; but generally there is an enlightened and serious attitude to the work and in the last twelve months I have seen some educational theatre projects that have been quite brilliant. If this kind of work is to be extended, could Theatre Schools consider providing a course of training for students attracted to this actor/teacher profession?

As I said at the beginning, my college in no way prepared me for teaching drama, apart from the encouragement it gave to formal play-production. The result has been that until I found the kind of job where I had time and opportunity to hammer out my own philosophy and practice of drama in education, with much more enthusiasm than understanding, I dabbled in all kinds of approaches, half-absorbed from casual short-course or conference contacts. I suspect that a large number of teachers in the profession have shared my experience.

But now fewer drama enthusiasts entering the profession know as little about educational drama as I did. Indeed, there appears to be a glorious harvest of drama-trained students leaving colleges each summer. (Unfortunately the amount of drama in schools does not correspondingly increase – even the best students cannot always cope with the very real lack of understanding among the rest of the profession.) It is, however, worthwhile asking the question, 'When a student has been trained in drama, what is the nature of his expertise? And does his contribution to the education of children differ in kind or in skill if he has taken drama at college curriculum level, main course, BEd, theatre school, supplementary course, advanced diploma or degree?'

There is not time to attempt an answer to these questions but it seems to me that, whatever kind of training a teacher has had, he should be equipped with the following resources:

  (i) He should know how to build mutual trust between himself and his class so that both can reveal feelings, enthusiasms, and interests with a large degree of honesty.

 (ii) He should have the kind of eye for really seeing what is happening when children are working at their drama, what is happening to the children as persons and also in terms of the drama created.

(iii) Having recognised what is happening at these two levels he should have the skill to help extend the quality of the drama along a direction that is in keeping with what appears to be the educational needs of the children at that particular moment.

How does a graduate in drama who goes into teaching receive training in these fundamental skills? How can the student in a College of Education acquire more than a few useful how-to-begin exercises in a curriculum crash-course? And what exactly are the priorities of all the other courses in between?

It is the role of a conference like this to ask the questions that will help us define our priorities.

Drama and theatre in education: a survey. In Dodd N, Hickson W (eds) *Drama and theatre in education.* Heinemann Educational, 1971.

A statement outlining the contemporary view held of drama in education in Great Britain

This is Gavin Bolton's attempt, written for a Belgian/Dutch audience at a conference in Leuven in 1981, to share the principles underlying his 1979 book Towards a Theory of Drama in Education *and the historical perspective in preparation for his 1984 book* Drama as Education *with a European audience. It was read in English.*

In this paper I shall briefly trace the changing philosophical positions held by drama educationalists in Great Britain since the beginning of the century, an historical approach which will provide a useful background against which our current attitude to the subject may be discussed in detail.

The word 'play' has figured largely in the terminology used by most of our pioneers. In so far as it is a composite word conceptually drawing under its umbrella many different kinds of activities related to 'as if' behaviour it may have been useful, but in so far as those activities have critical differences which remain blurred, the use of the term 'play' has been misleading. For instance, for many centuries prior to 1900 the theatrical use of the word, meaning a playwright's text, was traditionally understood in our public schools where the 'school play' was performed annually as an extra curricular activity. At the turn of the century, however, the word started to be applied to a method of classroom teaching. This was a dramatisation of subject-matter introduced by a Mrs. Harriot-Findlay Johnson in her state primary school and later called the 'Play-way' by Caldwell Cook[1] in his public school. Neither of these pioneers in using performance to the rest of the class as a method were challenging the traditional view of education in England as transmission of knowledge. They were attempting to make that transmission more palatable by the application of theatrical techniques, 'By doing things, and not by instruction'.

But the seeds of *progressive* education, an alternative to 'transmission of knowledge' which took fifty years to have any real grip on the educational system, could be observed in the claims that were made for this

12

new methodology as a means to personal development. The 'growth model' of education with its roots in the child centred philosophies of Rousseau and Froebel, attracted the theatre-trained men to education who from the 1930's onwards advocated a fundamental change in methodology from their performance biased predecessors. Peter Slade[2] and Brian Way,[3] while rejecting Cook's theatrical approach to learning (his play-way), nevertheless continued to base their philosophy on 'play' by which they meant the natural expression, often therapeutic in intent, and free from adult interference. Whereas Cook taught his pupils theatrical techniques, Slade and Way pioneered 'creative' or 'child' drama, firmly denying theatrical form to the pre-adolescent child. It will be seen that the term 'play' was now being used by opposing drama camps. The 1970's in England represent a time when drama educationists attempted to make sense of the resulting confusion, a confusion that was further aggravated by detectable contradictions between the stated philosophy of Brian Way and his recommended practice which utilised, as a means of achieving personal development, many of the concentration and sensitivity exercises Stanislavski used to train actors. It was as if Way, while attracted to the philosophy of self-expression, could not entirely shed his own theatrical training, nor dispense with the responsibility of the teacher in the child's creativity.

The educational drama philosophy that has emerged in the 1970's[4] can be said to harness Way's dilemma by reducing the polarisation between a 'theatre' faction and a 'creative drama' faction. It has also displaced the aim of 'personal development' held so strongly by both factions as a primary educational objective with a new attempt to relate dramatic activity to the pursuit of knowledge. I shall discuss this philosophy under the headings of: (1) 'Modes of acting behaviour', (2) 'The relationship of creative drama to theatre' and (3) 'Drama for understanding'.

1 Modes of acting behaviour

There are three basic modes of 'as if' behaviours which in their purest forms contrast fundamentally with each other in psychological terms. In less pure forms they overlap with each other, but it is easier to identify them for the time being as opposite poles of experience.

The clearest distinction can be made between dramatic playing and performance.

Diagram A

Dramatic playing ⟵————————————⟶ Performing

(Characteristics:
Experiential
Spontaneous
Existential
Not repeatable)
Private emphasis
on internal

(Characteristics:
Less spontaneous
Repeatable, public
Concerned with
demonstrating and
communicating to
an audience)
Emphasis on external

The critical distinguishing feature between these two modes is that of *intention*, between being in the 'as if' mode for oneself and one's fellow participants as opposed to being in the 'as if' mode for other people. In the former one submits oneself to the experience; in the latter one projects what one has already determined.

There is, however, a third mode which evokes a different mental 'set' from either of the other two – and this is the *exercise* mode where the intention is to *practise* something.

Diagram B

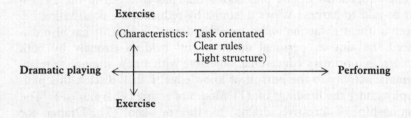

Exercise

(Characteristics: Task orientated
Clear rules
Tight structure)

Dramatic playing ⟵————————————⟶ Performing

Exercise

Now these three contrasted psychological behaviours – practising, communicating and experiencing – have different kinds of learning potential. It may be said, using the crudest terms, that whereas performing may *clarify* to the participant what is already known and exercise may *reinforce* what is already known, dramatic playing may *modify* what is already known. In other words playing is likely to have the greater potential for understanding new experience.

Each of these modes in educational terms has both strengths and weaknesses. (For instance, while dramatic playing may have a potential for learning new things because of its spontaneous, existential qualities, it may be less effective because it lacks the strong sense of purpose and tightness of structure of an exercise form). One of the features of our modern approach to drama in education is that we either find a dramatic form that combines at least two of these three modes (for instance, the existential quality of dramatic playing with the structure of an exercise) or employ within the same drama work a flexible sequence of performing ↔ exercise ↔ dramatic playing (in any order) so that all kinds of learning potential are harnessed.

2 The relationship of creative drama to theatre

The controversy over whether we should train children as performers has in the past given a disproportionate attention to that aspect of theatre to do with acting, to the neglect of the more fundamental elements of dramatic form. Examination of the internal structure of dramatic playing, exercise and theatre reveals that at this deeper level the three modes share the same core components: focus; tension; and symbolisation. These are the very tools with which the playwright and director manipulate their craft, tools which the youngest child entering an 'as if' form of behaviour unconsciously deploys in creating a fictitious context. In other words, *in this sense* the child is operating in dramatic form. Recognition of this view fundamentally affects how the teacher sees his craft. Our modern approach therefore includes acknowledgement by the teacher that although a theatrical presentation may no longer be a priority he has a parallel responsibility to the playwright or director. Just as they are concerned with focussing meaning, increasing and resolving tension and selecting symbols that resonate for the audience, the teacher must use these basic elements for the participants in the creative drama situation.

3 Drama for understanding

Historically, we have seen drama used variously for training in acting skills, transmission of knowledge, personal expression and development and therapy. We are now more concerned with making the themes of drama significant to the child. This is more than transmitting knowledge; it is a process of personally engaging with knowledge at either a contextual or a generalised level. By contextual I mean, for example, 'space travel'. By generalised I mean such themes within the context as

'people who might never come back'
'facing the unknown'
'team interdependence'
'when efficiency has to be 100%'
'personnel selection procedures'
'training of personnel'

These themes are clearly universal, going beyond the particularity of the context. There may be a third source of meaning – that which is unique to the individual.

The notion of levels of meaning in drama needs to be expanded upon here. Drama is the most concrete of the art forms. The meaning is created from the juxtaposition of two concrete events: the actual use of time and space by the participants; and the simulated use of time and space in a fictitious context. Whereas the actor walks across the stage four times, in the fictitious context the prisoner is pacing his cell. Whereas the child is bestraddling a stick, in the fiction he is riding a horse.

The relationship between these two concrete events can be described in two significantly different ways. One way is to say that the relationship is representational i.e. the actor 'stands for' the prisoner; the bestraddling child 'stands for' riding a horse. An implication of such a description is that there is some prior knowledge of prisoners or horses that becomes objectified by the use of the actor or the stick. I call this the contextual view of dramatic activity. Much teaching of mime in schools emphasises this view of dramatic action as accurate imitation of a physical reality. A more subtle, less extreme example is of the use of role-play that requires the child to imitate a stereotype attitude: an angry parent, a stern headmaster or a wicked step-mother.

A very different way of describing the relationship is to see it as a dialectic set up between the two concrete events, between the actor and prisoner, between the child and horse-riding. The meaning that emerges is the actor-in-the-prisoner experience or the child-in-the-riding experience. The meaning is unique to the interaction.

That both views can exist, at the same time, not only places drama at the opposite end of an artistic spectrum from music where there can rarely be a contextual aspect, it also places drama in a special relationship with the rest of the school curriculum, for most of our school curriculum is contextual, that is, it is concerned with the objectification of prior knowledge.

One of the paradoxes of drama then is that in so far as it is contextual its meaning is dependent upon a point of reference outside itself and in so far as it is unique its meaning is within the experience of the participant. Our primary objectives, then, are to help children experience drama in a way that engages their understanding at many different levels, the contextual, the personal and the universal. Sometimes, one of these rather than the others will be emphasised at any one time.

I have been discussing *primary* objectives in drama education. Many of the aims that we have held in the past – to do with therapy, training in skills of language and movement, interpretation of text, may also be appropriate, but the two objectives which a teacher has in mind most of the time are to do with finding significant meaning in the material of the drama and satisfaction from the work.

We are very much concerned, therefore, with using drama for *cognitive* development, harnessing the *affective* process to achieve this end. With this as our priority, the word 'play' seems inappropriate. The key phrases today are: modes of acting behaviour; dramatic form; and levels of meaning.

A statement outlining the contemporary view held of drama in education in Great Britain. In Goethals M (ed) *Opvoedkundigdrama*, 1982. (University of Leiden Press, Postbus 566, 2501CN, S-Gravenhage, Netherlands.)

References

1 Cook C 1917 *The play-way*. Heinemann.
2 Slade P 1954 *Child drama*. University of London Press.
3 Way B 1967 *Development through drama*. Longman.
4 Bolton G M 1979 *Towards a theory of drama in education*. Longman.

Freedom and imagination – and the implications for teaching drama

Gavin Bolton preceded his formal reading of the paper with a showing of his 'Outlaws' video (recorded by ILEA) in which he works with a class of ten-year-olds. His intention was to show this audience of, in the main, music, art and dance specialists from teacher-training institutions, how the processes of decision-making occur in drama. One of the dance specialists was afterwards heard to remark, 'That was not proper drama at all'.

The term 'drama in education', like the term 'play', has become a 'family' concept. It is difficult to define its essence. Drama in education is not the study of dramatic texts, although this could be part of it; it is not the presentation of the school play, although this could be part of it; it is not even teaching drama or teaching about drama, although this could be a large part of it. Essentially, it is a process, dramatic in kind, which focusses pupils' feelings and intellect towards educational goals. These goals are generally to do with the development of mind and specifically to do with understanding the 'content' of a particular dramatic experience. This experience is created by pupils and teacher together, working within the unit of a drama lesson or session in which often undifferentiated dramatic and non-dramatic elements (for instance, discussion or writing) are part of a total learning process.

It seems then that the drama in education process may only be distantly related to the art form of drama as the priorities given to education and learning and their implication for teacher–pupil interaction supersede the more normal considerations of the dramatists' and actors' crafts. Such a deviation from the norm affects this paper, for whatever is considered to be a proper discussion of Imagination and Freedom in terms of the dramatist, actor or spectator must give way to an investigation of these concepts as they relate to the teacher and the pupil.

Imagination is a psychological process which takes a particular form in dramatic activity. It requires that the participant consciously adopt an 'as if' mental set, simultaneously holding two worlds in his mind, the present or real world and the absent or fictitious world. What is expressed is the inter-play of these two worlds. When a child dramatises, say, being an outlaw the meaning for him is to do with himself in an outlaw situation. He is both participant and percipient. This is a special kind of awareness which, to borrow a phrase from Mr R.K. Elliott, allows the child to 'live it' and 'to fix attention on it' at the same time – an awareness with a potential for learning curiously ignored or underestimated by psychologists and educationists.

That 'as if' mental process is the source of dramatic energy. The different views held in the past of what direction this energy might take have often reflected educational trends, which variously have perceived drama as skill-training, drama as free creativity and drama as therapy. The orientations implied in these three trends might be described respectively as cultural transmission, natural expression and introspection. Without entirely dismissing these views, contemporary practice in drama education tends to promote a direction more analogous to progressive educational theories where learning is dependent upon the learner's interaction with the environment.

We can now offer a definition of dramatic activity that attempts to encompass process, direction and purpose:

Dramatic activity is a process of engaging with something outside oneself using an 'as if' mental set in order to activate, sustain or intensify that engagement.

The key word in this definition is *engagement* which implies a subjective/objective relationship at an affective as well as a cognitive level, a relationship that is both dynamic and rational. It involves not merely a gaining in knowledge of the world, but *an investment of oneself in the knowing*.

This view of drama as a mental activity of a special kind, brings it very close to Mrs Warnock's account of imagination:

For the imagination is the power to see possibilities beyond the immediate; to perceive and feel the boundlessness of what is before one, the intricacies of a problem, the complications or subtleties of something previously scarcely noticed. To work at something, to begin to find it interesting, this is to let the imagination play on it. To begin to explore something imaginatively is to begin to see it stretching out into *un*explored paths, whose ends are not in sight.[1]

In this quotation there is a suggestion of risk-taking, of engaging with a different perspective. In this sense drama is an act of imagination.

In claiming that drama enhances understanding we need to differentiate levels of knowledge. The most popular level of knowledge in our schools, knowledge of facts, is only minimally served by drama – although the growing interest in simulation games is perhaps an indication that this usage is not unimportant. Much more significant is that aspect of knowledge to do with values. In a drama about outlaws with a class of 9–10 year old pupils, for example, some of the children revealed a knowledge of at least two facts – that a famous outlaw was Billy the Kid and that he killed his father. Drama is only functioning at an imaginative level, however, when the children's minds become engaged with something beyond the facts. This process of 'going beyond the facts' can operate at two levels: it can focus on important consequences of the facts – in this case, 'What will happen to us outlaws if we get caught?' or, more subtly, 'What effect have our crimes had on our families?' and it can also focus on elevating the particular instance of dramatic action to a level of more universal implication, so that it can be understood as a symbol, for example, of 'those who carry a burden from the past', 'of those who cannot take freedom for granted', 'of those who cannot return home' etc. etc.

It is interesting that these kinds of concepts, so important to the understanding of life, become almost neglected by a school system dedicated as it is to the value-free 'detached' knowledge of subject disciplines. Even Mrs Warnock in spite of her declared interest in imaginative understanding, tends to be dismissive of this kind of common knowledge. It may be that she feels bound to make a stand against the radical platform from which a recommendation for the study of this kind of knowledge in the curriculum usually comes. She writes of Postman and Weingartner:[2]

> It is worthy of note, in passing, that the enquiry lessons quoted with approval by these authors almost turn out to be questions such as 'what counts as a rule?' Is there one and only one sense of 'right' and 'wrong'? 'Can there be different versions of the truth?' and so on.[3]

But although one might reasonably share her view that a whole curriculum made up of these kind of enquiries would be ridiculous, it is nevertheless part of the imaginative function to grasp the nettle of these basic values of life. Certainly a central characteristic of drama as an educational medium is that it can confront children with such values.

The personification in the last paragraph of drama as an active challenger to the pupil as passive victim inverts the usual metaphor of the pupil as active creator. There are three senses in which the participant is both active and passive. He is making something happen so that it can happen to him. Just as all art is a process of selecting constraints and submitting to them, so drama is a process of defining the rules of make-believe so that there might be a release into experiencing the make-believe. The second sense in which the participant is both active and passive has already been referred to. He is not merely a participant; he is a percipient, a spectator of his own actions and other participants' actions.

It is the third sense which requires our more detailed attention, for it is here that the educational purpose of the created product apparently limits the extent to which the participants can experience freedom. Because creative drama, as it is sometimes called, is a group activity, individual expression is necessarily curtailed by the need for group concensus, but a further form of constraint comes from the teacher whose objectives in respect of a particular created work may differ from and even be in opposition to the intentions of his pupils. Whereas the pupils, unless they are particularly sophisticated in drama, will tend to anticipate their drama as a sequence of actions creating a plot, the teacher's interest, as we have seen, is in implications and generalisations that might be drawn from the situation. Thus as the children make a choice of 'Outlaws' as their topic, their thinking is likely to be at a 'what should happen to the outlaws next?' level, while the teacher is searching to make available what he sees as a more significant meaning. Thus two opposing currents of structuring may be observed – the children may 'find gold' in order to get themselves out of a tight corner within the fiction; the teacher may work within the fiction to prove that solutions do not come as easily as that, or, if the children persist, he may try to hold up the action for reflection on the irony of having wealth without liberty. A popular way of describing these conflicting intentions is to say that in creative drama of this kind there are two plays going on at the same time: the play for the pupils and the play for the teacher. If the balance between these two plays is wrong, the drama will either remain at a superficial 'action' level or be so saturated with teacher's educational objectives that the dramatic excitement disappears.

Drama in education then is a process of negotiation between pupils and between pupil and teacher, each putting constraints upon the freedom of the other. But it is not intolerant of freedom of expression, for paradoxically creativity is liberated as the boundaries narrow. The teacher's responsibility is to deepen the level of meaning which the pupils might imaginatively explore.

In summary, I have suggested in this paper that a discussion of Freedom and Imagination in drama in education must give attention not so much to the crafts of the actor and playwright, but to the skills of the pupil and teacher in the context of a learning/teaching relationship. A contemporary view of the subject places emphasis on the participant's interaction with the objective world at a feeling/thinking level. The pupil *engages* with the value content of a dramatic context in an imaginative act. This kind of content often relates conceptually to the 'common' knowledge of life which so much of our subject-centred teaching neglects.

The freedom of the pupils is curtailed, however, in so far as the teacher structures the dramatic action towards this more significant level of understanding. But it is also enhanced by the imaginative act of holding in mind both the particular event and its more universal implications.

Freedom and imagination. Unpublished. (Paper read to Conference on Aesthetics and Education at Bishop Lonsdale College, Derby, August 1982.)

References

1 Warnock M 1977 *Schools of thought.* Faber, p. 155.
2 Postman N and Weingartner C 1971 *Teaching as a subversive activity.* Penguin.
3 Warnock M op. cit., p. 67.

Section One

On the nature of children's drama

Introduction

A note on dialectics

In introducing this section it may be opportune to attempt to make clearer one of the concepts which has become very important to Gavin Bolton in his writing about drama. This is the concept of a 'dialectic'. He often talks about a dialectic being set up between one thing and another. For example, in 'The activity of dramatic playing', he writes:

... it is the paradoxical nature of play and drama in allowing the participant to be both in and yet not in the symbolic situation, that critically affects potential for awareness. The activity is a metaphor relating two contexts, the actual world of the child as controller of events and the fictitious world in which events have control. The relationship is a dialectical one of controlling and being controlled. The experience *is* the dialectic.

When asked recently in an interview what dialectics meant, he gave this answer,

I know what it means to me – it means (and it may be that I'm not using it correctly) there is a relationship between opposites that allows for the seed of one to be within the other so that if you take two opposites like hot and cold and you wanted to demonstrate that there was a dialectic between them you would have to be able to demonstrate that within the hot is emerging the beginning of cold, that the hot anticipates the cold and the cold anticipates the hot. There is this continual mutual relationship.[1]

He goes on to say that he is using this as an analogy and a physicist may or may not say this is how temperature changes. But if we pursue the analogy it does hold a clear explanation of a dialectical relationship.

To apply this definition to the first quotation from 'The activity of dramatic playing' would be to see the activity as made up of two interconnected opposites. Out of the actual world where the child is controller can come the fictitious world where the events have control. And these two activities exist *at one and the same time*. This is the dialectical relationship.

The fundamental dialectical unity of opposites in drama is this one of the fictitious and the real co-existing at the same time as soon as the 'as if' mental set is engaged with, in this case through active role-play. Gavin

Bolton had identified this unity of opposites before he had the notion of dialectics. For example, in 'Drama as metaphor' (which appears in this section, p. 42), he describes drama as having two physical presents: the actual and the metaphorical. He says earlier in the interview already quoted, 'For some years I had been identifying dialectic(al) structures within drama without realising that I was applying Marxian theory. I recall an article by Marx making a great deal of sense to me at a later stage.'

The article which Gavin Bolton had been introduced to was, in fact, by Lenin and called 'On the question of dialectics'.[2] The first sentence of this reads, 'The splitting of a single whole and the cognition of its contradictory parts . . . is the *essence* . . . of dialectics' (p. 359). Now Gavin Bolton would not claim that he is a dialectical thinker, rather he could be seen as an empiricist who by the very close and brilliant study of one aspect of human behaviour – here acting – is forced to recognise that two opposites, being and not being, are co-existing at the same time. Gavin Bolton rather borrows as it were from dialectical logic this fundamental category that opposites can and in fact must co-exist as a unity. Kant, for example, says that 'Nature cannot abide antinomies', in other words, 'You cannot have contradictions in nature.' For Kant, something must be either one thing or another. It cannot be both at the same time. Only dialectical logic allows or rather insists that everything is made up of an identity of opposites. Lenin[3] goes on to explain, 'The identity of opposites . . . is the recognition (discovery) of the contradictory, *mutually exclusive*, opposite tendencies in *all* phenomena and processes of nature (*including* mind and society)' (pp. 359–60) [emphasis in original]. The dialectical thinker would seek to discover the essential contradictions in all phenomena which govern their *self-movement*. The mental reflection of these processes would be what cognition consists of. Gavin Bolton does not use dialectics in this way but rather uses it where he is able to identify two opposites occurring at the same time. For example, he says,

In *Towards a theory of drama in education*, it was important to me to make a distinction between two modes, a performing mode and a dramatic playing mode, the latter being spontaneous, existential, living through; the former being a mode to do with communicating to an audience so that they can have an experience. It was useful at the time to formulate these as two categories of behaviour in an attempt to help teachers to understand that sometimes children are in one, and sometimes in the other. Having made that distinction I am now ready to move on from there and recognise that it's not as simple as that, because now I want to make the point that the two represent a dialectical relationship, that within the performing mode is the seed of experiencing dramatic play and vice versa, that within the seed of dramatic playing is the performing mode, that each anticipates the other and therefore, speaking methodologically, a good teacher of drama may be sensitive to the ease with which one can move from one mode to another because this anticipation is already there.[4]

Papers in Section One

This section starts with an early paper of Gavin Bolton's, published in 1966, 'The nature of children's drama'. He points out that there has been agreement to abandon the scripted play but no clear agreement about what should replace it. He sets out to offer a perspective. It is the refinement of this perspective which has occupied him in all his subsequent writings. Here can be identified the seeds of all the major concerns which he has sought to elaborate and develop over the years.

At this stage he is using Piaget as his main theorist to argue that creative drama is built on make-believe play; he argues for drama as a social activity rather than the individualising drama that was being offered by Slade and Way; he argues for the children taking an active part in their learning; he points out that play and therefore drama are predominantly mental activities; he argues for the importance of choosing relevant action so that this will focus on universal elements in the drama; and finally he is anti exercise for its own sake.

He has made major changes in his thinking in three areas. In the first place he has left Piaget behind as his theoretical support and replaced him with Vygotsky. When asked recently to what extent Vygotsky had replaced Piaget for him, he replied,

Oh considerably, because Vygotsky says the kind of things that drama teachers want to hear about. If you listen to Piaget he really is not all that helpful to drama. For one thing, his developmental stages erroneously give the impression that young children are not capable of abstract thought – teachers using drama know different, for children can think abstractly *in context*. His book on play is still useful, it gives insight into things like first and secondary symbolism which is still relevant to drama. However, if you follow Piaget logically you would have to conclude that drama cannot be used as a tool in education because symbolic play, in his view, only reinforces what the child already knows – either reinforces or deliberately distorts. For him, play is only dealing with the past and cannot encounter.

anything new: you cannot learn through play, you can only reinforce what you already know. Now this is not really very useful to drama teachers who are trying to demonstrate that drama is a useful tool for new learning.[5]

In the second place, Bolton would no longer describe drama as a symbolic activity where symbol means simply one thing standing for something else. This denies the dialectic of both imagined and real being present at the same time. It is in this former way that the Schools Council Project *Learning through drama* (see p. 207) uses it with all the consequent weaknesses that are contained in that account of dramatic activity.

For Gavin Bolton 'symbolic' quickly became reserved for those actions or objects in the drama around which can accrue the central meaning of the play, and which can work affectively on the players.

Thirdly, and perhaps most significantly, Bolton no longer sees make-believe play as the natural and essential building block of educational drama.

... in my latest thinking I have removed that very aspect of play that I used to consider absolutely essential for good drama. The aspect of play that I saw was central to drama was this experiential one of living through an experience which is what children do when they are absorbed in their own play. It's an experiential mode, spontaneous and living from moment to moment. I always felt, until recent years, that in setting up drama in school, whatever the drama context, one was always trying to recapture that kind of living-through experience, there was always this spontaneous play element. I no longer think that it is as valid, because in recent years in the dramatic methodology I have been attempting to use, I see the activity of spontaneously experiencing a context as less and less important.[6]

What has replaced make-believe play is game play as has been pointed out in the general introduction, and spontaneous living-through has been mediated by distancing devices. It is interesting to note that in this article Gavin Bolton talks about personal and projected play and extols the virtues of personal above projected. Much later, he can be found saying,

Peter Slade wrote his theory of personal and projected play which many people, including myself, just did not see the value of, and dismissed it really as a fairly useless way of describing play activities. It's very interesting that no other play theorist actually used this kind of terminology or even made that particular classification. I have, in recent years, come to respect that classification, not because it is important to emphasise the *difference* between projected and personal play, but because it is more apparent to me that in certain kinds of drama work that we offer children, personal and projected play can be used at both one and the same time.[7]

The second article in this section is a previously unpublished 'aide-memoire' setting out Gavin Bolton's notion of the need for a second dimension to role. This has always been the way Gavin Bolton has approached what Dorothy Heathcote approaches through the notion of 'frame'.

In 'Drama as metaphor' Bolton extends his thinking in the area of drama as *not* doing. It is essentially an imaginative activity. What is important is how to obtain a release into an intense living through experience by using the actual symbolically rather than literally.

'The concept of "showing" in children's dramatic activity', while attacking teachers who only work in product, is interesting for the early emerging of an interest in game structure and drama. Talking of games in drama time, he writes, 'If only our teachers were trained to structure for such dynamic "living-through" experiences within the art form instead of out of it!' And, of course, this is precisely what he went on to explore, how game structure could supply not just a living-through experience but also a reflective experiencing as well. Really, the undercurrent of this piece is a shifting to recognising the importance of ways of reflecting on the product being produced while it is in process. 'It seems to me that attempts to encapsulate experience, in order both to look at it and have it looked at, might have potential for understanding that we have so far under-rated.'

'The activity of dramatic playing' is important for further development in the way dramatic playing differs from what Piaget calls symbolic playing. It is the structure and the focus on meaning which the teacher brings which heightens the activity from that of symbolic playing. In this article Gavin Bolton is firmly moving to the importance of game structure, 'I am more and more impressed by the logical connections between games and drama.'
And again

> ... because the teacher takes a large measure of responsibility for structure, dramatic playing undergoes a tightening of form that brings the activity *structurally nearer to games than to symbolic playing*. [Original emphasis.]

In 'Drama in education: learning medium or arts process?' Gavin Bolton delivers a riposte to Malcolm Ross who has accused him of devaluing the art form, and an answer to John Fines who has accused him of being too concerned with the art form. Ross is concerned that Gavin Bolton brings about direct emotional responses (reactive behaviour) rather than maintaining a concern for form and therefore a 'cool strip' (reflexive behaviour). What is called into question by Ross is the compatability of art and learning through the drama experience which demands a 'real' emotional involvement. Gavin Bolton sets himself out as first and foremost an educator and then proceeds to argue how the art form can be used for learning of a special sort which *necessitates* the use of emotion – but this is not 'raw' emotion but is already filtered by the make-believe situation. But the learning takes place *because* the children are freed to focus on enjoying the activity and are not *primarily* concerned with thinking about form, which remains the teacher's responsibility. He invites both Ross and Fines to join him in the middle ground where children can learn through 'the potency of a dramatic moment'.

References

1 Bolton G M 1983 Unpublished interview.
2 Lenin V I 1961 *Philosophical notebooks* (vol 38 *Collected works*). Foreign Languages Publishing House, Moscow.
3 Lenin V I ibid.
4 Bolton G M op. cit.
5 Bolton G M ibid.
6 Bolton G M ibid.
7 Bolton G M ibid.

The nature of children's drama

During 1964 and 1965, Gavin Bolton wrote to all tutors of drama in teacher-training institutions inviting them to set up a drama specialist branch of ATCDE. The first conference, financed by the University of Durham, was held in 1965 at St Chad's College. The first paper was well-received in spite of the rather primitive student accommodation and the tolling of the Cathedral bell every 15 minutes through the night!

A recent visitor to the north-east, commenting on the drama he had seen in schools up and down the country, said that the majority of lessons he had been invited to observe seemed to be getting children ready for drama rather than offering the children the experience of drama itself. I believe it to be a fair comment.

With wholehearted agreement we have condemned the scripted play as a vehicle for the young child's dramatic expression, but we cannot claim to have been equally positive in setting up an alternative. Indeed, it is a general vagueness as to what should replace the script that has resulted in all kinds of activities going on under the name of drama that bear little relationship to it. It seems to me that we have a long way to go in our thinking before we reach common agreement in defining the nature of creative drama. In this paper I shall make an attempt to communicate my own thoughts on the subject.

I begin, traditionally enough, with the assumption that drama in school develops from the child's natural play activity. Piaget[1] distinguishes between two kinds of play: practice play which is a purely sensori-motor activity repeated for the sheer pleasure derived from the action, and symbolic play, a make-believe activity in which a child evokes a situation not immediately present. He achieves this by impersonation and by using available objects or actions as symbols for absent persons or things. It is the make-believe aspect of play that provides the basis for drama.

The nature of symbolic play

The content of symbolic play operates at two levels: at the conscious level the child may be playing school by impersonating his teacher, but this is the outward plot, as it were, the means the child has chosen for expressing the unconscious level which may be a desire to exercise authority or a desire to manipulate the school situation into a more palatable form, or any other hidden theme.

A child will only resort to the use of symbols in his play when he is personally concerned about something; when motivation fades, he no longer needs to sustain belief in the situation he has created and he returns to the real world. I stress this because so often I have seen drama lessons where the principal motivation towards involvement has been the desire to please the teacher, so that children turn themselves into cats or soldiers or misers or Long John Silvers, one after the other, without there being any evidence of personal concern for these characters. Play is a serious matter: children rarely switch from one set of roles to another in a space of half an hour, and yet so many drama lessons invite children to work at this superficial level.

Piaget points out that a great sense of pleasure and freedom accompanies the young child's play, because he is creating a symbolic situation in order to relive his life on his own terms; in other words the make-believe is a pretext for the distortion of reality, but as the child emerges from the egocentric phase, play becomes much more an intellectual activity, so that the child uses make-believe at this stage of development as a pretext for learning about the world outside himself. It must, of course, be remembered that however anxious he may be to understand his environment, the act of personal identification, by its very nature, precludes complete objectivity. Indeed, in drama there is always some distortion of reality. The moment we draw upon real life or literature for our material, say, the seamen's strike or *Oliver Twist*, in the acting of these situations we straightaway create a viewpoint; we organise a few selected facts in highly selective fashion in order to make them fit the dramatic medium. I am not suggesting that ready-made material should not be dramatised – far from it: I am merely putting in a plea for a recognition of drama's limitations. If more teachers were aware of drama's distorting quality, they would not so readily slip into the educational howler of reading some exquisite poem which in itself gives the class a complete aesthetic experience, and then saying brightly, 'Would you like to act it?'

Educational elements in group play

When a child is of school age much of his make-believe play is a group activity. It is a positive sign of maturation when he is able and willing to sustain belief in symbols that have taken on a collective, social meaning (the chair that is magic has to be magic for everyone as long as the make-believe lasts) when he has to be both actor and spectator, always modifying his own contribution in response to the contributions of others. This group element generates other qualities that have educational significance; the interaction of members of a group results in an abundance of energy, a great deal of action, a great deal of talking (as much

talking about their playing as the talking that springs from their playing) a great deal of inventiveness, group responsibility and group
decision-making. Are not these qualities, particularly the last two – responsibility and decision-making – basic to the true function of education? And yet how many lessons do we see where the children feel
that they are responsible for the form the lesson takes? How often, in
practice, do we see children make group decisions? In my experience
many drama lessons put a full-stop to group creativity by carefully
planned schedules where the pupils, puppets in the teachers' hands,
behave as separate individuals in spaces of their own within different
contexts imposed by the teacher's voice every few seconds. I quote from
a lesson in *Child drama*:[2]

Average age seven years. (A class of forty-two children, in the school
hall.)

TEACHER   Turn yourselves into big, fat frogs.
          They leap about silently.
TEACHER   Now little baby frogs.
          As soon as there were signs of tiredness:
          Now all asleep.
          All lie down and relax.
TEACHER   Now show me how your father walks.
          The children do so, proudly.
          Now your mother.
          The mothers walk much faster.
TEACHER   Now a little baby.
          They waddle round; some crawl.
          Now show me how you come to school.
          Laughter. Then they walk slowly round.
TEACHER   Now, how do you go home.
          A roar of laughter and everyone runs round.
The lesson continues with the children being horses,
wheel-barrows, circus clowns, chariots, crocodiles, etc.

It was apparently only the third lesson with this class. Peter Slade
in his comment afterwards approves of this rapid fire of suggestions
from the teacher in the initial stages, saying 'It is all right as long as
you suggest what to do and not how to do it.' This is a fatal piece of
advice. It is true that some classes of young children at first appear not
to have any ideas, but lessons like the one quoted merely establish for

the children that the teacher has a constant supply of ideas that they could not possibly match. Surely if the children are not used to daring to make suggestions a teacher can disguise the fact that the ideas are his by judicious questioning like 'I don't know whether you will tell me that the story we are going to make up has to be about somebody kind or about somebody cruel.' This is such a simple, well-tried technique, but an absolutely vital one if from the start in the infants' school or any other school the children are going to shoulder responsibility as they do in their own play. But worse than Peter Slade's approval of the teacher's imposed suggestions is his admiration of the structure of the lesson. In an art lesson we do not ask children to do a lot of little sketches each period – we allow them to be creative; we give them all the time they need to work at one picture; we respect the seriousness of their work. I see so many lessons like the one I have quoted. Unfortunately, this lesson sample has been read by thousands of teachers all over the world, and we know from experience that many people who fail to understand the far-reaching significance of Slade's philosophy, are quite happy to seize on his illustrations of lesson as prototypes for all their future teaching, ignoring the context in which they were written, that of a drama adviser giving encouragement to any teacher who was prepared to break away from the formal tradition.

But many schools do provide opportunity for free dramatic play, play that can move in whatever direction the spontaneous whims of the children care to take it, within, of course, an agreed skeletal structure. We see this happening in the Wendy House activities in the infant school; or in its class equivalent where the teacher agrees that we are all at the seaside (and having agreed, she withdraws) or the children have all landed on a planet and are free to explore; or in the popular (sometimes over popular) small group activity of the junior and secondary school where pupils are left alone to make up their own plays; or at any unexpected moment in a more formal class play-making activity when complete involvement allows group spontaneity to take over, the children (or adults) 'living-through' an experience that only differs from child play in the sophistication of its content. These are precious, rewarding moments in the drama lesson, and, just as no adult, having watched a child at play, says 'That was good: do it again,' so the teacher should recognise that there are occasional moments in even adult play-making that cannot be recaptured.

But this is one of the exciting aspects of working in a creative medium – there is a constant oscillation between the subjective, intuitive response and the autonomy of an artistic form. It requires a high degree of sensitivity on the part of the teacher to recognise which pole the children's energy is moving towards at any one moment.

Drama as a ritual

I have described the spontaneous, open-ended activity of make-believe play and I have suggested that in certain ways we let this develop in school. But there is a valuable parallel activity in the infant and lower junior school that moves in a contrary direction to spontaneous play.

When I used to do drama regularly with top infants, I was always puzzled and disappointed that if the children asked to repeat a story they had made up and acted as a class, they would invariably fail to improve upon it for the second run-through, in spite of perhaps talking about 'how we can make it better' or even practising some of the movement.

If there was any change at all in my infant work it was nearly always for the worse – each run-through suffered a telescoping process, so that what had once lasted six minutes was reduced to two. I was also bothered by the cliché attempts at characterisation and the lack of precision in miming. Of course if I made it quite clear that the aim of the lesson was to please teacher, the children would, sometimes, oblige by speaking and moving in a way that satisfied me; I could force them to think of using the whole of their bodies to be tigers instead of simply putting up their hands as claws; I could force them to turn the magic key in the lock in an exact imitation of the real action. Indeed, it struck me forcibly that children of this age can do all this quite well if they want to. The question is, of course, why do they not choose the apparently better way?

The answer lies in the natural tendency of young children to ritualise. This never happens in their make-believe play, because they never know what is going to happen next; there is no sense of working towards a completion, no sense of climax and resolution. But when a story is presented to children as an entity, the 'living-through' takes place mentally when they first hear the story or when they themselves go through the process of inventing it. If they then proceed to act it, their purpose is quite different from when they play – the aim is to recapture something that is known. In the first run-through they translate the story into physical terms and thereafter each repeat is a condensed version of the previous one, with actions and speech reduced to a series of shorthand signs that are merely points of reference to the story. If having a feast is part of the sequence, children who are perfectly capable of giving a precise imitation of the eating process, simply resort to raising a hand to the mouth.[3] What in fact appears to be rapid deterioration to the teacher has become a ritual packed with inner meaning akin, not to make-believe play, but to children's street games like 'Ring-a-ring of roses' or 'What time is it Mr Wolf?'

When these episodes are crowded with archetypal characters from fairy-tales and myths, the children are brought closer to apprehending the ineffable, the quality and depth of the experience being reflected in the complete absorption of the children when they come under the magic of the story's inner texture.

I suggest, therefore, that for children up to mid-junior school level (please do not take these age divisions as rigid) there are two distinct kinds of dramatic activity, the opposing tendencies of spontaneity and ritualisation. As children mature the desire to ritualise a story fades, so that a willingness to work within a set structure now combines with the personal involvement and meaningful detail in acting that characterises spontaneous play. In other words, at this stage, the best of both worlds can be achieved, although as I have suggested before, the extremes of either pole never completely disappear – there will be times when children will be inclined to over condense and at other times they fall back on free play, losing all sense of shape, of time or of a previously planned sequence.

Make-believe play as part of thought structure

In order to clarify the nature of drama at this more mature level, I need to turn to one more factor in the nature of child play that is, I believe, of tremendous significance.

We need to examine play as a mental activity. Piaget regards the make-believe symbol as part of the structure of the child's thought It develops at a time when verbalised thought is in embryo, so that the manipulation of make-believe symbols is the only mechanism the child has for thinking with any precision. All thinking is a symbolic process: when a child begins to control his environment by make-believe behaviour, he is employing the most primitive form of symbolism; when he uses his own body in order to be someone else, he is working at the most concrete level that symbols can operate. This is the significant factor in what Peter Slade calls personal play: it is the lowest level of abstraction in thinking, and as such it nourishes and revitalises the more abstract thought processes that multiply as the child matures. In most other symbolic forms – painting, music, speech, the written word, there is a projection of the sensori-motor and emotional elements. In personal play the actions and emotions are contained within the symbol. Now, as we have seen, spontaneous drama stems directly from make-believe play, and right through to the art form of theatre the manipulation of symbols at a concrete level is a characteristic that distinguishes dramatic activity from other forms of artistic expression.

Drama operates at a concrete level

If we, here and now, decide to dramatise the voyage of Columbus, we cannot get on to our feet without translating this abstraction into a particular event or a particular aspect of the voyage. It may be the physical suffering of the crew is something we would wish to draw attention to. We read in the accounts that there was a shortage of fresh water and food. This phrase 'shortage of water and food' is quite clear in its meaning when we read it, but quite inadequate for the purpose of acting; even if we translate it to 'the men were hungry and thirsty', it is too general a term to be really helpful. If required to by the teacher, children will often attempt to portray hunger and thirst with a lot of stomach clutching and writhing, which may be adequate and expressive at the more abstract level of dance, but drama needs to be more specific. If, however, at this particular moment in time, each of us queues up with his bottle for the day's water ration and for the allowance of three mouldy ship's biscuits, and if, as we watch with suspicious, unwavering eyes to make sure that the supplies are equally divided, we are working out in our minds how much we are going to eat and drink straightaway and how much we shall try to save in our secret store until a time when there are no supplies left – we are working at the concrete level that the medium demands, the level of relevant action.

I have used this incident as an illustration of the concreteness of drama, but it also serves as a pointer to the kind of drama I believe top juniors are ready for. At this concrete level children enter into other people's experiences and gain insight into another point of view, into other attitudes, into another set of values: the experience of the particular feeds their understanding of the general.

What is the role of the teacher here? This is play-making at its highest level, where the success of the action depends primarily on the quality of the children's thinking. The teacher has the dual responsibility of

(1) helping children to identify with the situation (for instance well-fed children of today cannot evoke the reality of starvation point without considerable mental effort) and (2) guiding towards the selection of the particular moments in the historical sequence or story that will carry the greatest significance for this particular group of children: if the Columbus story is used to illustrate how the problem of hunger and thirst and mutual distrust are eventually outweighed by the communal fear of the unknown, then queuing up for a ship's biscuit and hiding it in some secret place is an appropriate way of beginning, but if the story is to illustrate the crew's mounting hatred of their captain then a completely different set of concrete actions is required. A good playwright will know just what situation and what moment in time will best convey his chosen theme. Left to themselves children are merely capable of following through a story sequence at the 'what happened next' level. If they are to have the deeper experience that only comes when characters, emotions, dialogue and actions are integrated by their high degree of relevance to a particular abstract theme, they need to rely heavily on the teacher's guidance. But teacher's guidance is of little value if the pupils do not feel a personal concern. Something in the Columbus voyage must elicit a personal, emotional response, so that the children are ready to identify themselves with the situation. This is why it is so difficult to work with mixed classes, particularly at the secondary level, as themes that naturally arouse the interest of both boys and girls are difficult to find.

If the children's interest in a particular piece of dramatic work is sustained over a number of days or weeks, then development may appear in many guises: in their thinking, their talking, their acting, their property-making, their respect for each other's view-point, their sense of artistic discipline, their desire for further factual knowledge, their writing, their painting. I believe that drama has done its work if, for example, children spend a whole lesson talking about their play (indeed how many real experiences do children share in school that are worth talking about? – one sees so many false 'discussion' lessons where from the very beginning there has been no personal involvement). Drama has done its work, too, if they spend a whole period doing further research in the library or, at the other extreme, if they spend time improving a piece of drama work ready for showing to the class next door: children often need that feeling of completion that can only come from the presence of an audience; as long as the emphasis is not on communication but rather on inviting people to look in at their work, there is much to be gained from the occasional experience.

Movement and drama

When so much of the drama in our schools is based on movement training, I feel that this paper should include my views.

When, in his play, a child is jumping, running and stretching for no other purpose than for the pleasure of doing so, he is involved in what Piaget calls practice play. Not only does he acquire skill in a repertoire of actions, he also, through experimentation with his body in space, extends his physical resources. It is particularly this extension of physical resources that we are concerned with in our movement work in education. We help the child to be more objectively aware of the dimensions of space, aware of the varying speed and quality of movement with which he can control space, aware of the emotional qualities that colour movement. It seems that all the various branches of learning, whether they be concerned with the physical and emotional qualities of words in a language lesson or appreciation of the movement implicit in a painting or the intersection of different planes in mathematics, may draw upon the experience of the movement lesson. There is no doubt that drama in particular is enriched by movement work, but I would suggest that it is a mistaken notion to assume that they are so closely allied that movement automatically merges into drama. The starting point of make-believe play is the child's wish to leave the real situation and to create a different one, but in the sensori-motor exercise of practice play the child is well satisfied with the real situation and is set to explore its possibilities. There is always a sensori-motor element in make-believe play, but, as Piaget has pointed out, it is always subordinated by the symbol. Can we not have both movement and drama running as two parallel activities in school? It seems to me, as far as I am able to judge the overall picture, that most of the movement training enthusiasts in the country pay lip-service to drama.

Before I finish let me make certain that my point of view is quite clear. It must not be assumed that because I have criticised certain methods that I would never employ them. In order to achieve the overall aim of helping children to enter other people's experiences, it may be necessary, for a short space of time, to use any of the devices I have condemned. I may be faced with a class of adults for whom a few minutes of movement before they start their drama is a useful unwinding process; it may be that the movement required in the play about landing on the moon is well worth practising at length; it may be that the miming required for the play about the machine belt in a factory breaking down is so complex that the acting will never get off the ground until appropriate miming exercises have been worked out; it may be that the threat of a thunderstorm or examinations inhibits concentration so that a few easy exercises may help; it may be that I am a student straight from college and I need the security of having a class spaced out with each individual on his own and a list of itemised activities in my hand. And, finally, there are times when it is necessary to tell children exactly what to do and how to do it and these times are more effective because they are rare.

In all creative activities there are occasions when helping the child to analyse the techniques of self-expression enhances the quality of his work. In our English teaching we have realised that there is a place for language and punctuation exercises but that they cannot replace creative writing; we have realised that the speech exercise is no substitute for real talking situations. I submit that the poor quality of much of the drama work in schools stems from our failure to make a distinction between the exercise and the creative activity, and when the visitor I referred to at the beginning talks of children 'getting ready for drama' what he has seen is an overdose of the Punctuation, the Grammar, the Spelling and the Handwriting of drama instead of the real thing – a shared dramatic experience.

The nature of children's drama. *Education for Teaching* (Journal of the Association of Teachers in Colleges and Departments of Education, 1966. (151 Gower Street, London.)

References

1 Piaget J 1962 *Play, dreams and imitation in childhood*. Routledge and Kegan Paul.
2 Slade P 1954 *Child drama*. University of London Press, p. 192.
3 Langer S K 1963 *Philosophy in a new key*. Harvard.

Further notes for Bristol teachers on the 'second dimension'

The 'second dimension' was an expression I kept using during the weekend's work. I hope these notes will help to clarify the various points I tried to make. I shall illustrate from the lesson on 'Camping' with the Secondary class of children.

The single dimension offered by the children is 'Campers'.

Before they get on their feet, the teacher must create a second dimension – *zealous* campers, *unwilling* campers or, as it turned out in this lesson, *novice* campers. This second dimension has a treble function:

(a) it supplies the link between the child's life experience and the context of the first dimension. (Children who have never camped will bring only second-hand knowledge of camping but all can bring first-hand knowledge of 'zealous' or 'unwilling' or 'novice');
(b) it supplies the universal link between 'campers' and 'mankind' so that the activity is always 'bigger' than the first dimension;
(c) it provides a potential activating agent for drama to develop, for the second dimension often implies a tension or problem to be resolved.

During the weekend the injection of a second dimension was used in two different ways. Notice the difference between children pursuing occupations of novice campers and later being faced with 'you're the worst lot of campers I've ever been in charge of'. Although the latter appears to be an extension of the former, there are the following important differences:

1(a) The first is an ongoing situation, its success depending upon each child's own emotional and perceptual recall.
  (b) Its success does not depend on group interaction.
  (c) From the teacher's point of view it has allowed action to start, at the same time providing an opportunity for observing the class.
  (d) It *may* become the context for development as drama; it *may* supply the theme that will ultimately be the principal area of learning for the children.
2(a) The injection of the second dimension by the teacher in role (or by any other means) provides a sudden change of situation re-

sulting in an accompanying increase in quantity and quality of the emotion (the tight corner!)

(b) Educational drama has started because the new dimension has supplied the impetus for organic growth out of the implicit conflict and because the new theme of 'coping with an authority situation' is sufficiently worthwhile for these children to apply their minds to.

In the brief exercise I set you at the beginning of Saturday afternoon we were concerned with setting up (1) rather than (2) where (1) permits a sustained exploratory action with emotion on an even keel. There are times when a teacher prefers this as a beginning to anything more obviously 'dramatic'.

Hence the distinction we need to draw between

(1) 'nurses round an operating table who care about their patient' and
(2) 'nurses who suddenly recognise the patient on the operating table'.

It seems to me that (2) is a plot injection that not only makes greater emotional demands but also tests belief in the situation. Similarly,

(2) 'The hungry gypsies catching sight of someone bringing in a rabbit' is much more demanding than:
(1) 'The hungry gypsy queuing for and then privately chewing his ration of meat'.

Further notes on the 'second dimension', 1972. Unpublished.

Drama as metaphor: a different perspective on the nature of children's creative drama

Introduction

The idea for the above title came from an article by Dr Ann M. Shaw[1] where she says (p. 85),

> . . . I consider improvisational drama to be richest in import for the child when it is defined and practised in such a way that it includes both the process of making metaphors and the metaphor made.

It is the aspect of children's drama concerned with 'making metaphors' that I am interested in pursuing in this paper.

My definition of metaphor is:

> The meaning or meanings that are created by the juxtaposition of two seemingly incompatible contexts.

The metaphorical expression 'That chap is "on the rocks"' is an example, in a literary form, of two such contexts – money and a sinking ship. The financial context could be said to be the *actual* context of the unfortunate man to whom the expression applies. The ship on the rocks is the *imagined* context. The created meaning stems from the *relationship* set up between the two.

Similarly in drama a relationship is contrived between an actual context (the participant operating in a physical environment) and an imagined context (a make-believe situation that is evoked by the participant's actions, words and use of properties, etc.). Thus the situation of an under-fed young actor in a back-street rehearsal room with a paper tissue in his hand can coincide with the situation of an overweight, gouty landowner waving a lace handkerchief from his carriage window.

In this paper I shall argue that the quality of the metaphorical meaning created is dependent on (1) how the two contexts inter-relate; (2) the degree to which the make-believe context sustains a universal implication; and (3) the degree to which the actual context is deployed symbolically. I shall confine the discussion to work with children, as the final purpose of the paper is to suggest that failure to understand drama as metaphor has often led to the wrong ordering of priorities in our drama teaching.

The make-believe context – second dimension controls the area of meaning

'Let's be pirates, Sir.' In fact children cannot be pirates; they can only be pirates who have to keep their eyes skinned because danger is round the corner, or pirates who must find the treasure before dark, or pirates who want their fair share of the loot, or pirates who find it difficult to move quietly because of their wooden legs! and so on. Whether employed unconsciously by the children or deliberately by the teacher this second dimension is a pre-requisite of any make-believe action.

It is the second dimension that represents the chosen meaning. In an intellectual discussion about pirates a group of children may verbally cover many facets of the concept. In play and in drama a choice has to be made. A child cannot give 'keeping eyes skinned', 'being short of time', 'wanting a fair share of the treasure' and 'keeping quiet with a wooden leg' equal priority. He may pursue the one that most satisfies himself or the group or his teacher. Other facets may later become relevant and there may be a re-ordering of priorities as the playing or drama proceeds but only one aspect can be uppermost at any one time.

An examination of the function of this second dimension reveals that it has a dual significance. It is both personal and universal. The following table may illustrate what I mean by this:

	Personal	Universal
Pirates who have to keep their eyes skinned for danger	The child may draw on what he knows of anticipating danger or a threat	The drama may become about people who never feel safe
Pirates who must find the treasure before dark	The child may draw on what he knows of being short of time	The drama may become about people who work to a dead-line
Pirates who want their fair share of the loot	The child may draw on his experience of sharing and not trusting	The drama may become about people who distrust each other
Pirates with a wooden leg	The child may experiment with modification of physical control	The drama may become about people who are physically restricted

43

It is the third column, the universal, that allows children to share the same drama experience with each other. It is the second column, the personal, that brings for each child a *reality* to the pirate make-believe. As I said earlier, children cannot be pirates, but they can be people who anticipate danger, who are short of time, who can't trust others and who adapt their physical movement.

It is important to notice that the last one, the modification of physical movement, is of a different order of experience from the others. One purpose of this essay is to express the view that whereas each of the first three experiences could stand alone as a sustaining force in both personal and dramatic terms, modification of physical movement or its equivalent is insufficient, in itself, and that it needs to be accompanied by or replaced by a different quality of experience. A class of six year olds can only find this quality of experience if 'having a wooden leg' is transformed, for example, into 'the noise our wooden legs are making will cause us to get caught' so that 'getting caught' experiences are what each child can draw upon.

I am hypothesising, therefore, that central to any make-believe experience is the recall of past experiences. It is not necessarily the actual events that are recalled. It is the relevant feeling that is evoked. The child does not bring to the fore of his mind all the precise images to do with incidents in the past when, say, he could not trust others to share fairly, but he does evoke the kind of feeling (and consequently the *meaning*) that belongs to those events. Whatever surfaces as a result of tapping past experiences, whatever form it takes – imagery, verbalisation, feeling, etc. – it is a representation of past events; any new thinking or feeling will be affected by the representation.

The actual context – the symbols define new meaning

The new thinking and feeling is stimulated by the actual physical context. If the make-believe world is about 'non-trusting' pirates the actual world clearly carries no such meaning. And yet the way its resources are used will very much effect the created meaning. Let us look at some possible resources: the teacher may have supplied an old box disguised as a treasure chest; the miming of the digging may be carried out with care; voices may be roughened; patches and head scarves may be worn; and the teacher may have even stuck on a sound effects record of breakers on a seashore.

I would like to suggest that although these devices are often essential for 'getting things started', for aiding belief, for encouraging commitment, they do not necessarily feed into the drama, the metaphor. The activity of drama operates on a different plane of experiences from the actual context and any devices, properties, features or actions employed have to take on a different quality of meaning for them to feed into that experience. If the sound of the seashore and the head scarves are merely *signs* that we are on the seashore and that we are pirates, their function is limited because the meaning is limited. On the other hand, if the box is not simply a sign of treasure but a *symbolic representation* capable of many levels of meaning then the children grappling with those meanings emotionally and intellectually are working in metaphor. The direction the meanings take will depend on what inner feelings are being tapped. In our example of pirates who cannot trust each other to share the loot, the box may stand for 'the end of a long trail'; 'a test of trust'; 'claiming one's rights'; 'a chance to buy freedom', etc. In other words, the *meaning* is created from an oscillation between some feature or features of the actual present and the memory bank of feelings, which, as we have seen, are both personal and universal.

Let us look at some of the implications of this hypothesis. Supposing in our example of pirates one of the features of the actual context is very careful miming by the children of digging a hole. I would maintain that no matter how skilful the children may be in imitating the action of digging, this alone does not qualify as a drama experience. The digging must essentially function as a symbol, representing the appropriate feeling and attitude of the pirates in that particular 'non-trusting' context, and not necessarily resembling the external features of the action. In other words, the emotional loading of the action must be true to the context; the physical use of time and space does not have to be.

Implications for teaching

The above paragraph may well startle many teachers who place an emphasis on the value of accurate miming as part of drama education. Indeed in hypothesising that drama operates in a metaphorical mode, I am to some degree removing it from the immediate world of sensations. I remember when I first started teaching reading an article that advised teachers of drama that if during a single lesson 'all five of the senses had been covered' this guaranteed a good lesson. Much of the literature on teaching drama supports the notion that exercises giving practice in perception are useful aids to drama experience. Indeed I have never heard this challenged until recently Mike Fleming, a higher degree research student at Durham University suggested in his thesis that 'moving around the room with eyes closed does not in itself help someone to know what it is like to be blind'. It seems to me that this observation is valid in that the exercise, while useful in giving the participant a crude understanding of visual deprivation, needs to be extended considerably if the concept of blindness is to be tackled seriously. Indeed if it is to move onto a plane of drama rather than remain as an exercise, restricting the sense must somehow acquire a symbolic meaning beyond the immediate sense experience.

Thus the notion that drama is dependent on imitation is not valid. Much energy has been misdirected into 'getting it to look right', so that actions have been perfected, sound effects have been made impressively real, costumes have been authentic, all on the assumption that the nearer the actual context can get to the imagined context the better the drama will be. Thus a teacher feels compelled to suggest that children 'build a ship' to start their drama about the sea or believes that Wendy House play is promoted by the close simulation of a kitchen. I will go so far as to suggest that, paradoxically, when the drama experienced is distanced from the actual, the more 'real' it will feel to the participants – more real and, of course, more significant. It will feel to the child that it is actually happening in the same sense that a child playing a game of football feels that it is actually happening although it is 'just a game'; he is not acting; he is not pretending; he is not demonstrating; he is living-through an event of heightened significance. He will feel real and perhaps intense emotion*; he will think on his feet in action, making decisions and solving problems.

The problem for the teacher is to find a way of helping the child to tap his store of past feelings and to use physical resources as symbols. For those teachers who like to give their children practice exercises, perhaps it is this area of 'finding many meanings' that could most usefully be explored.

Drama as metaphor. *Young Drama* 4(3), June 1976. (Thimble Press, 'Lockwood', Station Road, South Woodchester, Glos. GL5 5EQ.)

---

* For a discussion of the part played by emotion in drama, see the paper read by Gavin Bolton at the American Theatre Association Convention, in Washington DC, August 1975, published in the *Canadian Child and Youth Drama Association National Newsletter*, February 1976. (see p 89 this volume.)

Reference

1 Shaw A M 1975 Co-respondents: the child and drama. In McCaslin N (ed) *Children and drama*. David McKay, New York.

The concept of 'showing' in children's dramatic activity

Of all the topics that continually recur in our MA (Ed) Drama Course discussions, the old hoary one of the value of drama as process or product is the most persistent, so I thought I would like to put into print my latest thinking on the subject.

When a child hangs a painting on a classroom wall, he is not only sharing it with others, but sharing it with himself. What was originally an experience of a process from the inside has become an experience of a product from the outside, a psychological shift and a shift in time. The extent of the psychological shift is dependent on the degree to which he anticipated the change of perspective. It seems reasonable to assume that a child totally absorbed in gaining moment-to-moment satisfaction from the process will have an experience different in quality from the child who intermittently or concurrently perceives what he is creating as a product in the making. This movement from process to product is a complex change in perspective which appears to be even more complicated when applied to dramatic activity, because of the elusiveness of the product. This paper will attempt to identify the principal factors involved and to discuss some of the educational implications.

Even the child totally absorbed in the process is ambivalently in both an active and a passive mode: he is actively taking a brush, dipping it in paint and making contact with the paper and then subjecting himself to whatever experience the images on the paper offer him, until he, in turn, takes over control again and adds more to his painting.

Dramatic activity and child play (indeed, it could be argued, everything we *choose* to do in life) have this dual characteristic of controlling in order to be controlled. A child in play bestrides a stick in order to give himself a cowboy experience. He can say both 'I am making it happen' and 'It is happening to me'. It is this latter experiential aspect that opens the child to new learning both in play and in drama. But a significant feature of drama is that this active/passive mode may be shared unevenly among the participants: the leading 'cowboy' calls 'away men!' and the rest spring to their horses. Some degree of controlling is retained by even the most passive: the 'cowboy', unexpectedly shot by an 'Indian', still has vestigial control over the style of his death spasms, or, more importantly, some autonomy over whether to continue to abide by the rules of the drama game. The point that is relevant here is that the relationship between the active, instrumental and the passive, experiential is variable. Many actors can contribute to this movement within the active/passive mode. For instance, if the teacher is in a dominating role in the drama: 'I am the sheriff; hand over your guns' each child in the class is more likely to feel 'It is happening to me' than 'I am making it happen'. On the other hand, when a child chooses to 'show' his drama, the reverse is more true, for 'showing' by definition implies a special kind of 'making things happen'. This paper attempts to assess how this and other characteristics of make-believe action are affected by a product orientation.

Let us isolate a comparatively simple example from child play for analysis, that of a child who, in playing on his own, impersonates driving a car like daddy. It is not unreasonable to assume that all symbolic play carries at least two meanings: (1) the objective context, in this case daddy driving a car, and (2) the subjective value or mixture of values the child places on the objective context, for instance that it is fun or heroic or alarming or important to be daddy driving the car. Further hidden meanings are possible where the choice of context is almost arbitrary, where the meaning really is 'I want to be free like daddy or have power like daddy' – or it may reveal even more sinister views of daddy! That the child's external actions are all to do with driving a car may have less significance than the child's feelings about being daddy. On the other hand the child may simply love cars and be repeating past car experiences as closely as he can remember. Thus it becomes clear that the relationship between objective and subjective meanings is variable according to where the emphasis is placed by the child. But supposing his mother comes into the room and asks him what he is doing, to which he replies 'I'm daddy driving the car. Watch me' I maintain that should the child now attempt to repeat his previous actions the experience is a fundamentally different one. It is affected by the two crucial requirements of repetition and communication. The 'meaning' of the experience must now tilt towards the objective context whatever the previous personal emphasis. The instrumental aspect of the active/passive mode is increased, for any 'it is happening to me' experience is replaced by the pragmatic need to 'make it happen to me – again'. Thus the immediacy and spontaneity of the 'living through' quality is reduced. The purpose has changed from intrinsic satisfaction derived from the action itself to extrinsic satisfaction derived from the new social context. The direction of the activity has changed from being intra-personal to extra-personal. Structurally, it must also change from what was symbolic, elliptical and condensed to the grammatical precision of a collective sign system. In other words, action is a form of language and, like language, its structure changes as it moves from a personal to a collective mode. Finally as a mental operation it has also changed from the intuitive to the rational. I think a tabulation of these changes would be helpful.

Table one

	A Process	B Product
	Child alone	*'Look at me'*
Purpose	Intrinsic satisfaction	Towards extrinsic satisfaction
Meaning	Variable between subjective and objective	Towards objective
Direction	Intra-personal	Extra-personal
Mode	Active and passive (instrumental and experiential)	Towards active (towards instrumental)
Mental operation	Intuitive	Towards rational
Structure	Elliptical	Towards precision
Mediation	Symbol	Sign
Form	Metaphor	Explanation of metaphor

It is suggested that the above table represents psychological and structural changes that take place when a child enters the make-believe context with the intention of 'showing' to someone not in the make-believe. But what happens when more than one child shares the same plane or drama? Is there not then a move towards the explanatory or demonstrating features of the product column for the participants to communicate with each other? Certainly a greater degree of objectivity is required than for the child merely playing on his own. The make-believe must have some meaning other than each child's private interpretation; otherwise the children, although playing side by side and apparently sharing the same context, would virtually be playing on their own – as indeed one can observe in the play of some children in nursery school or even in a drama lesson. But, when they do share, are they 'showing' each other as in the 'look mummy' example? Is one child in the make-believe play an audience for the other? It seems to me that the principal distinction between the two lies in its form, the last item listed in the above table. Drama is a metaphorical form in that it is created by the juxtaposition of two concrete contexts: actuality and fiction. The actuality is that the child is a three year old boy sitting on a chair holding his arms in front of him and moving them in a circular fashion; the fiction is that he is daddy driving a car. The meaning of the experience is dependent on a dialectic between these two contexts. Now whereas a group of children jointly playing or doing drama share that meaning from within the metaphor, any observer does not have that privilege: the audience is outside the metaphor and 'look mummy' may precede an intention to *explain* it. Indeed this is what actors do for the audience in theatre. A fuller picture can be gained by inserting a third, middle, column to our categorisation, taking up a middle position in every sense.

Table two

	A Process	B Process	C Product
	Child alone	*Group of children*	*'Look at me/us'*
Purpose	Intrinsic satisfaction	Intrinsic satisfaction	Extrinsic satisfaction
Meaning	Subjective/object-ive	Subjective/object-ive	Objective
Direction	Intra-personal	Intra-personal	Extra-personal
Mode	Instrumental/exp-eriential	Instrumental/exp-eriential	Instrumental
Mental operation	Intuitive	Intuitive/rational	Rational
Structure	Elliptical	Elliptical/precise	Precise
Mediation	Symbol	Symbol/sign	Sign
Form	Metaphor	Metaphor	Explanation of metaphor

It seems from the above table that the psychological and structural differences among individual play, shared play or dramatic activity and showing to an audience may be both complex and significant; and yet one of the interesting features from our point of view is that the same outward actions (as for example driving a car) could obtain in each case. So, to the untutored eye, the behaviour of the child, although internally differently orientated could appear to be unchanged. As teachers, we need to recognise the subtle distinctions. Even the most experienced observers might find it difficult to discern whether a particular child is working principally in columns **A, B,** or **C.** The presence or not of an audience would not necessarily give the observer a clue. Many groups of children in my experience can become so absorbed in their improvised work that they are working in column **B** in spite of the presence of an audience; it is as if a child has said 'look mummy' and then forgotten that she is there. Similarly, many other groups of children behave (and indeed are trained to behave) as if they are showing – even when there is no-one watching; such children can spend their school drama lives always behaving at column **C.**

It is this latter kind of drama that gives me cause for concern. One sees, particularly in our secondary schools, a perpetual working in product rather than process. Teacher and class may discuss a significant (often socially significant) topic such as immigration, and the class are required in their groups to enact what they know about it. But from the beginning, like the child who knows before he puts brush to paper that his painting is for putting up on the wall, the column **C** explanatory, instrumental mode of action is adopted in order to 'make a statement', to show the rest of the class. Any attempt to work in column **B** is eclipsed by the need to work for product. So these pupils never *experience* immigration; they simply demonstrate what they already know.

It seems ironical that secondary drama teachers do in fact often give over a great deal of drama lesson time to an experiential mode, but they tend to use a non-drama form to achieve it – *games*. If only our teachers were trained to structure for such dynamic, 'living through' experiences within the art form instead of out of it! My view is that games have gained in popularity because they achieve the very personal and group involvement that drama is failing to give. The potential in drama is often not tapped because teachers do not know how to tap it. So one can often observe *real* experiences in the first half of drama lessons and then a change over to the instrumental, 'making a statement' or 'demonstrating' drama in the second half.

It seems to me however we should not allow this obviously unsatisfactory use of drama (unsatisfactory that is when it is in *regular* use) to detract from the possible value of column **C.** Firstly, I should emphasise that although I have categorised the three columns for the sake of simplicity they represent not so much categories as directions, and that in my view there can be a fluidity of movement among the three directions *within the same drama experience.* Secondly, although I would regard column **B** (sharing) as the most educationally significant dramatic mode, it is possible and indeed desirable that there are times when the children can more easily and perhaps imperceptibly slip from column **B** to **A** and from **B** to **C**. In this way the children can at times find meanings that are deeply personal and are not amenable to objectification and at other times they can, as it were, put their pictures on the wall, so that they can both reflect at a distance on the product they have created and also have the feedback on what their drama has meant to someone else.

It is possible that in the past our reaction against formal performance (about which I still have reservations where young children are concerned) has caused us to reject 'showing' altogether. It seems to me that attempts to encapsulate experience in order both to look at it and have it looked at, might have a potential for understanding that we have so far under-rated.

The concept of 'showing' in children's dramatic activity. *Young Drama* **6**(3), 1978.

The activity of dramatic playing

In this chapter I propose to conduct a theoretical analysis of a certain kind of dramatic activity in schools. It is an attempt to analyse the *activity per se*. The function of the teacher will be discussed in so far as the teacher controls the activity in terms of its potential for learning. Regrettably, because the subject is so vast and complex neither methods of teaching nor implications for teacher-training can be included in the discussion.

Three kinds of dramatic activity

The Schools Council Secondary Drama Project[1] team usefully coined the phrase 'acting-out' as an umbrella term to cover seemingly countless varieties of dramatic behaviour to be found in schools. A popular way

The activity of dramatic playing

of categorising acting-out is to use the criterion of *outer form*: movement; mime; dance-drama; role-play; improvisation; scripted-work; performance etc., but I find it more useful to classify the activity according to its *orientation*.

There are two basic polarities in dramatic activity: (1) moving in a direction of 'being' or 'experiencing' and (2) moving in a direction of giving someone else an experience, i.e. performing. The former tends to be characterised by a spontaneous, existential quality that is perhaps found at its most intense in children's playing; the latter tends to be characterised by a 'demonstrating' 'calculating the effect' quality that is found, par excellence, in professional theatre. But just as there is an incipient degree of 'demonstrating' at the heart of a child's play, so vestiges of 'spontaneity' can linger in the most rigid theatre performance. These two orientations can be seen, therefore, as a continuum rather than as divisions.

Towards experiencing $\longleftarrow$ ——— $\longrightarrow$ Towards performing

Whether the children in school are using mime or movement or improvisation the drama work will have one or other of these basic orientations, unless it is directed towards the third form of orientation – *exercise*. Here the purpose is primarily neither experiencing nor giving experience: it is practising. Usually a skill that is felt to be appropriate to drama (at any point on the above continuum) is isolated for training e.g. sensitivity; concentration; group awareness; voice skills; movement skills; acting techniques etc., may be practised.

Notice the classification I have made implies a relationship between intention and quality of experience:

1 Orientation towards experiencing – a quality of spontaneity.
2 Orientation towards performing – a quality of demonstrating.
3 Orientation towards exercise – a quality of practising.

It may be that in isolating *quality* I have successfully determined the most fundamental criterion affecting different educational drama practices, for a basic difference in quality implies a basic difference in learning potential in each kind of activity. A justifiable inference might be that the first orientation leads to 'discovery' learning, the second to 'communication' and the third towards an acquisition of skills. But quality is not the only significant aspect of the three orientations. The outcome in terms of learning derives from equally significant factors such as teacher function, meaning and structure.

The whole of the school drama scene is so complex that I propose to confine this examination to the first of these orientations[2] – *towards experiencing.* I shall call this kind of school drama 'dramatic playing'. Our findings may, at least by implication, throw some light on the significance of the other two. Reference has already been made in the second paragraph to children's play. Indeed a tradition of English writing on educational drama, started by Caldwell Cook[3] and Peter Slade,[4] has made the linking of the two a *sine qua non.* But for me it is not a matter of following faithfully in the paths of pioneers. I consider an understanding of the relationship between play and drama to be critical to a theoretical basis for drama in education. Certain characteristics essentially found in play are also central to the activity of dramatic playing. I shall discuss them using the following dimensions:

1 Quality of experience, already touched upon above.
2 Awareness.
3 Meaning.

1 Quality of experience in play and dramatic playing

What is this quality of spontaneity that characterises the experience? It is a sense of the immediate, of being in the here and now. It is both an active and passive mode, both controlling and being controlled, both making it happen and submitting to it happening. For example, the host gives a smile of welcome to set the tone of a greeting and at the same time responds to the hand proffered for shaking; the swimmer agitates the water for propulsion and at the same time submits to the water so that this body floats. In other words the quality of spontaneity is what we experience a great deal of our waking time: living actively and passively in the present. My suggestion in the second paragraph therefore that this spontaneous quality is perhaps found 'at its most intense' in children's play, hardly seems to make sense when spontaneity clearly belongs pre-eminently to 'living' rather than to a specially contrived activity known as 'playing'.

Thus we come straight away to one of the many paradoxes of the subject under discussion. It used to be assumed by many theorists that play implied freedom. Indeed according to John Wesley it is on these grounds that the activity should be spurned: 'He that plays as a boy, will play as a man,' he warned! but in fact as Vygotsky[5] has pointed out, 'Play continually creates demands from the child to *act against impulse* i.e. to act on the line of greatest resistence' (my italics) and yet I shall persist in identifying the quality of spontaneity in this very activity that goes 'against impulse'.

An explanation, which may also hold true of some dramatic playing, is that play activity both constrains and liberates. The constraints are in the form of rules which require a disciplined commitment; the subsequent release into freedom is an experience unhampered, as Dearden puts it, by the 'prudence and obligation' that belong to ordinary life. 'Play stands apart from the web of purposes which make up the serious, and in this sense is self contained'.[6] Thus in a sense play allows a spontaneity that is, if you like, in a purer form than in everyday living because it is liberated from the moral and legal consequences that normally temper freedom of response. To summarise the paradox: it is a self contained non-serious activity the very separateness of which permits a serious commitment to its specially contrived rules. It is this submission to the rules that liberates the participant into the freedom of spontaneous behaviour.

This quality is not a characteristic of all kinds of play, however, any more than it is shared to any significant degree by the other two orientations of drama. Piaget[7] distinguished three categories of play:

Games: where there are socially determined rules e.g. playing tennis
Practice play: where some action is repeated for its own sake – practising a tennis stroke
Symbolic play: where an absent or fictitious context is represented e.g. 'pretending' to play tennis

Practice play, by its repetitive nature, implies non-spontaneity, but its difference from symbolic play and games lies deeper than that. It has to do with the degree to which it is a self-contained activity. In fact, although it can be seen as contrived it is not as separate from the normal 'web of purposes' as the other two. Thus practising a tennis stroke does not have the *special* quality of spontaneity of a tennis game: 'This is it now' might describe the feeling that colours the game, whereas 'getting ready for it' is more likely to describe the predominating feeling behind the exercise. I stress this of course because of the parallel difference we find in school between 'dramatic playing' and 'exercise drama'.

The reader may be puzzled by my reference to games when clearly it is symbolic play that is closest to drama. This essay may well to some extent challenge that view, for I am more and more impressed by the logical connections between games and drama. Vygotsky makes the interesting point:

Just as we were able to show at the beginning that every imaginary situation contains rules in a concealed form, we have also succeeded in demonstrating the reverse – that every game with rules contains an imaginary situation in a concealed form.[8]

We may not wish to go all the way with Vygotsky in finding a concealed imaginary situation within every game – I find it very difficult to discern make-believe in, for example, cricket, apart from the agreement to identify with two opposing sides – but we can agree to an important similarity between games and symbolic play in terms of self-containment, and the special quality of spontaneity, i.e. a 'living-through' that is freed from the normal pressing needs of living.

One of the obvious differences between symbolic play and games is that whereas in the latter the rules are social, collectively agreed before the activity starts, in the former they are open to negotiation. In symbolic play the rules affect a greater number of levels of spontaneous behaviour from the purely physical to the deeply imaginative. On the other hand spontaneity has a greater chance of breaking down in symbolic play if the rules are too vague to be trusted. That the negotiation often requires such fragile handling clearly has implications for the teacher working in dramatic playing. It is no wonder that so many drama teachers fall back on drama games which give the children an active spontaneous experience without the risk of inadequate negotiation of rules. Often children who commit themselves freely to 'living-through' in games will not trust the drama context to the same extent.

2 Self-awareness in play and dramatic playing

I suggested earlier that spontaneity in play implies both a passive and an active aspect – both 'making it happen' and 'having it happen', as it were. But the question arises to what extent is a participant *conscious* of controlling and being controlled. Can he in fact *knowingly* say, 'I am making it happen; it is happening to me'? Spontaneous action in real life seems to vary in the degree to which a participant is conscious of his behaviour i.e. the extent to which one is, say, talking as opposed to being *aware* that one is talking. Usually the circumstances have to be rather special for one to become a spectator of oneself in this way – an interview situation is an example of where this may happen. Indeed in such an example we may say that an interviewee's 'self-consciousness' is not allowing him to 'be himself'.

Are play activities likely to fall into line with non-play activities in this respect? One can certainly visualise the footballer, who, because his girl-friend is watching, fails to play his normal game out of sheer 'self-consciousness', or the tennis player who during a game is self-consciously attempting to employ a stroke he has not yet quite mastered. Indeed even in symbolic play and certainly in dramatic playing the presence of an audience may, under some circumstances, shift the experience into a 'self-conscious' performing.

But is 'self-consciousness' the same as 'self-awareness'? In the examples I have given I have implied a distortion – a movement away from the normal behaviour in an interview, a game or in symbolic playing. Self-awareness, on the other hand, implies a heightened awareness of a moment of living that remains unspoiled by the act of observation. We can probably all recall some moments and have forgotten many others when we have, as it were, 'caught sight of ourselves'.

I shall now argue that the nature of symbolic play, and, subsequently, dramatic playing, is such that opportunity for this kind of self-awareness is increased. It seems to me that because the child is his own agent contriving his own 'self-contained' situation, he can claim with some force: 'I am making it happen, so that it can happen to me'. Thus he has a vested interest in the activity which no doubt invites a special attentiveness to what is happening within it.

But there is more to it than that. Again, it is the paradoxical nature of play and drama in allowing the participant to be both in and yet not in the symbolic situation, that critically affects potential for awareness. The activity is a metaphor relating two contexts, the actual world of the child as controller of events and the fictitious world in which events have control. The relationship is a dialectical one of controlling and being controlled. The experience is the dialectic. It is this act of both contriving and submitting to a *metaphorical* context that gives symbolic play and drama, and indeed all art forms, a richness and intensity that sharpens awareness.[9] Vygotsky makes the point that 'the child weeps in play as a patient, but revels as a player'.[10] It is this juxtaposition of two affects, of the fictitious world and the actual world, that invites heightened attention rather than the total absorption as in weeping in real life.

But heightened attention to what? It seems to me that we cannot discuss the possibility of awareness without attempting to specify what is being perceived. *Self-awareness* supplies an answer, but we perhaps could be more precise. I prefer to talk about the MEANING of the experience for it is the dialectic between the *self* and the *fictitious context* that gives the experience meaning. Thus any perception is of 'the-self-in-the-fiction'. The participant is not aware of some general self, but of a particular self in a unique relationship. That relationship is the meaning of the experience. But let us give this problem the detailed examination it deserves.

3 Meaning in symbolic play and dramatic playing

Vygotsky[11] has pointed out that play is a step in the direction of abstract thinking, where the meaning created is something other than the actions and objects present in the child's immediate field of perception. Let us picture two three year old children playing at riding a horse. One, astride a stick, is dashing in mad circles around the garden. The other, perched on a high kitchen stool is jogging up and down on it. In these examples, the meaning is to do with horses; the objects and actions are a stick and a stool and running and jogging. Vygotsky writes 'In play, action is subordinate to meaning, but in real life, of course, action dominates over meaning'.[12] It seems clear then that one of the purposes of play is seeking of meaning. It will be useful here to analyse further the factors that might contribute to the meaning created by the two children in the illustration.

Although both children might well describe what they are doing as 'playing horses', in fact, their experiences are significantly different from each other. The aspect abstracted by the first child (running around in circles) is one of speed and/or direction, the second child (on the kitchen stool) has abstracted height and/or being jogged. The meaning created might then be tabled like this:

	Child A	Child B
Context	Horse	Horse
Abstraction	Speed/direction	Height/jogging
The action and object employed	Running astride stick	Jogging on kitchen stool

But this is only half the picture. Something has given the two children the energy to set up these actions. There is an affective, motivating factor which brings another dimension to the meaning. The abstraction on the second line of the above diagram we will call the 'objective' aspect of the meaning in order to distinguish it from this second source of meaning, which we will term 'subjective'. Let us confine ourselves, for the time being, to child **A**. What are some of the possible range of feelings that might have prompted the 'running astride a stick' action?

Child A's motives

I like the sensation of riding a horse
I like to ride a horse at speed
I would like to be a fast horse
I'm a cowboy on TV
I would like to ride away
I am scared of horses
....
I like rushing around
I like showing off
Teacher says I am a fast runner
I'm like my dad
I know it's really bedtime

Any one of these motives or combination of them may give the impetus to the playing. A more definite meaning is often implied in the motives as I have described them, for example, 'I like rushing around' may imply a feeling of 'it is *exhilarating* to rush around', 'it is *joyful* to rush around' or the more ambivalent 'I'm a bit *nervous* about it but I think I like doing it'. On the other hand, 'I'm like my dad' may imply more than that he has a horse-riding father; it may more specifically imply a feeling of 'dad is *powerful*', 'dad is *fun*', 'dad is *important*' or 'dad is *frightening*'. Note that I have described these implications as 'feelings of'. In other words they are 'felt values' given to whatever the context is. It is these felt values that contribute to the child's subjective meaning in playing and are a central feature of the activity of drama.

Child **A**'s subjective meaning, then, may stem, say, from a combination of the following felt values:

1 It is fun to ride a horse at speed
....
2 It feels important to be like dad
3 It feels risky but exciting to carry on, although it's bedtime

} Subjective meaning

Notice the dotted line in each of the two lists. I have classified the motives and values into two kinds. Above the line are those motives where the selection of 'horse' as the topic is highly relevant, whereas below the line alternative actions and objectives might have served the purpose just as well. We have then a greater degree of interdependence in some cases between the subjective and objective meanings. For instance: 'I like rushing around', does not *necessarily* require that he be 'riding a horse', compared with, 'I'm a TV cowboy'. On the other hand, 'I know it's really bedtime', is simply using horse-riding as a pretext. This becomes important later in discussing dramatic activity. Let us see what child **A**'s diagram will look like with a few subjective meanings added.

Child A

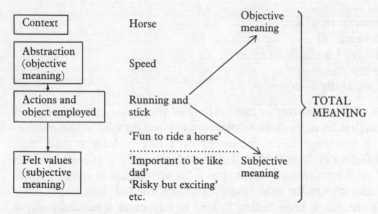

Notice how the action and object, although subordinated, as Vygotsky suggests, nevertheless control the meaning both in its subjective and objective aspects. For suppose that child **A** who 'wants to ride a horse at speed' is confined (because it's raining outside, poor chap!) to child **B**'s kitchen stool, that particular object is certainly going to restrict his capacity for 'speed' experience. Similarly, his drive to be like dad may be somewhat thwarted if the new physical conditions (the kitchen) do not have 'dad' associations for him.

We seem to have established so far that symbolic play is concerned with creating meaning that is a variable mixture between subjective and objective. The meaning is both controlled by and freed from the action and objects.

But I still haven't answered the question posed at the end of the previous section. Although I have attempted to outline a model to explain the way meaning evolves in symbolic play, I still have to relate this to the claim that the child is experiencing a 'heightened awareness'. In what way is the child aware of the meaning that is created? Certainly the meaning accessible to our hypothetical child will have but a slender connection with the examples given above. They are merely theoretical, hypothetical samples which are not describing a play activity, but the author's *notion* of a play activity. And the notion of a play activity is expressed in a written, discursive form that has nothing to do with play. Thus although a reasonable interpretation of a particular playing activity might be that: 'She is taking a long time undressing her doll because she wants to delay going off to bed herself', the meaning for the child herself *lies within the action and the images in her head*. Greater awareness therefore implies, to use Bruner's[13] terminology, an enactive and iconic knowing not amenable to verbal or other symbolic explicitness. To put it crudely, she understands what her fingers tell her. If there is some kind of change, it is a differentiated understanding at an intuitive level, which may or may not result in her recognising her own true motives. The 'discovery' learning may be no more than a reinforcement of what she already knew about the order in which clothes come off!

Which brings us a bit nearer to a discussion of some of the ways in which dramatic playing moves away from symbolic play. So far, by selecting the dimension of quality, awareness and meaning we have been able to treat the two activities as if they were the same, but whereas one might be impressed with the potential within a self-initiated playing activity for a particular pre-school child's growth in intuitive understanding, it surely cannot be that dramatic playing in school is simply a perpetuation of child play. Many play theorists, Vygotsky included, argue that, developmentally, the older school child does not require this action-based activity. So let use examine what dimensions we have to consider when we look at educational drama as an activity apart from play, still confining the discussion here to the orientation I have called dramatic playing.

Dramatic playing

(a) Appropriateness, integrity and collectivity

We have seen in our hypothetical illustrations of symbolic play that the relationship between subjective and objective meanings may vary according to the degree to which it is important to the child to imitate the external world. Thus a child proving to himself what a good car driver he is would be likely to give more attention to physical detail than an 'escaping robber' who happens to have seized a car for his getaway. This variable emphasis on accuracy of representation is found, of course, in drama too. In the early days of drama teaching we used to think that accurate simulation was a top priority; we failed to recognise that it depends on the *meaning* of the experience. Thus one might find a class enacting a story about body snatchers whose divided fears between the imminence of the law and the supernatural are such that they fail to take the right body, simply using *token* gestures to represent digging with spades, as compared with another class who were in role as expert gardeners teaching the new apprentices. Both forms of action could be considered appropriate.

On the other hand, suppose one of the boys who elected to role-play a policeman arriving on the scene, did so with a 'mock' seriousness or an openly flippant attitude, then in so far as this runs counter to the meaning of the experience as it is understood by the rest of the class, you could say that his behaviour was inappropriate. Thus in drama it is the *collective* meaning that dictates appropriateness. Similarly, if the second class had pre-decided that the 'apprentices' were totally committed to learning the trade and one of them clearly shows from his behaviour that he could not care less, his contribution too could be described as inappropriate, for in terms of the drama he is breaking the agreed rules.

Could the two boys' behaviour also be described as lacking in integrity? On the surface yes, but supposing they do not know what their behaviour is communicating – like 'Smiler' in Wesker's *Chips with everything*, whose compulsive smile was always misinterpreted by his superiors as disrespect; or supposing they are intellectually incapable of grasping the rules; or emotionally frustrated at failing to find the rules credible; or, in the case of the apprentice gardener, wishing to break the agreed rules in order to move the drama on? One of the difficulties for a teacher of drama is deciding the extent the above types of inappropriate behaviour should be tolerated and contained by the drama, because the recalcitrant individual is, by his own light, behaving with integrity.

Such tolerance may invite drama that is therapeutically beneficial for the individual, but in terms of the drama and education, the work for the group may become undermined. And here, of course, in speaking of the activity as 'work' we have moved away from playing. Indeed in playing, connotations of wish fulfilment and personal satisfaction, rather than appropriateness may prevail. But in the reference to 'the work' there is a hint that some created group entity exists. This links with Dearden's comments about the non-seriousness of play. It is significant that when he talks of the arts, he feels compelled to qualify his position:

> Before leaving the question of what play is, however, something ought to be said about an important class of activities which on the face of it do satisfy the criteria suggested, yet which we should not call 'play'. These activities are the various arts and sciences when they are pursued quite apart from any obvious applications which they may have to the serious business of living. On the face of it, therefore, they could well be non-serious, but a closer look shows this not to be so. Though they often do give satisfaction to those who pursue them, the reason for pursuing them as worthwhile in themselves is rather that they seek to establish or to create something of objective value, whether this is some mathematical proof, scientific law or object of aesthetic merit. They are to be assessed not primarily by the satisfactions which they give, but by impersonal criteria of truth and of merit. Furthermore, though not themselves dictated either by prudence or by obligation, and hence not in that sense serious, they do have a very intimate connection with the serious in that they explore aspects of the conception of ourselves and of our situation which is the background against which our objective evaluations of seriousness are made. They are concerned with the various sorts of 'reality' which are presupposed in asserting the validity of all such judgements. The similarity of these activities to play, therefore, is no more than apparent.[14]

Now we may not feel that drama of the dramatic playing kind is in the same class as a work of art. Nevertheless I maintain there is an important shift from playing to dramatic playing that qualifies the latter for consideration in terms of 'the impersonal criteria of truth and merit'. Significance in drama in schools should not be confined to personal satisfactions but the meaning of what is created should have some kind of universal application.

The recognition of universality of an experience suggests a generalising, conceptualising requirement of the participant that goes beyond the intuitive, discovery learning of play (beyond, but not independent, let me emphasise). It also implies teacher intervention. We are now moving into an educational process where teacher expertise is crucial if the activity is to be seen as more than 'just playing'. I shall now proceed to discuss the teacher's function in so far as it affects the structure of the experience.

(b) Structure[15]

It is perhaps in terms of structure that dramatic playing differs fundamentally from symbolic play. Geoff Gillham[16] has usefully coined the phrases: 'the play for the teacher' and 'the play for the children' as a way of describing the double negotiation that goes on between the children's goals and the teacher's educational objectives. In other words the meaning which the teacher wants to draw out from a context is not necessarily the meaning immediately available to the children themselves. Thus a teacher's responsibility, if drama is to be used as a medium for learning, is to structure the experience so that learning can take place. But he must find a balance between 'his play' and 'theirs'. An example for me a short while ago occurred when a group of adolescents chose to make a play about a drug-ring. Now I immediately structured into that dramatic context an exploration of how entering this kind of legally and morally doubtful commitment can conflict with the way one might normally wish to be open in one's relationship with close friends and family: the adolescents experienced their own domestic 'cover-up' as a lead into but, more importantly, as a microcosm of the larger scale 'cover-up' they had chosen to be involved in. They were still able to pursue 'the play for them' the drug-ring activity, but it was now coloured by the more universal reference to do with deception etc. On the other hand, if a teacher gets the balance wrong, very little can be learned. When I worked, a week earlier, with a class of first year secondary children who chose 'killing scientists', I so loaded the intellectual requirement of 'my play' with the problem of assessing which invention has done most harm to mankind, there was a danger that the only one having the dramatic experience was the teacher!

Unless the teacher can 'fold in' his meanings into the children's meanings, nothing worthwhile will happen. The chief means at his disposal are structural. We have earlier established that a quality distinguishing symbolic play and dramatic playing is the spontaneity that is released by the mutual negotiation of rules. I will now argue another paradox: that because the teacher takes a large measure of responsibility for structure, dramatic playing undergoes a tightening of form that brings the activity *structurally nearer to games than to symbolic playing*.

The Dutch anthropologist, J. Huizinga,[17] makes the following interesting point about games. He says they demand 'order' and their elements, which also belong to aesthetics, are 'tension, poise, balance, contrast, variation, solution, resolution, etc.'[18] But these are the very elements of theatrical form. Thus it can be argued that as dramatic playing moves in structure nearer to a game, so it is also nearer to theatrical form. Indeed, in so far as it is the business of the playwright to create tension and contrast – and I would add *focus*, for it is the focus that defines the rule – so it is the business of the teacher to negotiate these elements with the children.

In summary, the teacher's function in drama is to 'fold in' a level of meaning above, beyond, wider than or deeper than the level readily accessible to the class themselves. One of the most effective ways he has of doing this is to tighten the inner structure while retaining the spontaneous existential quality or mode of the 'play for them', thus achieving a quality of living through within a theatre form.

Learning in dramatic playing

This last section, while discussing potential learning from dramatic activity, will also be a kind of summary of what has gone before, for it is the preceding analysis that has guided me to certain conclusions about learning.

It seemed that symbolic play, a self-initiated activity, is a kind of 'standing outside' what one has already experienced in order to 'discover' what it means. Three kinds of understanding seem possible: an intuitive grasp of facts, a development of skills and a recall of feeling about something. In our earlier illustration of the boy riding a stick, he could be, for example (a) reminding himself of what he knows about horses, (b) practising running fast in a circle, or (c) testing his attitude to his father. The *meaning* of the experience is a compound of the child's attitude/physical running/horse context any aspect of which may be emphasised at any one moment, but each is coloured by the others. The meaning then is unique to a particular feeling/action/mental imagery experience. This it seems to me is a reasonable description of the intuitive thinking process of symbolic play. Theorists like Piaget see this as an egocentric form of thinking, distorting reality. Others, like Smilansky,[19] for example, perceive it as a process of imitating reality. We have noticed earlier in this chapter that there appears to be a variable dependence on accurate representation of the objective world.

Now if we move away from play towards dramatic playing, an

educational arena which a teacher must enter, how does this affect the natural thinking process of symbolic play? A great deal of play reinforces what a child already knows. A drama teacher may help a child to new knowledge by offering a new context or by giving practice in new skills, but I suggest that the most significant change in understanding through drama must be at the subjective level of feeling. By feeling I do not imply untethered emotion, but as mentioned earlier in this chapter, a 'feeling-value', i.e. a feeling tied to judgement. Piaget states it quite dramatically:

> We do not love without seeking to understand, and we do not even hate without a subtle sense of judgement.[20]

It is in this area of feeling-value, or attitude, that a drama teacher's responsibility lies when he is negotiating meaning. Whatever the topic i.e. the context for the drama, the teacher is concerned with refining in some way the feeling-judgement the children bring to it. The refining may take the form of a clarification, a broadening, a breaking of stereotyped thinking, a challenging of prejudice, a questioning of assumptions, making the implicit explicit, seeing something in a new light. Thus it may be that as a direct result of a drama experience, some children in a class might for the first time realise that being an historian is like being a detective or that scientists' persistence in examining what is natural is a way of ignoring what is supernatural, or that motherhood is a mixture of joy and pain or that freedom has limitations or that policemen are real people with houses and families or that heroes are not without blemishes, – and so on.

Differentiated understanding then implies that whatever feeling appraisal a child brings to a dramatic metaphor (unless what he brings is lacking in integrity in which case drama cannot even start for him) his judgement becomes modified in some way by the dramatic experience. But does differentiated understanding imply an explicit generalisation as listed in the previous paragraph? For if it does it means an intellectual shift, as Bruner[21] puts it, from the left hand to the right hand. Is this the learning objective in drama to reach cognitive explicitness, to see the particular action of the drama experience as an instance of a broader category, something labelled and classified? Does the pupil literally say to himself: 'Ah! I now know not to include heroes in a category of perfection'?

The answer it seems to me is both yes and no – more no than yes! To objectify experience is what we do in most subjects of the curriculum. It is an important way of handling knowledge. It seems to me therefore it is of educational value to identify what one has learnt through drama in these objective terms that can, at least partially, make one's experience available to others and for one's own intellectual recall.

It is this 'partially' that challenges that conclusion, for we have to consider to what extent the limitations of abstracting only what can be made verbally explicit have in reality removed the experience. The meaning embodied in the drama experience is a personal meaning. A child may conclude that being an historian is like being a detective, but it is *himself in that conclusion* that is the meaning. The statements about historians, scientists, motherhood, policemen and heroes are only objective out of context. Implied in their meaning is the feeling of the child who makes the discovery. It is uniquely his knowledge. The initiative process that we discussed in symbolic play essentially retains its power in drama. I believe it may be useful for children of all ages to engage in an intellectual explanation of an experience, but it is those meanings that are not amenable to a discursive form of communication that give differentiated understanding through the dramatic art form its essential identity. Although a participant or an observer may, as I have done above, intellectually pinpoint a particular attitude or feeling appraisal, such a labelling has to be seen as a recognition of a door to be opened to things that cannot be labelled. But it is my view that unless the teacher, at least, recognises which door he is trying to open, in other words unless he goes through some labelling process, he may simply allow drama to do what play does most of the time: reinforce what the child already knows – the meanings beyond the door do not become available.

Which brings me to the aspect of the activity that could be described as the principal feature of dramatic playing: the symbolisation process.[22] I emphasise *process* to distinguish from the way Piaget and the Schools Council Drama (Secondary) Project use the word symbolic. They both use symbol or symbolic to refer to an action that represents something else. This perfectly valid use, however, is not particularly helpful for describing those significant moments in drama when there is an enriching of meaning – when, to use the same metaphor, the children 'go through the door'. It is a fascinating feature of educational drama work that, although it may be necessary as I have suggested for the teacher to identify the door with an intellectual label, once identified, it is non-intellectual theatrical symbol with its potential for crystallising as opposed to conceptualising meaning, that will take the children through. Indeed perhaps this is one of the marks of the good drama teacher, that he can both identify the door and then work the magic – thus employing two entirely different thinking processes.

Dramatic playing, in its most pedestrian moments, will involve actions and objects that have for the participants just a single, collective, unidimensional, functional meaning; in its most heightened moments the actions and objects will accrue for the participants many layered, personal as well as collective, non-functional as well as functional meanings. Put crudely, the children will have gone through the door. It is not my place here to discuss how this might be done, but to draw attention to its significance for learning. In the discussion on structure, I tried to establish that it is the teacher's responsibility to change the form of symbolic play by injecting a tightness of structure, employing such basic theatrical devices as focus, tension and contrast. I will now add to this list the making available of symbols. A teacher can only *make available*. He cannot guarantee that a particular symbolic action or object is going to resonate meanings for the participants. He can do no more than be sensitive to the potential.

Mary Warnock, in summarising Kant's view of imagination, claims that:

> What we appreciate or create in the highest art, is a symbol of something that is forever beyond it.[23]

This, then, is the other *partial* answer to the overall picture of learning through dramatic playing.

Conclusion

The reader may have wondered why I chose to confine my discussion to just one aspect of drama in schools – I have neglected drama towards performance and drama training in skills. I hope I have now made it clear that in terms of learning potential, dramatic playing has the greatest educational value. Its strengths, it seems to me, lie in the unique relationship it offers in combining theatrical structure (not outer shape, of course) and a quality of spontaneous living that belong to both symbolic play and to games.

The activity of dramatic playing. In Day C, Norman J (eds) *Issues in educational drama*, Falmer Press, 1983. (This article was written much earlier than the publication date, probably in 1978.) Also write to:

Malcolm Clarkson, Falmer Press, Falmer House, Barcombe Cross,
Lewes, Sussex.

References

1 McGregor L, Tate M, Robinson K 1977 *Learning through drama*,
  Schools Council Drama Teaching Project (10–16). Heinemann.
2 Bolton G M 1978 The concept of 'showing' in children's dramatic
  activity. *Young Drama*, **6**(3): 97–101. (The reader may refer to
  this for further discussion on the relationship between dramatic
  playing and performance.)
3 Cook C H 1917 *The play-way*. Heinemann.
4 Slade P 1954 *Child drama*. University of London Press.
5 Vygotsky L S 1976 Play and its role in the mental development of
  the child. In Bruner J S *et al. Play: its role in development and
  evolution*, Penguin Educational, pp. 537–54.
6 Dearden R F 1967 The concept of play. In Peter R S (ed) *The
  concept of education*. Routledge and Kegan Paul.
7 Piaget J 1972 *Play, dreams and imitation in childhood*. Routledge
  and Kegan Paul.
8 Vygotsky L S op. cit., p. 543.
9 Bolton G M 1976 Drama as metaphor. *Young Drama*, **4**(2): 43–7.
  (For discussion of the metaphorical nature of drama and its
  implications for teaching.)
10 Vygotsky L S op. cit., p. 549.
11 Vygotsky L S ibid.
12 Vygotsky L S ibid., p 551.
13 Bruner J S 1974 *Beyond the information given*. Allen and Unwin.
14 Dearden R F op. cit. p. 85.
15 See Bolton G M 1979 *Towards a theory of drama in education*.
  Longman.
16 Gillham G 1974 Report on Condercum School Project by Live
  Theatre. Unpublished.
17 Huizinga J 1949 *Home Ludens*. John Wiley, 1970 (first English).
18 Huizinga J ibid., p 29.
19 Smilansky S 1968 *The effects of sociodramatic play on disadvantaged
  pre-school children*. John Wiley.
20 Piaget J op. cit., p 207.
21 Bruner J S 1962 *On knowing: essays for the left hand*. Harvard
  University Press.

22 Bolton G M 1978 The process of symbolisation in improvised drama. *Young Drama*, **6**(3). (For further discussion of symbolisation.)
23 Warnock M 1976 *Imagination*. Faber, p 63.

Drama in education: learning medium or arts process?

The occasion for the reading of this paper (1982) was the second of a series of major annual conferences inaugurated by NATD. The first address, given the year before, had been published as 'Heathcote at the National'.

Things are happening in the drama educational world. The alarm is being sounded. A call to arms! The battle cry can be heard from Chichester to Exeter. Forces are gathering; manoeuvres are under way. At last a bit of excitement. After all these dreary years of Schools Council eclecticism and blandness, people are taking sides, declaring loyalties, waving banners. And somewhere in the middle of the battle-field, trying to run hard to get out of the way but not sure which way to run for safety is *me*. But swords are not very sharp and the war cries are perhaps not so much a threat as an invitation to join the ranks. However, I want to stay where I am, and this paper is to be a justification for trying to be loyal to both camps at the same time while denying the prerogative of one over the other. Let me paint the scene of battle.

John Fines, in addressing a group of teacher-trainers in September, speaking with a strength of conviction that sent them all scribbling in their note-books, pronounced, '"As-if" is possible wherever you go in education, and . . .', he added with a 'mock' cutting glance in my direction, 'you do not have to put the word *drama* in it'. As an historian who has discovered the 'as-if' game can be played successfully in the classroom when the teacher wants children to get to grips with people's attitudes behind historical events, Dr Fines with his colleague Ray Verrier[1] has made a strong case for the use of 'dramatic method'. He knows that the educational value of his method is unchallengeable and is both astonished and disapproving of the move I have been making in recent years towards emphasising the importance of dramatic form. He certainly thinks that my attempt to analyse form is a waste of time. And he would be shocked at my recent recommendation that all teachers of drama should be trained in theatre arts.

But it has been my turn to be astonished. As a postscript to a paper I read at an Exeter conference on Aesthetics last summer, Malcolm Ross[2] seems to be holding me responsible for all that's wrong with drama. He condemns my practical work on the grounds that it is over-emotional, manipulative, thematically-centred and anti-theatre. In respect of the latter he writes:

> Many drama teachers take their lessons and inspiration from the theatre (the writings of Brook and Grotowski for example) rather than from educational sources – and with drama in education in such difficulties they'd probably be right to go on doing so. It's certainly high time the wrangle between theatre and drama was wound up. Drama in education is a doomed mutant unless it can draw life from the theatre. (p. 152)

It is difficult to grasp how Malcolm Ross can argue the above point in opposition to my paper which includes the following assertion:

> The history of drama in education in this country had polarised between the two camps, between what was called 'creative' or 'child' drama and 'performance' . . . It seems to me that these factions, in emphasising differences at a peripheral level of skills, are failing to recognise the common ground between them. Indeed I would like to argue that most drama teachers of whatever persuasion are at a fundamental level using the same dramatic form. The 'clay' of drama is the same for the teacher, the pupil, the playwright, the director and the actor . . . Regrettably we do not train our teachers to know the basic feel of that clay and yet this is what they should be passing on to their pupils – the essence of dramatic form. (p. 142)

Does this really seem that I am anti-theatre? But he also suggests that I am manipulative (yes I agree and I have never claimed otherwise), too concerned with issues and themes (I would have thought I am in good company here – many playwrights and directors share such a concern) and that my work invites emotionally reactive (to use his terminology) rather than reflexive behaviour (I need to answer this one at length) and also that I work at the wrong pace! Let us look further at what he says:

> I feel drama in education is often too dominated by concern with themes and topics to the neglect of medium control; is too extravagant and excitable, often on account of some commitment by the drama teacher to giving the children a good (i.e. 'hot') time in every single lesson . . . Drama in my view needs to be much cooler, and the work much more respectful of the intensely complex nature of the medium. It needs to run more slowly and temperately. (p. 149)

I never thought the day would come when I could be accused of working too fast! It is ironical that the most common complaint I receive from teachers is that they bite their finger nails down to the quick in their frustration at the diffident, exploratory, reflective legato of my work with children. They have also often expressed exasperated concern at the lack of excitement in the work. Indeed, taking the sensation out of what appears to be a sensational topic is one of the things I might be considered to be good at! For many years my concern has been to help children find awe in the ordinary.

So does Malcolm Ross know anything at all about my work and the kind of educational drama I stand for? I cannot think that if he has come into contact with it he has understood it. And yet he does have before him the paper I read in which I described a class of fourteen year old Manchester boys choosing the topic of 'the city of Manchester preparing for a nuclear holocaust' which, in terms of 'ordinariness' centred on things like 'how deep will the air-raid shelter have to be?' and the victims of radiation years later being spoon-fed by a nurse. Malcolm Ross, in his postscript also gives a practical illustration from his own teaching, showing us how drama *ought* to be handled. He works with a group of two, making the point that three people, two participants and an observer, make an ideal grouping. I cannot think, however, that his particular example helps him to make the contrast with my work that he wishes to underline. For he exercises the teacher's right as manipulator by offering the group a script (*Dr Faustus*). And the central idea of the work, using the Helen of Troy scene, revolves round the notion of 'intercourse with the dead' (his words). Is this not a *theme* and is not intercourse with the dead a wee bit *sensational*?

But no doubt he would argue that whereas his group's work was emotionally cool, mine was not. He seems to be able to detect that whereas in my work the participants have emotions which are bad, in his work they have something much superior – *feelings* which are, of course, good. To use his terminology my classes respond reactively, his reflexively. I have looked up what he means by reactive behaviour. In his book, *The creative arts*,[3] he gives a list of examples of such behaviour:

> Reactive expression releases energy. Reactive expression serves to re-
> duce an uncomfortable state of arousal to a more tolerable level. We
> all respond reactively to situations, to frustrations, anger, anxiety,
> disappointment, fear, sudden surprise. We lash out physically and
> verbally, we run away, we run amok, we gasp, we groan, we roar with
> delight or rage, we flash our eyes, raise our voice, wring our hands,
> hide the face we have lost or are in danger of losing. (p. 41)

Is this what Ross thinks goes on in my lessons? But the theory he has
bound himself to does not seem to recognise the importance of any kind
of spontaneous emotional response. I would like to know how in his
session on *Faustus* he managed to avoid it for it seems to me that far
from avoiding it he *used* it. Before the group of three worked on the
text they 'doodled' using their bodies experimentally in space. He explains as follows:

> I watched and listened and helped them select what turned out to be
> the 'holding form' for the rest of the day's work. This was a simple
> encounter situation in which the girl moved towards the man who
> prepared to embrace her only to find her walk on 'through' the em-
> brace. The event occurred fortuitously and was selected from much
> else on the grounds that both actors and observer sensed its dramatic
> quality and possibilities. (p. 151)

I would like to know how they can 'fortuitously' experience a
thwarted embrace without an emotional response of something like frustration, embarrassment or amusement. It seems to me that such for-
tuitous occurrences give a drama lesson its richness. It is the excitement
of that shared moment that can be harnessed and recaptured when they
turn to the text – surely a process of working in drama that we learnt
at our mother's knee. Why does Malcolm Ross need to try to establish
his method as an alternative way of working? Any teacher who has an
enlightened approach will use this among many approaches.

I find a lot of what he has to say just balderdash. Which is a pity,
because underneath it all I have some respect for what Malcolm is trying
to say. John Fines, who does know my work well, its strengths and its
weaknesses, has expressed alarm because he is afraid I am in danger of
identifying too closely with the Ross-type philosophy of arts education.
I can respect John Fines' challenge and wish to take it seriously. I want
to take Malcolm Ross seriously, but I think I feel insulted by his post-

script to my paper because he has chosen to ignore one of the threads of my argument which was to point out that in drama in school (and here I am quoting from the last line of my paper): 'At its most profound, through the art form, our deepest levels may be touched as we engage with what is outside ourselves' (p. 147). Indeed, you would not know from Ross's criticism of my paper that for most of it I was attempting to establish the importance of dramatic form. What he does not like, of course, is that I also state quite categorically that for me good education is what I am interested in first and foremost. Whether it is conceivable to see art and learning as compatible is something I propose to take up now.

This is a huge topic and because so much of the Ross postscript is concerned with quality of feeling, I have decided to look at the relation between Art and Learning through the particular focus of Emotion. I shall outline a model which challenges Ross's theory not by finding some logical flaw in it – I am not good at that – but by posing an alternative model which draws heavily on what I see happens when children participate in drama. I cannot offer it as evidence only as a hypothesis.

One of Ross's major worries has been that drama in schools operates at an excitement level which can at best be unproductive. (It is a pity, I think, that the only drama lesson described by Robert Witkin in *Intelligence of feeling*[4] was one that got out of hand.) However, I wish to argue that built in to the dramatic mode are a number of safety valves which are worthy of our detailed attention.

I have for some years now been gnawing at the notion of distinct kinds of acting behaviour and on my visit to Australia three years ago I tried out a paper rather weirdly titled 'Emotion in the dramatic process – is it an adjective or a verb?'[5] [See p. 100] (I have not been invited back to Australia!) Only recently have I come across – or rather, it would be more accurate to say that Ken Robinson[6] put me in the direction of an author, Alan Tormey,[7] who also uses a grammatical analogy, and although he is a philosopher he uses a number of references to the acting process in order to illumine his elegantly argued thesis on the nature of *expression*. His thesis is that there is a double valence to behaviour – expressive behaviour *and* representational behaviour. Expressive behaviour implies a state of emotional arousal; representational behaviour does not – it merely 'detaches the surface of expressive behaviour'. Both are present in the actor simultaneously.

Before adapting his thesis to my own ends I need to explain what he means by expression. As I intend to make it the very basis of my dramatic model, we need to understand the precise way in which it is being

used. Expressive behaviour is verbal or non-verbal. It points simultaneously in two directions: towards some state of emotional arousal in
the person (say, anger or wonder or pleasure); and towards what he calls
an intentional object, something outside the person to which the state
of arousal is prepositionally related. (I am angry *over* an act of injustice
or I wonder *at* the sight of Niagara Falls or I am pleased *with* my garden). We might well be inclined to call this intentional object the *context*
of the emotional arousal for it is the cognitive relationship with a particular context that gives the emotion its particular characteristics.
There is really no such experience of an emotion called anger – there
is only *my* anger, in *this* context, on *this* particular occasion. Notice also
that expressive behaviour in this definition does not distinguish vol-
untary and involuntary behaviour. If I blush with embarrassment at
being caught in a lie, my response is just as expressive as if I complain
to a neighbour about a noisy dog. Both entail a subjective-objective relationship. Expressive behaviours then by this definition are very common, occurring from minute to minute within our day.

Now a further dimension which is critical to this thesis, is the *mode*
of the expression. This will obviously vary according to whether what
is occurring is entirely for oneself (subjective) or whether it involves
someone else. Angrily banging the door to when my son has left it open
for the umpteenth time is different from complaining to him about it
over lunch. Both are expressive, but quite different in form. On the
other hand the action of banging that door to can itself have two importantly distinct orientations. If I angrily bang that door long after my
son has departed, the experience is one kind of expression, but if I was
to bang it knowing full well he would hear it, that is a different mode
of expression. Although the action is the same the *intention* is different.

A few weeks ago my wife and I were leaning over a parapet looking
down onto a jetty where a deep-sea diver was getting into his skins in
order to untangle some rope which had got caught underneath a moored
fishing vessel due to depart. The diver had obviously been 'called in'
to solve the problem. He looked none too happy and gave a great sigh.
A moment or so later he suddenly caught sight of us watching – and
he gave another great sigh. But this one was different, for having been
absorbed in what he was doing, he suddenly saw himself as an *object*
of our attention. He responded accordingly and 'placed' his sigh in our
direction. It was a calculated, 'public' action, a 'depicted' or 'performed'
sigh. He had moved from subjectively experiencing to objectively representing. I do not know whether it was the 'same' sigh in physical
terms, whether for instance it involved the same volume of breath ex-

halation, but I do know that the intention and effort and therefore the *meaning* had changed. I want to suggest that whereas the spontaneous, private first sigh was *occurring*, the second calculated public sigh was descriptive. The first was expressive of his state of experiencing, to use a grammatical analogy, a verb; the second was *descriptive* of his state of experiencing, an adjective. The first was fluid and not easy to recapture; the second was static, conventional and accessible to repetition.

Was the second sigh phony? In one way it was not because it represented a state of feeling that he was actually experiencing, but there nevertheless was an element of deception in that he was pretending the sigh was spontaneous, experiential, subjective. It was in fact adjectival – demonstrating *how* he felt – but he wanted us to believe in it as a verb, a spontaneous occurrence. It was an instance of contrived spontaneity. When I bang the door in my son's hearing, it may be purely subjective because I am oblivious he is there; on the other hand I may be doing it knowing he is there and in all honesty demonstrating my anger to him; I may, however, intend to demonstrate but want him to believe it was my subjective reaction, as if I did not realise he was there – thus another example of contrived spontaneity. Only in acting is contrived spontaneity legitimised and seen as having integrity.

The actor offers us the adjective – and we, the audience, see the action as a verb, as someone's experiencing. But it is the character's verb, not the actor's, for dramatic behaviour is holding two worlds in one's head at the same time, what Augusto Boal[8] calls 'metaxis', a continual change of state, a dialectic between the actual and the fictitious. In actuality the actor adopts the demonstrating or describing mode, but he portrays or depicts the character's spontaneous experiencing.

In a sense, the art of acting is the art of contrived spontaneity, but there is a related characteristic which has repercussions for the drama teacher. Although I as a father may have feigned spontaneity, at least it was an expression of my anger; I *was* feeling angry. Now for the actor there is a critical difference: he is not angry; he is not *expressing* anger; he is portraying the character's expression of anger. The character's actions, not the actor's, imply some emotional disturbance in relation to some object in the character's fictitious world. It is Lear who is raging at the storm, not the actor. The *substance* of the actor's expression is his concern with effectiveness in representing Lear-raging-at-a-storm. But the *mode* of that expression is, like the second sigh, adjectival. The actor is seeing himself as an object of an audience's attention; he 'places' his presentation in their direction; his presentation is static rather than fluid; accessible to repetition, descriptive rather than experiential and, we can now add, in Tormey's terms the actor's behaviour is *not expressive* because the substance of what is being communicated to the audience is not expressive of the actor's ongoing emotional state. Tormey does not intend this conclusion should diminish the actor's achievement, rather the reverse, for as we shall see he wishes to make the point that all art is detached from expressive behaviour in the way it has been defined. This is not its weakness but its strength. For one of the features of expression is that some aspects of the subjective experience remain hidden from the observer. There is always a subjective aspect of my experiencing which I cannot communicate when I feel angry, sad or satisfied about something. In art, Tormey argues, there is nothing hidden; there is no inner consciousness that is not available to the observer. It is all there – on the canvas, in the musical rendering, on the stage – provided the observer is sensitive enough to respond to it. A play expresses, not the actor's or the playwright's emotional state. It expresses itself. Furthermore, what one character expresses is but one property of a complex whole. As Tormey puts it:

> We may, given the circumstances of the action of the drama, be justifiably certain that the cries of the protagonist are an expression of remorse, but this leaves unanswered the question of the expressive properties of the *play*. The drama itself may project pity, horror or contempt towards the remorse of the protagonist. (p. 139)

Thus what a play is about may be different from and even contradict a character's expressive behaviour.

On the basis of this theory as I have so far presented it, actor-training is concerned with developing skill in representation, a process of describing a character's emotional state. A director's responsibility lies beyond that to the overall meaning of the thing created, the play itself. The play must effectively express its own meaning.

Now what are the implications here for educationalists? Given the view that Malcolm Ross holds that drama is a performing art so that what is created must ultimately be shared with an audience, '. . . where interaction between maker and audience is part of the expressive process itself, the audience being integral to the medium',[9] one can perhaps understand how this allows him to see dramatic action as detached from emotion, for according to this model acting is a matter of demonstrating feeling not suffering it. When he talks of a 'cool' approach, emotion becomes some past reference point, projected through the medium of the character's gestures and words. When he talks of concentrating on the medium itself he means the technical craft of depictment and the director's overview of what is being communicated. He closes his postscript with what really amounts to his credo:

> Above all we staked our work on the inherent, inexhaustible and sufficient interest of the *dramatic* problem. (p. 152)

And all this makes sense – provided one chooses to confine dramatic educational experience to this narrow view. I have made the point that in the postscript he does not really answer the central thrust of my chapter. The answer is he cannot. His view of drama is exclusive – there is no place for my conception of the subject.

For him, as for Tormey, an art product is about itself. And education in the arts, while putting one in touch with one's feelings, is not concerned with direct expression of them. Nor can it be concerned with learning about subject-matter. Such a pursuit is irrelevant if we are to let the art product 'speak for itself'. I find this persuasive. In using drama to get children to look at issues we may well be deflecting the child's attention from the arts process and indeed be failing him in his aesthetic education.

Arnaud Reid[10] attempts to define aesthetic attitude:

> What is called the 'aesthetic' attitude or interest in an object, is sometimes described as a 'disinterested interest'. This is intended to mean that the object is attended to, and in some sense 'enjoyed for itself', for its own sake', for the qualities it possesses in itself as apprehended, and arouses our attention and interest. It is called 'disinterested' not, of course, because we are uninterested, but because it excludes extraneous or irrelevant interests, such as the interest in increasing our factual knowledge, or improving us morally, or in making a good investment by buying a picture. Aesthetic interest might, incidentally, achieve some or all of these other things: but aesthetically speaking they are irrelevant.

This appears to put most of what we do in drama in schools in a most unfortunate light. After this no one is going to rally to John Fines' banner! If you have been using drama to teach Road Safety to your infants, or what it is like to carry the burden of responsibility to your juniors or corruption in society today to your CSE drama group you'd better write yourselves off as artistic failures and take up plumbing!

But hold on a minute. Let us at least look at what does go in the way many of us teach drama – we may find we are not as far astray as it appears. Let us begin by examining our practice, noting in particular those aspects which differ markedly from Malcolm Ross's views.

First of all let us take self-expression in Tormey's sense of the word. We do encourage children during drama actually to feel sad about something in the fiction, or to be pleased or curious or disappointed or magnanimous or frustrated or amused or even angry. These are not the raw emotions that worry Ross for dramatic activity by definition is reflexive – any emotional disturbance is projected through the 'as-if' and raw emotion is tempered. But it is also a subjective experience with some facet of the disturbance remaining hidden. It is the emotional engagement with something outside oneself, filtered through the make-believe that has such a powerful learning potential. For instance, the child who in the drama experiences, perhaps for the first time, the pain, the effort and the joy of standing up for himself and not giving in to his peers, and who finds that because he is labelled John Smith, Explorer and the others in the class fellow adventurers, has personal resources he did not know were there for John Smith, *schoolboy*, must go through that pain and triumph over peer pressure. Other aspects of the curriculum (literature, for example) might 'tell' him about those feelings, but in drama he 'engages' with them – in a way he cannot do in real life. Nor would he reach the same change in understanding if he were required in drama to 'depict', for depiction or description tends to convey what is already understood rather than open up new meanings. There is, however, a built in protection in the 'as-if', protection from the exigencies and immediate confrontations of the actual present. The effect is not necessarily to reduce or water-down the emotion, but to liberate it, so that John Smith may allow himself an emotional struggle he would not be prepared to cope with in the rawness of everyday living. Thus emotion in drama may be deeper, more intense than in 'real life', because it is safer.

Acting behaviour in this kind of work is experiential: it is the verb, not the adjective. In this it differs fundamentally from what the performer is doing. However, we need to modify our position here, for the way I have argued so far has suggested that the verb and adjective of expressive behaviour are mutually exclusive. This is not absolutely correct as we know, for instance, that certain actions can function as both without their external features changing – the sigh, for instance, was an example of this – but more importantly many instances of acting sustain a dialectic between the verb and the adjective.

I would like to put the point that performance for an audience *requires* description, while accepting that to varying degrees, varying in intensity, varying from actor to actor, from performance to performance, from style of play, from style of production, etc., etc., the actor may be expressing actual feelings. I would also like to claim that in drama work with children, whereas the nature of the work *requires* real feelings, it may also to varying degrees be descriptive. (Indeed because drama is social, a certain amount of describing must be going on – to *each other*.) That the expression of emotion is often qualified by this kind of dialectic is yet a further move away from the raw emotion of reactive behaviour.

Indeed many drama teachers have realised that where a topic is too 'near the bone' for a particular class – say, 'facing death' or 'street violence' or 'experiencing failure' – 'depiction' rather than a spontaneous improvisation may be both safer and more thoughtful.

One of the techniques used by drama teachers in recent years has been 'teacher-in-role', which Malcolm Ross sees as dangerously manipulative – like a teacher putting a stroke onto a child's painting. I can understand him seeing it that way as that is what it sometimes looks like. But I want to suggest that 'teacher-in-role' is no more manipulative than showing the children a painting or stimulating them with a story or inspiring them with music, for 'teacher-in-role' is equivalent to what Ross calls 'realised form'. Teacher is never *in* the experience – she is always in the descriptive mode which automatically puts the pupils in a *spectator* relationship to her contribution.[11] This provides yet another qualifying factor to the rawness of emotion. What the teacher does in her role is often very exciting for the children, but it is the excitement of a collective audience and collectively they can harness that excitement for their own actions, just as they would if teacher had read an exciting story.

And yet, of course, the purpose of 'teacher-in-role' is also to heighten the engagement of the children and direct interaction, too heavily handled by the teacher, can spill over the boundaries of fiction. But these occurrences are relatively rare. (I can recall two occasions – one some years ago when I with too much suddenness frightened a class of four year olds, and more recently with a group of Cleveland headteachers, I misjudged the distress level caused by a particularly strong use of teacher-in-role.)

To summarise, I have suggested that in children's drama a number of distancing processes are going on that protect children from reactive behaviours. One is that make-believe is essentially reflexive – I can channel my feelings *through* the role I am playing. The second is that it is never entirely experiential – there is in all dramatic playing at least an element of 'describing' or 'showing'. And thirdly, when 'teacher-in-role' is adopted, she is always 'describing', never experiencing with the children.

This may be fine as far as it goes, but I have avoided the apparently unanswerable challenge that we are depriving children of the aesthetic because so much concentration is on understanding not aesthetic form, but a drama's subject-matter. We busy ourselves with learning areas, objectives, concepts, generalisations and all the paraphernalia of educational respectability. Teachers of the other arts eschew such practice, for they know they are concerned with something different. Why is drama out of step?

I want now to suggest that we only appear to be out of step, for the whole practice of drama in schools is based on an assumption, using Arnaud Reid's definition of the term. It is an assumption made by the children, not the teacher. *The children's assumption is that the activity is 'for itself'.* Indeed if this were not the case no drama would ever get started, for it is this pleasure in making believe for its own sake that provides the critical motivation for doing it. Take it away and nothing can happen. This applies as much to the executive trainee, subjected to role-play simulation as to infants playing at witches. The executive must enjoy it for itself as he does other 'play' experiences such as cards, golf or fast cars. Teachers nowadays rarely talk about drama in this way, but even if they do not acknowledge the 'play' element in their drama work, they must at least subconsciously be catering for it. John Fines prizes this. He knows that drama has to have the fun of playing a game. When he was recently broached by a worried headmaster about how much history he thought a class of children had learnt, the answer he wanted to give was something like: 'Can you not see that these children within their drama were more animated in their conversation with each other than ever before? Who cares about history?' John is more than content with the joy of the playing.

But the drama 'game' can be a very sophisticated one as children who work with John Fines and Ray Verrier discover. It is often set in quite an elaborate historical context requiring intellectual discipline and style in communication. He has no interest in keeping the game of drama at 'Snap' when they can cope with 'Monopoly'. The game's the thing and, *incidentally*, they will learn a great deal about Monopoly!

However determined the teacher may be to enrich the drama, he must always respect – indeed he has no choice but to respect – that the game is theirs and the practice of it *is satisfying in itself*. To re-quote Arnaud Reid, 'This is to mean that the object is attended to and in some sense 'enjoyed' 'for itself', 'for its own sake' . . .' (p. 4). Thus the play impulse, as Schiller[12] has urged is the very basis of aesthetic experience and art and this same basis is the *sine qua non* of drama.

Now when children play they do not usually 'perform' their playing. Whether they are in role as a goal-keeper, a cowboy or a 17th-century Puritan, they express themselves experientially. They do not describe or demonstrate these roles; they experience the passion of them. There is, as Vygotsky[13] has pointed out, a 'dual affect': '. . . the child weeps in play as a patient, but revels as a player' (p. 549). It is the revelling which sustains the notion of dramatic play for its own sake and because of this once more tempers the rawness of that passion in that process. It is this passion that the drama teacher can harness for educational ends. Drama, like literature, stands apart from the other arts in the sense that it draws directly on the world for its substance. The careful organisation of that material by the teacher makes the 'game' more elaborate and challenging. During the process of enjoying the drama the child's view of the world may be changed, but this can only happen because the child's need for satisfaction in doing drama was met.

Where the teacher doing the structuring has a strong sense of theatrical form, the playing can become something more than sophisticated interaction. Through careful selection of focus, tension and symbol,[14] the dramatic playing may be such that the playing experience becomes elevated to high drama, not achieved technically through participants' performances, but because their collective expressive behaviour is wrought by theatrical form. Drama is more than a performing art, dependent upon a final interaction with an audience. Drama can be a group celebration to which there are no witnesses.

John Fines is right to promote the 'play-way' to education, but if he denies the value of drama as a subject in its own right, then I think he is wrong to do so. Malcolm Ross is right to recognise the importance of drama as a performing art, but he is wrong to see it as exclusively this. I invite them both, occasionally, to join me in the middle of the field, where children can learn about themselves and the world around them through the potency of a dramatic moment.

Drama in education: learning medium or arts process? In *Bolton at the Barbican*. NATD Publication, 1982. (NATD Publications, Peter Noel-Storr, 26 Canonbie Lea, Madeley, Shropshire.)

References

1 Fines J, Verrier R 1974 *The drama of history*. New University Education.

2 Ross M (ed) 1982 *The development of aesthetic experience*, Curriculum Series in the Arts, vol 3. Pergamon Press.

3 Ross M 1978 *The creative arts*. Heinemann.

4 Witkin 1974 *Intelligence of feeling*. Heinemann.

5 Bolton G M 1978 Emotion in the dramatic process – Is it an adjective or verb? *National Association for Drama in Education Journal* (Australia). **3** (Dec.): pp 14–18.

6 Robinson K 1981 A re-evaluation of the roles and functions of drama in secondary education with reference to a survey of curricular drama in 259 secondary schools. PhD thesis, University of London.

7 Tormey A 1971 *The concept of expression*. Princeton University Press.

8 Boal A 1981 *Théâtre de l'opprimé*, Numero 5. Creditade: An 03.

9 Ross M op. cit.

10 Reid A L 1982 The concept of aesthetic education. In Ross M (ed) *The development of aesthetic experience*.

11 Fleming M 1982 A philosophical investigation into drama in education. PhD thesis, University of Durham.

12 Schiller F 1965 *On the aesthetic education of man* (trans R Snell). Frederick Ungar, New York. (First published 1795.)

13 Vygotsky L S 1976 Play and its role in the mental development of the child. In Bruner J S *et al. Play: its development and evolution*. Penguin Educational.

14 Bolton G M 1979 *Towards a theory of drama in education*. Longman.

Section Two
Drama and emotion

Introduction

The question of why emotion is an important part of the learning process is addressed more fully in *Towards a theory of drama in education*:[1] 'drama for understanding' being in essence a process of cognitive/affective appraisal of the objective world. In these papers Gavin Bolton focusses his attention on the process of emotion in drama, and problems arising out of that process.

The greatest of such problems in Bolton's view arises not from dangers of too much emotion but from there being all too little:

> And yet the sad position is that in its own way drama has become yet another subject that trains children to avoid their feelings. *This is the greatest abuse of all.* (his emphasis)

But are there some emotions which are harmful to children? The teacher has a duty to protect children, but protect them *from* emotion or protect them *into* it? The question still divides drama teachers to this day. While the early essays reflect comparative uncertainty, by 'Emotion in drama' Bolton transforms the question into an emphatic statement: painful emotion

> *is not in itself harmful.* (his emphasis)

I propose to introduce 'Emotion in drama' (the last essay in this section) first, because of the richness and importance of the ideas it contains, particularly to do with protection, and then trace the development of those ideas through examination of the other two.

Emotion in drama

This most remarkable essay was written primarily as a result of Bolton's dissatisfaction with the view of emotion in drama put forward by Robert Witkin in *Intelligence of feeling*. However, it moves beyond mere argument with Witkin to an important discovery (or rather re-discovery – the original term appears to have been coined by Peter Slade); that of the concept of 'projection'. Projection is the degree to which the medium of the product in an art form is different from the actions involved in the process affecting intensity of emotion likely to be made available – 'high' projection in the form leading to less intensity; 'low' projection leading to greater intensity, thus:

> More people weep in the theatre than in the art gallery.

86

Drama, Bolton suggests, is a complex form where many different degrees of projection are available.

A second important discovery is that projection influences not only intensity but also *quality* of emotion. Up to now he had felt there were only two controllable components of emotion in drama: (1) what Vygotsky calls 'dual affect', and (2) intensity. 'Dual affect' is the tension which exists between the concrete world and the 'as-if' world, sometimes leading to contradictory emotions (enjoying/crying over a book); intensity simply being the strength of these emotions. In identifying a third, quality, he also discovers that all three components, dual affect, intensity and quality are in a more complex, even contradictory relationship than he had been hitherto aware of:

> Thus our 'haunted house' list is not straightforwardly a matter of intensity. It becomes modified and indeed turned upside down by the other two factors.

His resultant list of projections possible around a 'haunted house' theme bear interesting comparison with Heathcote's 'conventions' contained in 'Signs and portents?'[2]

But is he by this rejecting 'living through' modes of dramatic activity? Although the list of 'Don'ts' (occasions when *not* to use 'living through' modes) has grown to nine, projections seem to be a radical shift of emphasis but

> may only be *preliminary* steps towards the direct experiencing

i.e. an important and complex device for protecting into 'living through'.

Finally, in reaffirming that feeling response is modified by the process of cognition (cognitive/affective *appraisal*) he not only rejects Witkin's view that feeling is merely 'disturbance transformed', but he advances his thinking on emotion in drama into the mainstream of psychoanalytic thought, notably that of Jung.

Drama and emotion – some uses and abuses

Much of this essay is concerned with the allied problems of protection into feeling, and achieving intensity of feeling. 'Dual affect' is here termed 'first and second order emotions', while the illustration of it is interestingly a 'haunted house' drama.

Three devices for achieving intensity attract Bolton's attention: 'finding the universal', 'using the existing emotional network', and 'conning', which receives (albeit guarded) approval in some circumstances. A contradiction is revealed by this because at the top of his list of possible requirements for protection is:

1 The children should know it is make-believe.

This, merely a *possible* rather than an *essential* protection is in marked contrast to his current thinking where he *insists* upon this requirement, not only on the grounds of protection, but also to validate the experience as drama, consequently placing an absolute rejection upon conning. 'Using the existing emotional network' also appears to run the same risk as conning of the breakdown of the modification of emotion via the dual affect. In 'Emotion in drama' many of its features appear to be rejected in his list of deciding when not to use direct experiencing.

This essay bears fruitful comparison with 'Emotion in drama'. Whereas here he is predominantly concerned with *intensity* of emotion in drama, the later essay identifies that emotion has different *qualites* too; while some of the solutions to the problem of intensity in 'Finding the Universal' are an embryo form of the concept of projections of the later essay.

Emotion in the dramatic process – is it an adjective or a verb?

The central idea in this essay is that emotion which is described or 'portrayed' (adjective) does not exclude and is not inferior to emotion that is *felt* (verb) as he had hitherto believed, but rather is recognised as being in a *dialectical* relationship to it (i.e. that each one *includes* and may be transformed into the other).

The moderation of the 'living through' experience by 'emotion as an adjective' is not just a revaluing of theatre form in drama, it is an important step towards projections. In 'Drama and emotion' Bolton refines the concept of emotion further, appearing to reject the idea of two kinds of the one thing, emotion, in favour of a dialectic between two different things – *disposition* (adjective) and *emotion* (verb), after Gilbert Ryle, the philosopher.

The essay also contains a comparison of the structures of dramatic playing and 'game'. In game, he observes

children are their own agents in setting up the experience

and can 'switch on' and 'switch off' more easily than in dramatic playing. These ideas about autonomy and manipulation, made available by game structure, which he here appears to overlook, have received Bolton's renewed interest and revaluation in recent times.

References

1 Bolton G M 1979 *Towards a theory of drama in* Education. Longman.
2 Heathcote D 1982 Signs and portents? *SCYPT Journal*, No. 9, April.

Drama and emotion – some uses and abuses

This paper was read in August 1975 at the American Theatre Association Children's Theatre Convention where Gavin Bolton was given a special award for his services to child drama. It represents his attempt to answer Dorothy Heathcote's critics. Earlier that year a most vituperative article had been written by the English/Canadian pioneer of creative drama, Margaret Faulkes, condemning Dorothy Heathcote's work (the 'cancer' example referred to in the text was a lesson taught by Dorothy Heathcote). Margaret Faulkes was the 'horrified observer' who took the child out of the room.

Whether we are talking about real life situations or creative drama situations, the kind, degree or quality of the emotion expressed is dependent on the meaning abstracted from the situation. If, in real life, an adult finds himself perched unexpectedly on a narrow ledge overhanging a precipice, he may experience sheer terror. On the other hand, a circus trapeze artist in that same position or even a young child who has not yet found anything alarming in his environment, may experience quite different emotions according to how he interprets the situation.

Because an event can carry several meanings for any individual observer, it is not often that only one emotion will be experienced. Indeed, some contradictory emotions may be felt at the same time. If a boy who is making his first crude attempts at diving off the side of the pool suddenly becomes aware that his friends are watching, he may feel both embarrassed and flattered by their attention. He may be fearful and yet determined; he may feel scared and yet enjoy feeling scared.

Sometimes an individual may not experience different emotions, but differing qualities within the same broad band of emotion. Let us suppose that a woman sees her child with a badly cut hand. She feels considerable concern, but because of the many meanings available to her, her reaction is, in fact, a mixture of different levels or kinds of concern.

Concern A: How to deal with the bleeding
Concern B: About her own ability to cope in this situation
Concern C: That her child has been careless again
Concern D: That her child has been disobedient again
Concern E: At the enormity of responsibility in being a parent

It is important to notice that Concern A (How to deal with the bleeding) is different from all the others. It relates to the practicalities of living and carries its own kind of feeling quality. The mother in the illustration, however, is capable of reading several meanings and consequently responds with a corresponding complex of emotions. It seems then that every new external event is capable of two kinds of interpretation. One is an immediate, practical interpretation with a simple direct response which is often quickly modified by a second category of interpretation dependent on perceiving the event in symbolic terms.

My hypothesis, therefore, is that whereas in real life an event is open to a totality of meanings, in creative drama, one of those meanings – the here-and-now, the immediate, the practical meaning – becomes partially redundant, and consequently the emotion related to that particular meaning becomes modified and may even disappear.

The 'practical' meaning of our illustrations is not likely to be accompanied by any kind of spectacular emotion (unless of course this particular mother could not stand the sight of blood) but there are instances in life when the immediate reaction is a more violent one: the fist to the jaw in reaction to an insult; the witness's scream of alarm as a car knocks down a child; the panicking search when a wallet is lost; the terrified flight from the stranger in the dark. These emotionally-charged actions are not part of a drama experience. Drama does not require that people actually faint, that they scream themselves into an hysterical ecstacy, that they hit each other in rage. It does require a no less real but a different order of emotions: children should experience a deep concern, a genuine elation, a feeling of anger. Providing the response is to the symbolic situation, then all the emotions that belong to living, that playwrights have handled as their stock-in-trade, are the proper stuff of creative drama experience, whatever the age of the child (I shall be discussing this further).

But let me follow my hypothesis more closely. Imagine two little children playing with their dolls. The one who is limiting her experience to whatever is immediate in the situation may be fascinated by the softness of the doll's hair or may express curiosity that the eyes open and shut. Compare this with the other child who has reached beyond the immediate of a toy called a doll, to developing a highly emotional mother/child relationship. She is experiencing what I am calling a second order emotion, an emotion responding to the symbolism. Now although the *stimulus* has been the doll, the *source* for the symbolisation has been the child's inner self, feelings embedded in her personality, her attitudes, her values.

It seems then that it is useful to think in terms of two main interdependent categories of affect in drama:

1) Response to the immediate meaning of a concrete event. It becomes partially redundant.
2) Response to the symbolic meaning which feeds the drama more strongly than the actual context.

A good example of these operating in a group make-believe situation was when I observed young children playing at ghosts to a point that reached some depth. In order to get an immediate feeling of fear, they put themselves in complete darkness. The reaction was a mixture of genuine fear coupled with the fun of frightening themselves. Had this continued the experience would have had just a single meaning, a 'being frightened in the dark' meaning, which would have been less than drama. But they worked hard at this 'ghost' idea, recalling intellectually and emotionally what they knew of a world of spirits, of invisible things, of dangerous things, of a world that broke the normal physical laws. And a new kind of fear and wonder overlapped with the simple fear and excitement of being in the dark. The second order of fear was no less real: it had been initiated by the superficial fear of the dark but had become enriched by a collective memory of things 'of which we are afraid' which in the make-believe were now called ghosts. And yet alongside this was the accompanying feeling of enjoyment which they never lost and the feeling of security that they only had to switch on the light and the spell would break. It is interesting that the second order emotion was still dependent on the sustaining of the initial external stimulus and that the original fear of the dark operated, albeit vestigially. It appears that however symbolic the drama activity is, something in the environment keeps it tied to the concrete. It may be necessary, therefore, for a teacher in setting up drama to darken the room, or use attractively coloured robes or a shield or a bandaged finger or appropriate sounds or shock tactics to set off a ripple of automatic emotions. Indeed such devices may have to be retained throughout or introduced when belief is flagging. The greater problem for the teacher is how to tap the inner resources of the children so that these external stimuli become partially redundant. It is not the purpose of this paper to discuss how a teacher should promote a drama experience but there are three fairly common ways of achieving an intensity of experience which are worth looking at closely. The first is the way already referred to, where going beyond the concrete requires that fundamental feeling memories are tapped in a way that can be shared, i.e. finding the deeper response that is both personal and universal.

The second, equally valid, if not over-used, I shall refer to as 'using the existing emotional network'. The third I call 'conning'.

Finding the universal

It is often very difficult to achieve the intensity of feeling that is necessary for good drama. It is dependent on each participant drawing on relevant affective memories. It is not always possible for a teacher with a class of thirty to find just the second dimension that will ensure this kind of probing. I can recall working with a class of twelve year old boys and girls who wanted to make up a play about the Plague of London. To my astonishment the central theme of death was treated with delicious levity. Bodies, curled up with laughter, were dragged along across the highly polished hall floor, a sensation in motion that apparently was so enjoyable that the dead got up and died all over again. No attempt by me to tap any inner understanding of death stood any chance. And why should it? I had failed to find any way into the drama that could collectively have real significance for that particular age group. It was not until the second lesson when I knew I had to find a way of retrieving a desperately weak teaching situation that I found a way of opening up the theme of death for twelve year olds. And this was through the use of pets. In my reading before the second lesson, I discovered that during the Plague, orders were given for all pets to be destroyed. So, invited by me to feed their pets, to talk about them, to put them to bed, the children were interrupted in their activities by teacher (in role) putting up a notice in the market-place: ALL PETS TO BE DESTROYED IMMEDIATELY. SIGNED LORD MAYOR OF LONDON. The seriousness was now there. I had tapped an appropriate universal, that aspect of their inner feelings that as a group they were prepared to have exposed. We had moved into the Plague obliquely: for children or adults to cope with people dying as part of their drama there needs to be a trust of each other, a trust of the teacher and a trust of the medium they are working in. None of those were present in that first lesson. By moving to off-centre in the second lesson, I was allowing them to test the ground. Perhaps by the fifth lesson, had the work continued, they may have been ready to extend their understanding of the central theme.

The existing emotional network

The above is an example of a teacher searching for a way of making personal a context that is out of a group's experiences. One way of bringing depth of emotion to the drama without finding out how each individual may relate to a theme is to utilise how the individuals relate to each other. Irrespective of the theme the teacher can tap the existing network of relationships within the group or the underlying attitudes of the group. To some extent this is always being done, albeit unconsciously, by the teacher. But a teacher can deliberately harness the group dynamism which is always there ready to surface when required.

Sometimes it takes a simple form – group members have a great respect for a particular leader – or more complex – the girls and boys despise each other; or individuals seem to be in competition with each other or there is a fight for leadership or their mood is anti-authority or their thinking is over-intellectual. By using this existing emotional layer so that the emotional qualities required of the drama coincide with those that already exist not too deeply under the collective surface of the group, the teacher is transforming what is often present as an interference factor into a useful tool. He will not always utilise this net work. Indeed he will sometimes deliberately work against it, especially if he feels there is something undesirable in the network as it exists. Sometimes the existing and simulated networks become entangled as in the following example:

The class of mixed ability eleven year olds in choosing to 'do a shipwreck' showed a determination to race through the complexities of boarding, sailing, sinking, nearly drowning, escaping from sharks and landing on a handy desert island with gusto but with no thought, in spite of my efforts to improve the significance of one or two moments.

In the second lesson the pattern of thoughtless action would have been repeated, but I was this time equally determined that some reality be injected into the make-believe. Slowly the island became a real place of refuge with agreed physical conditions that presented problems to do with keeping warm at night, protection from wild animals, sources of drinking water and food. Two thirds through this lesson a lookout 'spotted' natives. I watched the boys (not the girls) switch immediately to a 'kill the indians' stereotype mental set. I just about managed to avoid a wholesale slaughter taking place there and then by (in role) reminding them they had said earlier that most of their pistols and rifles had been lost in the shipwreck.

Emotionally, the boys were back in the 'fun' activity of the first lesson. I felt that for a class of normal eleven year olds drama must be more demanding than such superficial action routine required. In preparation for the third lesson, therefore, I built in the corner of the hall, a simple 'place' which, with a few artefacts such as a wooden bowl, a large shell and woven material, could be interpreted as a tomb or a shrine, a hiding-place or a dwelling. When the boys started to prepare their battle with the natives they could not ignore this 'place'. Such was the 'killing natives' instinct of the boys that when one girl suggested it was a temple, one boy blurted out, 'If it's a temple, they'll come here to worship and we'll 'get' them as they come round the corner'. In role I simply held up the wooden bowl and asked, 'The people we're going to kill – have they made these things?' The consternation of the boys became even more marked when I took on a different role as a 'native' spokesman wanting to be friendly. Consternation turned to anger when the 'women' supported the idea of friendly communication. This is a good example of the feeling content of the make-believe spilling over into the actual situation. In the drama the 'men' were angry with the 'women' for making friendly overtures to the 'natives'; in actuality the boys were angry with the girls for supporting teacher, who had clearly changed the play!

To call what followed a 'discussion' would give a totally false impression. Boys and girls, sometimes in role, sometimes out of role, at great excitement pitch went through a long process of angrily accusing, blaming, justifying, defending and eventually in milder mood, evaluating, tolerating, regretting and acknowledging. I was thrilled at their apparent gradual understanding of what they had felt and why, only to discover that the adults who had been watching the lesson were nearly as angry as the boys had been: they rounded on me at the moment the children left – for allowing children to get so angry, showing sides of their natures that were best left at home and for not letting the children enjoy the natural course of their drama – killing natives!

What the observers were recognising of course was that anger is the kind of emotion a teacher automatically quells for everyone's safety. What they failed to acknowledge was that in this case the make-believe was always a modifying factor. The actual and the simulated became temporarily confused; they did not become one and the same thing.

I am not suggesting there are no dangers in using the existing network. One such abuse occurs when the children themselves take advantage of the situation by deliberately using the simulated context in order to reinforce some undesirable aspect of their existing network of relationships. A teacher must always be on the look-out for this kind of manipulation and protect the child concerned in one of the following ways: (i) by anticipating the manoeuvre, or (ii) using the drama to raise the status of the victim, or (iii) reducing the status of the offenders, or (iv) exposing the problem. I can vividly recall an instance with a mixed class of 16–18 year old adolescents who took an intense dislike to a very bright and articulate member of the drama class – largely because she was so obviously more bright and articulate than they were. In a series of five daily sessions, in the early stages of which the group demonstrated their animosity by using the drama to score points against her, the teacher was able gradually to control the drama situation in a way that allowed the problem to be exposed and then discussed openly and amicably outside the drama.

Conning

Earlier in this paper I hypothesised that whereas in real life situations a totality of meanings may be available, in drama it is important that the most concrete meaning should be allowed to atrophy. One kind of drama structuring that gives me some concern is where the children are brought to a point of not being able to distinguish in *any way* between the fictitious and the real.

I am not talking here of those occasions when there is some temporary confusion. We all know as adults the experience of being so absorbed in a book that even though we have laid it down, the world in our mind continues for a time to seem more real than the one we are rejoining, and we have probably all experienced as teachers having children in the class who are reluctant to stop talking in role immediately the drama is finished, as in the 'killing natives' example. No, I am referring to those occasions when actuality and make-believe have become for some children completely indistinguishable – usually as a result of a 'con trick' by the teacher.

It may, for example, be justifiable for a teacher, wrongfully to accuse a class of adolescents of some fictitious misdemeanour in order that, later, its members may reflect on their reactions; in other words for the class temporarily to assume 'it's for real', but the length of time the teacher persists in this 'con trick' will be dependent on (a) the established pupil-teacher relationship, and (b) the age and maturity level of the class. The kind of activity I am referring to is well expressed by a headmaster writing in a school magazine:

More in Fun than in Earnest

Last Saturday we had a completely new experience at the school – exciting, amusing, yet at one or two points devastating. We had agreed to a visit from a group of five players or actors from Edinburgh Theatre Workshop. Just prior to their visit they proposed a harmless deception, to which we also agreed: one of the members would arrive disguised as a school inspector and proceed to inspect the school; only the staff to be in on the secret; the kids to act as they saw fit, believing it was, in fact, a man from the ministry.

Things went magnificently: total reality. Unfortunately the inspector began to speak about closing the school because dormitories were not up to regulation standards. A special meeting was called in the library, the inspector was introduced, then ensued a crowded meeting at which the kids reached such levels of feeling (passion, in fact) and speech in defence of their school that there can seldom have been more powerful argument on behalf of their school by any group of pupils anywhere, any time. The inspector had a hard time justifying his conclusion.

The climax was yet to come: a 'visitor' (one of the theatre group) taking the side of the kids, suddenly attacked the inspector with his fists – very realistically. In an instant three of the biggest boys in the school hauled him off, saving the inspector from violence. Only then did the actors, the inspector and the 'hippie visitor' declare themselves. Cheers all round. Unfortunately some kids had lived through the rather traumatic experience of having their school threatened – several were in tears.

The following hour made amends: all the actors put on a show of clowning and acrobatics in the big shed, and all the kids joined the circus. Some doubts remain as to the wisdom of such a procedure.

I think the device of 'conning' is a useful one for a drama teacher to have up his sleeve, to be used sparingly, economically and only if he is sure it is appropriate to the children's needs. How could a visiting theatre team possibly know that the use of such a powerful weapon was suitable at that time, in that place, with those children? Often as teachers we don't know either and we take risks accordingly, but I still have to be persuaded it is necessary for a theatre team to take those risks.

This brings me to a central issue in this paper: are there indeed some emotions that teachers should help children to avoid? Supposing a child is upset during a drama lesson, do we automatically assume that such an emotion is harmful? An interesting example occurred a couple of years ago in a lesson where nine year old children and a group of adults shared the same make-believe situation in which it was desperately important to make some special plants grow (the adults were the 'plants'; the children were responsible for them). The teacher structured the situation so that most of the 'plants' died. One child wept at the death of her plant. One horrified observer immediately took the child out into the fresh air to comfort her. The teacher's intention had been to help these young children understand that wishing and trying hard enough to make something happen does not necessarily bring it about. The observer's intention was to obstruct the child's learning of that hard fact of life.

It seems to me that in this case the teacher's intention was justified but before I could be sure of my judgement in this (I was not present), there were certain questions I would need to ask. I propose to discuss these in detail as I believe they are relevant to many situations.

Was the teacher failing to operate at a symbolic level so that the children were responding emotionally to a totality of meanings including the concrete one of believing they had *actually* killed the plants and the women? In other words, was the particular child's emotional upset of the *first* order of emotion, reacting to the symbolic meaning of the situation, perhaps to the pain of a new understanding of life's trials? It seems to me that Peter Slade, the pioneer of child drama in England, was so right when he pointed out to us twenty-five years ago that drama gave the child a chance to do the illegitimate legitimately. It seems that these children had the chance to face failure without failure's consequences, within the safety of the make-believe. It is this ambivalence – of being hurt yet not hurt; surprised and yet not surprised; saddened and yet not saddened – that is central to the child drama experience.

Another vital question that needs to be asked is whether there were any protective elements in the teaching situation to counter the distress. It seems to me that if none of the following were present then the observer had some cause for concern:

1 The children should know it is make-believe.
2 Whatever the major emotional response the final one should be of satisfaction in having created a make-believe.
3 If the emotional experience has been exciting then time and opportunity after the make-believe experience for containing, reordering, rechanneling or reflecting on the experience must be allowed for. The form this period of emotional adjustment takes may vary from discussion of individual feelings to deliberately talking about something else, from sitting quietly saying nothing to changing one's shoes, and in terms of time from half an hour or more to a couple of minutes.
4 The children should feel the situation is 'safe' enough for their feelings to be exposed. (Children are their own judges of this – rarely will children take this kind of risk if they do not feel secure.)
5 There should be a trusting bond (this does not necessarily have anything to do with how long they have known each other) between teacher and class. The teacher must indicate clearly that he identifies with the feelings expressed. If the make-believe world has been upsetting, the world he offers must be reassuring.

I have recently had a teaching experience that indicates only too well the kind of harm that might be done when that reassurance is missing. I was working for five days with a group of adolescents who were so 'theatre arts' trained that in everything they did they fell back on cliché-ridden acting. On the fourth day, therefore, I asked the teachers watching to split the young people into very small groups and through the use of their own very powerful role-playing challenge the adolescents strongly enough to make them start 'living-through' the make-believe instead of 'pretending'. In my enthusiasm I forgot to remind the teachers that they must not drop their normal function as teachers. What followed was perhaps one of the most anxious moments of my career. The role-playing of the adults was so strong and so effective in the terms I had asked for that here and there some of the young people were being overwhelmed, crushed, well nigh emotionally hammered to the ground. Fortunately we were able to recognise what was happening before it had gone too far and by dint of role reversal an equilibrium was achieved.

What had happened in fact was that the students had seen the teachers as an extension of me and offered to the teachers the trust that I had built up over four days, more than they would normally have offered acting with strange adults. Additionally, the teachers had seen themselves temporarily as actors, leaving their normal sense of responsibility for the teaching side to me. When the students experienced deep emotion there was little support in the return to the normal world; little assurance; little understanding. The circumstances of this lesson were unusual but useful enough to remind all of us that neither children nor adults can be left high and dry immediately after an emotional drama experience.

Because this paper has been about emotions, I may have given the impression that it is possible in practice to isolate emotion from intellectual activity. This is neither possible nor desirable. Indeed not only must cognitive activity complement emotional activity, in most drama experience reflection on what has been learned is essential if the emotional experience is to be codified and made available for future reference. Expression of emotion alone has no educational or any other kind of value.

In children's drama work, therefore, it is important that the thinking and feeling are right. So much drama I see expresses a kind of generalised excitement with little conceptual underpinning. Nearly as bad is the kind of drama that operates at an intellectual level without any real feeling. It seems to me that when drama operates at its best, thinking and feeling must be compatible with the symbolic meanings of the context, which brings me to what I consider to be the most harmful abuse of emotion in drama. I am referring to the kind of dramatic activity where children suffer overlong exposure to the trivial, where children are taught over a long period of time that drama is exercises, a series of sketches that have to entertain, an acquisition of techniques that avoid exposure to real feeling, where the only emotion felt is a sense of fun. It seems to me there is a strange contradiction in our attitude to drama. Teachers are often proud of what the subject can offer compared with the more formal aspects of the curriculum. We claim that it is the only aspect of the timetable really concerned with the whole person. And yet the sad position is that in its own way drama has become yet another subject that trains children to avoid their feelings. This is the *greatest abuse of all*.

Drama and emotion – some uses and abuses. *Young Drama* 5(1), 1977.

Emotion in the dramatic process – is it an adjective or a verb?

Gavin Bolton read this paper at the INSEA conference in Adelaide, 1978. This was the first occasion when the International Association for Education in the Arts widened the scope of its interests to include drama along with the visual arts and music. The 'big guns' of the Congress (2,000 delegates) were Professor Richard Courtney, Robert Witkin, and Elliot Eisner.

In England there is an ambivalent attitude towards emotion in education. Much of the literature of teaching drama claims that drama is significant because it allows children to get in touch with their feelings; it deals reputedly with 'the heart' whereas other subjects are confined to 'the head'. However, if in practice, feelings should actually get themselves expressed we, even drama teachers, find it singularly alarming. It seems to me that on the one hand we boast of drama as a powerfully effective medium and on the other hand we spend a great deal of time and effort finding ways of reducing its potency. Indeed the emotions that would be regarded as the stock in trade of the playwright: awe; grief; anger; anxiety; love, hate and fear, are somehow considered improper for children to handle.

Teachers have acquired at least three ways of avoiding such 'improper' feelings in their drama. First, and this is very popular, is by turning drama into such a quick-fire series of cameo exercises that there is not time to feel anything at all. Secondly, to confine the subject to 'nice' feelings like fun and joy and hope, or thirdly – and I shall give this some attention – to use the emotions solely as adjective. In this way the emotion becomes safely descriptive like other adjectives. So just as one can portray a poor man or a hard-working man so one can act a sad man or an angry man or a frightened man. This third 'avoidance' device is as old as the school play.

Now I am not as old as the school play, but I am pretty old . . . in drama teaching! So I could be classed as one of the original 'emotion avoiders'. I did not realise in the early days of my teaching of course that I was avoiding anything; that there was anything to avoid! For it seemed only obvious to me that feeling in acting was descriptive. So I trained my seven year old class for their school play to look sad, happy, murderous or even surprised. ('Surprised' was always a bit difficult – it's a matter of popping one's eyes and holding one's hands out flat, at the correct angle or course! Some children never got it no matter how much I showed them!) When I went on drama courses and learned that the school play was somehow or other inappropriate for young children I switched to the new fashion called 'creative drama'. One of the things it required me to do, was to narrate exciting stories (a tambourine in my hand for sound effects) while children switch on their 'scared' look. 'Plucking up courage (their courageous look) they entered the cave slowly, their eyes peering into the dark (some of them are not peering), their eyes *peering* into the dark; and, then, suddenly (they get ready to be surprised) there is a distant light; (they *are* surprised!) It is high up in the roof (heads raised); they can feel a warm glow on their faces and as they stretch their arms towards it (a good class this) there appears in the middle of the glow a vision. They are transfixed with awe (none-too-good on awe; must bring that into the next story) and then . . . it has gone . . . and slowly they left the cave.'

As a teacher attempting to follow this 'creativity' trend away from a theatre orientation, I was prepared to shed the script, even do away with rehearsing, manage without an audience, but I still assumed that emotion was descriptive, a feature, a characteristic to be adopted by the children and made explicit to each other and, of course, to the teacher. I thought I was in creative drama, but all I was doing was asking children to behave as if there was really an audience there. Indeed one can see in British schools a great deal of so called improvised drama where the participants are clinging to 'describing' techniques as if they were describing life to someone else rather than *experiencing* it.

This *experiencing* is the key to the dramatic educational process. In order to move away from the descriptive – I had to see the emotional element as existential, as 'living through', as happening in time, indeed as a verb. It seemed that no longer in acting out the Bible story of Joseph would the children portray jealous brethren, but would during the dramatic playing *become* jealous, no longer in acting out a haunted house drama would the participants portray scared intruders, but would *become* scared.

In switching to this new notion of experiencing I at first made the mistake as others have made of now assuming that all I had to do was to set children free, not appreciating that if they were to have significant feelings these can only be wrought from significant thoughts, that feeling and thinking are aspects of the same mental operation. I also made the mistake – and this brings us to the central topic of this paper – of holding two other misconceptions:

1 I assumed that because experiencing (emotion as a verb) appeared to have superior potential, there was no place now for emotion as an adjectival function. I did not see that the two modes may be at times mutually dependent.
2 I also assumed that the experiencing of emotion implied freedom of expression. I did not see that significance of experience is often dependent upon finding an appropriate form.

These two points then, the relationship between emotion as a verb and emotion as adjective and the relationship between emotion and form will provide the basis for this paper. Some of it is going to be pretty heavy going, I'm afraid. If you are bored, please make a note that 'being bored' is exactly what I mean by experiencing emotion as a verb!

The relationship of emotion as a verb to emotion as an adjective

In order to establish more precisely what I am talking about by experiencing emotion as a verb I can illustrate from the popular children's game 'What time is it Mr Wolf?' When young children play this game they can experience some very strong emotions for instance of anticipation, fright and relief. It is happening to them, they are actually experiencing those feelings but is not the anticipation, fright and relief of real life, because they are their own agents in setting up the experience. So it is accompanied by the pleasure of being in control. It is this controlling in order to be controlled that epitomises the game experience and separates it from real life experience. The participant can say both 'it is happening to me now' and 'I am making it happen'.

In a game of this kind then the emotion can be very intense at the moment of its happening and seem no less real, but it is nevertheless tempered by the participants agreement to enter the game. (This incidentally is why I am not keen on the use of 'conning' by drama teachers or TIE groups because there is no such agreement). Now if drama has the same requirements as the game, then, the participants must actually experience some emotion that is relevant to the chosen context. It is for this reason that teachers who encourage their classes to act-out the most dramatic physical calamities in life: shipwreck; plane crashes; mountain falls; houses on fire; car accidents etc., find they have such phony drama on their hands for the direct *experiencing* of these events is almost unattainable in dramatic form.

But the emphasis I have now placed on the importance of emotion as a verb is not the full picture. So far I have spoken in somewhat derogatory terms of emotion as an adjective, implying that it could be relegated to anything old-fashioned in dramatic activity.

We however need to take a second look, for it will be found that in many instances the business of *starting* the drama process is dependent on finding an adjectival, descriptive emotion. Whereas participants in a game can 'switch on' to playing it 'one moment I am not playing chess the next moment I am playing chess' and all that is required of me is a gathering of concentration and a directing of energy, in drama nothing of significance can start until an appropriate feeling quality has been found. The fictitious context, the characters or even the plot and theme may be pre-decided, but they only become meaningful when a feeling that belongs to the context is evoked. This evocation often demands hard work. Twelve year old children starting a play about people dying of plague are going to find it very difficult to bring to their dramatic actions the required feeling of sadness or fear or bereavement. Nine year olds, about to cross a precipice will be hard put to switch to an apprehension of danger. Similarly adolescents may fail to identify with the puritan zeal of seventeenth century Salem. And yet drama cannot start until some appropriate identification is found. For it is often this beginning feeling quality that gives the metaphor its initial meaning: it is descriptive – adjectival, no less. In the plague, the precipice adventure and in Salem the actions of the participants must identify sad, apprehensive or puritan qualities or something approximating to them.

To the question posed by the title of this paper then, is emotion in drama a verb or an adjective, the answer is that it may be both. An initial identification of feeling that is adjectival may be a necessary first step before emotion as a verb can take over. If in turn the process becomes product, a performance, once again the feeling becomes adjectival so that the members of the audience can go through *their* living-through experience. Leaving performance on one side, for although a very important aspect of drama it is not what we are discussing here, it seems that the teacher in the classroom may be faced in terms of affect with two phases.

1 Searching to identify an appropriate feeling quality – it is adjectival, fixed in time, and

2 The feeling quality giving way to the fluidity of a process, moving in time, a verb.

Now what does this all mean in practice? Supposing I announce now that all of us in this hall are about to do an improvisation under my guidance about Viet Nam refugees waiting for a boat to be taken to freedom. The appropriate feeling quality might be that you are anxious about the immediate and long-term future or it might be that you feel dejected and humiliated by all that you have had to suffer so far. How do you suddenly switch to those feelings? For after all, as far as I know you are a happy band of carefree Australians! So how do you become a group of anxious, dejected refugees? Some of you being of an obliging turn of mind, may put on your 'worried look'; some of you may be so acutely embarrassed that you either avoid each others eyes or become witty out of role or giggle; others may be so offended by my arrogant assumption that you would all be prepared to go along with my whim to have a large group improvisation that your only concern is how best to reach the nearest exit; others who have done a refugee improvisation before may be keen to show how good you are at refugee improvisations! My guess is that it would take a long time to find any integrity of feeling. You may of course go through the motions; I may have said, in role, 'all line up for your bowls of rice'. So you may all, even within your varying moods, look as though you are part of the fiction – after all, embarrassment can look a bit like humiliation, anxiety about doing the drama may look a bit like being an anxious Viet Namese. Even the man who really wants to escape from the conference hall may unwittingly be feeding in to what the drama is supposed to be about. The giggles perhaps could be ignored, the wise-cracks however would stick out like a sore thumb. My responsibility, as a leader of the group would be clear: I would try to find ways both inside and outside the drama to coax, persuade, lead or even shock you into sharing some feeling qualities that fit the queueing up for rice. One way within the drama is to convince you of my utter belief in the fictitious situation. Another would be to put you through a series of actions that make very safe unspectacular demands on you, so that imperceptibly you acquire appropriate feelings. Another way outside the drama would be to read you some particularly moving account of an actual refugee event so that an appropriate mood might be created among us. Yet another way out of the drama would be to convince you that if only you are prepared to trust me in this you will have the dramatic experience of a lifetime! Yet another would be to become the heavy handed teacher and remind you that you are supposed to be experienced drama specialists and surely if you have any professional attitude at all . . . etc., etc.!

Whatever device is used by the teacher or yourselves, success is dependent upon the recall or evocation of a relevant feeling. Only then can drama begin. If this is not achieved the experience is meaningless. Unfortunately in England we find ourselves working with many classes who for one reason or another fail to get beyond this first phase. They only have the experience of searching for drama, not drama itself. Now if in our refugee improvisation we do find integrity of feeling, then we can be released into experiencing, into 'living through' and submit ourselves to changes in emotion as things happen to us i.e. emotion as a verb. Dramatic playing would have started.

Finding integrity of feeling, however, is not just dependent on a group's willingness to co-operate: it is to a large extent dependent on the relationship of the actual emotional network of the group and the feeling that is required by the fiction. It is possible that the mood of depression or apprehension that sits on you when I announce cheerfully we are about to do our immigration improvisation can gradually and subtly be harnessed to approximate to the drama's requirements. But supposing I chose not immigration but a beach party where the wine has flowed and everyone is high, given your actual mood of depression integrity of feeling I suspect would be much further off! Indeed if we were really going to work at this I think I would be tempted to make our start 'the morning after the night before!' and gradually work our way back to pitching the improvisation at the more extrovert level of feeling matching 'a party spirit'. This device of moving obliquely into a highly charged situation is fairly common. Recently I worked with a class of thirteen year old children who asked for their drama to be about anti-social behaviour in school, but they were so inhibited by the large number of people watching us that I selected for our starting point a school staff meeting *about* lack of classroom discipline allowing their actual feelings of constraint to find a logical outlet within the fiction. We reached the anti-social behaviour by the third lesson. In other words, what started as finding the adjectival attribute of a 'worried staff', could lead step by step to the experiencing of disruptive behaviour.

But tapping a group's emotional resources, whether they are hidden and have to be worked at or are just under the surface and readily available for transferring to the fiction, is barely half the story. Drama is not a mere release of emotion. The expression of emotion some people claim is cathartic. This may be so but this has little to do with drama as an art form.

The relationship between emotion and form

I have quite deliberately used an illustration as alarming as the emotions implicit in anti-social behaviour in school in order to drive home my point that experiencing emotion as a verb is not in *itself* significant or even desirable.

I have already tried to establish that the game differs from dramatic playing in that the starting point, the switch from real life to the game, does not, as in the case of some drama, have to be worked at. Another difference lies in how the 'rules' are evolved. In games they are socially predecided. The rules themselves only become a matter of tension if someone is trying to break them. In dramatic playing the rules are open to negotiation during the action. This can put not only an extra strain on the participants, but expose them to a greater feeling of risk, for the outcome may not be known to them beforehand as it is to a degree in the game.

When we say that dramatic playing is metaphor, we mean the participant is involved either simultaneously or intermittently in two concrete worlds; he is operating in the fictitious context but the only physical and mental resources available to him are in the actual context. It is the dialectic between the two contexts that uniquely defines dramatic activity. Picture a child, who in order to create a fictitious concrete world of a king ascending to his throne before his people, actually mounts the school dais and sits on a school chair. He actually selected a chair with a high back and is fleetingly rather pleased with the effect of his choice.

But the fictitious world reminds him that he is having to face a lot of people who are demanding that their king should answer their problems – and he is beginning to feel burdened by this responsibility. 'My people!' *he announces*, but he may actually be *thinking* 'John Smith is grinning and is spoiling our play'. He is living in two worlds at the same time. In drama we require a heightened awareness of the interaction of two worlds, not an avoidance of the fictitious so that nothing is felt, nor an escape into the fictitious so that everything is felt but nothing is understood. The emotion that is experienced then is really a compound of emotions that is prompted by both the contexts.

Thus the basic structure of drama itself tempers the emotional release, but there are other restraints. I pointed out earlier that when a child enters a game, he is both controlling and being controlled, but in fact although he is controlling in so far as it is his decision to enter the game, it is the explicit socially ordained rules that dictate the nature of the experience to a large extent. Now as has already been suggested in dramatic playing, because the child is negotiating his own rules he has greater autonomy. However, if the dramatic playing is to move into an art form autonomy is more apparent than real, for the formal elements may take over as the rules have taken over in the game.

These formal elements are the elements of theatre. I do not mean by this the actor's function of communicating to an audience but a playwright's function in creating theatrical form through the use of focus, tension, contrast and symbol. These elements are the structural equivalent of the rules in games, not simply another means of constraint, but the very source for giving the experience significance. So as we become released into experiencing Viet Nam refugees or as the thirteen year olds become released into experiencing anti-social behaviour, we and they are simultaneously seeking and working within dramatic form.

The experiencing of emotion as a verb, as has been said, is not in itself significant and yet children left to themselves may indulge in just that. It is here then that the responsibility of the teacher lies. He must either take over the role of the playwright (I am here talking in terms of theatrical structure not about writing scripts) or he must guide the participants' paths to work to that end. A scene of 'anti-social behaviour' must not simply be an imitation of a sequence of violent actions – imitation is not drama. The dramatic use of tension, contrast and symbol must raise the level of the meaning of the experience, so that every action, every object takes on meaning beyond what is functional to the universal; thus the paradox of drama can be achieved: its meaning is both dependent upon and yet independent of the concrete context.

Thus we have distanced the emotional content of drama a long way from the raw emotion of day to day life. In the past we distanced it by removing it, or by demonstrating feeling rather than by experiencing it. All the passions of the soul, dark and light, are available for the child to explore but only if distanced by form. We want the experience to be intense, concentrated and significant. When the experience is over he may still be angry, elated or sad – we know what it is like when a closed book or yesterday's film lives on for us, but such feeling lives on without the practical, particular consequences of life's trauma. We can in our own time and in our own way reflect upon our feelings and our new understanding without the pain and thrust of actuality.

In summary then there are two qualities of emotion that can be identified in dramatic playing: a static feeling quality that may give integrity to the beginning of the process – I have called this the adjective; and the changing emotion experienced once the feeling quality is established

– I have called this the verb. This latter may match emotion of real life in fluidity and intensity, but it is tempered by:

1 the accompanying pleasure in creating a fiction,
2 by an awareness of being in control,
3 by the universality rather than the particularity of meaning, and
4 by the distancing that characterises all dramatic form.

We need not be afraid of emotion in the classroom, provided it is mediated by form. What should give us cause for some concern are the number of activities that go on in schools under the name of drama which fail to help children get in touch with their feelings. This is the real abuse of the art form. It is only through feeling that we can achieve change in understanding. The principal educational purpose of drama is change in understanding but that must be the subject of another paper.

Emotion in the dramatic process – is it an adjective or a verb?
National Association for Drama in Education Journal, vol 3, Dec. 1978. (Australia.)

Emotion in drama

This article was written in 1981 for a seminar with Gavin Bolton's MA students and represents a 'preview' of his chapter on emotion in Drama as education.

It is difficult, even with a class of articulate adults, to discuss in retrospect the emotional aspects of a shared drama experience. One reason for this is that we lack an agreed terminology, so that the participants in the discussions are left wondering whether they have really understood each other. Another equally significant reason is that many of us are either incapable of accurately perceiving our own emotions or disinclined to report them with any degree of honesty. A third reason may be that there is little to discuss, for a particularly 'intellectual' group of people may have spent their time in the drama session working hard at avoiding emotional engagement. This latter is true of many in our teaching profession who feel threatened if they are required to contribute more than their professional selves to a project, or, who, practised in being articulate about the objective world, feel totally inadequate when they are required to work even partially from a feeling impulse. Such people have paid the price of formal education to which Robert Witkin[1] so elegantly refers:

> If the price of finding oneself in the world is that of losing the world in oneself, then the price is more than anyone can afford. (p. 1)

There are indeed those who find ways of doing drama without finding the world in themselves.

Writers on affective education generally have noted this kind of acquired avoidance. R.M. Jones[2] refers to children whose whole mental development has been diverted unilaterally towards objectification. Using Bruner's[3] terminology of private and public forms of representation, he draws our attention to 'Children who have not grown beyond enactive and iconic representation but rather have grown around those modes of knowing, and cannot return to them' (p. 194). Witkin,[4] in laying the blame for this state of affairs at the feet of people like ourselves, teachers and educationists, does not criticise our intentions, but our ignorance:

> The repression of subjectivity in our age has served only to render its periodic outbursts sharper than ever. . . . This is all the more so because in the severe objectification of our existence the repression has taken a peculiar form. We have not denied the claims of feeling. On the contrary, we have solemnly endorsed these claims. Our problem is that we have forgotten what they are. (p. 12)

There is some truth in this, although teachers who see their subject as a vehicle for self-awareness or others for whom the main purpose of drama is cathartic release, or yet others who (by way of distinct contrast) train their pupils to 'act' a range of emotions through appropriate self-expression and gesture would no doubt protest that feeling is the very currency they are handling. Indeed I think there is some justification in the view that its importance is recognised more by drama teachers than teachers of other arts because of drama's obvious closeness to the action of life. And yet the situation described in the first paragraph above still obtains, for our conviction has outstripped our understanding of the function within a dramatic experience.

In this chapter I shall examine briefly how educationists have regarded emotions before examining in some detail the theoretical contribution to the arts made by Robert Witkin in his seminal publication *Intelligence of feeling*. It causes me considerable embarrassment when I have such respect for the author to have to say that I think his book does a disservice to drama in two ways:

(a) that it does not really find a way of accommodating drama into its theoretical framework as comfortably as for the other arts and
(b) that its illustrative references to drama lessons are of such an extreme or negative kind that they are likely to be misleading.

In order to bring out my arguments in support of point (a), I shall have to draft out a rather different model of emotional behaviour which attaches more importance to emotion as part of dramatic experience.

The literature on emotion offers a bewildering range of terms, for instance, affect, feeling, feelings, emotions, emotional drives, impulses, sensations, mood, tension, passions, disturbances and agitations. As to be expected writers take specialist perspectives reflecting philosophical, biological, neurological, psychoanalytical and cognitive interests, and select the vocabulary of emotion that best fits their specialism. Educationists who show interest in emotion have to cope with not only the bewildering variety of approaches and its concomitant confusion of word usage, but also with a well-entrenched suspicion of emotion as an inferior, regrettable aspect of the human condition which because of its connection with animal instincts, irrationality and/or the deep subconscious should be repressed, ignored or even denied. Such an attitude dies hard as Bloom *et al.*[5] discovered when they attempted to encourage teachers to open the 'Pandora's Box' of the affective domain of educational objectives. Yet thirty years earlier MacMurray[6] had been claiming, for instance, that rationality can be applied to emotional as well as intellectual behaviour. He writes:

It follows that none of our activities, not even the activities of thinking, can express our reason unless the emotions which produce and sustain them are rational emotions. (p. 24)

One of the dangers of battling to erode entrenched attitudes is that protagonists may be driven to take extreme positions. John Wilson[7] for example must have raised not a few eyebrows among his colleagues when he suggested that understanding one's emotions is central to religious education. Nor is the following statement by A.S. Neill[8] likely to find many adherents, I think:

I hold that education should concern itself with the emotions and leave the intellect to look after itself. (p. 1552)

Now art educators are in a peculiar position for they, traditionally, have been expected to pose as guardians of emotional development. People who object to the notion of emotional development as central to education might well be prepared to acknowledge a function of the arts as that of 'safety-valve', a view no doubt influenced by the affinity Freud observed between the neurotic and creative processes. But arts educators generally do not wish to be thrust into the therapy role, and yet they often see their subject as dealing with deep personal expression. Ross[9] for example, draws heavily on a psychoanalyst's (Winnicott) thesis of creativity. Ross writes:

Ultimately, the potential space survives as the site of all creative and cultural experiences – Winnicott mentions in this connection 'adult play', artistic creativity and appreciation, religious feeling, dreaming, the arousal and loss of affection, imaginative living and creative scientific work. As teachers of the creative arts it is precisely into this area of the potential space that we should be prepared to draw our pupils and step ourselves. (p. 6)

Implications here are that we are to be in touch with what may in school be regarded as taboo matters – religious feeling, dreaming and the arousal and loss of affection – and that there is a risk which teacher and pupil must take together. For Ross this still does not amount to therapy. One may detect a certain ambivalence in his denial: 'The expressive arts in school are not about reactive expression. Nor are they 'basically' therapeutic in the sense of compensating for or relieving the damaging consequences of chronic emotional deprivation' (Presumably there is some other sense in which he sees them as therapeutic.) He continues, 'Nor is arts education concerned with the purging of otherwise socially disruptive energies.' (p. 42). I share both Ross's views and the ambivalence with which he expresses them. We are not primarily concerned with art as treatment, although art therapy can be invaluable in helping sick people in special situations, and, as every teacher knows, even in the so-called 'normal' situation, for particular children the arts experience may be an escape or a cathartic release. But the teacher in the classroom is not a clinician monitoring his class in terms of potential sickness. This is not to deny however that a sensitive teacher may well be able to use the arts to help a distressed child. The point is that this is not a teacher's priority. R.M. Jones,[10] interested as he is in feeling in education uncompromisingly warns:

Let us enter it as a fundamental rule, then, that cultivation of emotional issues in classrooms, whether by design or in response to the unpredictable should be means to the ends of instructing the children in the subject matter. (p. 137)

Robert Witkin[11] would argue that Feeling 'is' the subject-matter of the Arts, but, as we shall see, he is using the term in a special way which had very little meaning for me as a practitioner of drama when it was first published. I have had great difficulty in matching Witkin's theory, based on a Piagetian model of interaction, with the experiential knowledge I have of my subject. Perversely, I could make sense of it when he applies it to the other arts, but not when he describes the practice of drama. The initial block came about, I am sure, because my perspective on the process of emotional engagement is inevitably quite different from Witkin's overview as an observer. Emotion is indeed the currency a drama teacher is handling because any imaginative act, as Margaret Sutherland[12] explained, is 'necessarily' accompanied by emotion.

In fact, we give a kind of reality to imagined creations by feeling these emotions; in a way we live an imagined situation because it affects us emotionally. (p. 5)

But having (successfully, I hope) 'unblocked' or as Dorothy Heathcote would put it 'cracked the code', I am left with the impression, as I have already indicated, that this theory does not fit the practice of drama, or rather, that his interpretation of its application to drama is erroneous.

It is necessary, however, to pave the way for a discussion of *The Intelligence of feeling* by selecting a model for describing emotion in drama that does work for me in my practice. In doing this I am aware of two distinct drawbacks (a) the model I have to offer may not fit other kinds of drama practice, in which case its usefulness will be limited, and (b) I shall be indulging in the questionable game of selecting from other authors' writing and picking up other writers' terminology as and when they appear to suit my case. But as I have not come across any other attempt to provide a rationale on the topic of emotion specifically related to drama, I propose to go ahead inspite of its shortcomings.

Dispositions and emotions

I like to use the term *emotion* in connection with a 'change' of psychophysical state. Gilbert Ryle[13] uses the image of 'eddy' in a stream, where there is a boulder in the stream interrupting its natural flow or the convergence of two opposing currents. An *emotion* is a resulting disturbance. Ryle's metaphor extends to what might be described as characteristic tendencies, the natural continuous flow of a stream being equivalent to what he calls inclinations or what I prefer to label as *dispositions*.

Dispositions give direction to behaviour and are identified by such characteristics as punctuality, tidiness, jealousy, pride, modesty, fear of heights and pessimism. We would say that given certain circumstances a person is prone to behave in a certain way, although we would not necessarily imply that such a person is conscious of his own disposition. He may be jealous, proud or modest without realising it. Such propensities can also be said to vary from weak to strong. Emotions, on the other hand, are relatively sudden occurrences which may vary from calm to violent: such states as humiliation, anger, shock, amusement, joy, embarrassment, etc. When a disposition is frustrated or overstimulated in some way, then a disturbance (in Ryle's metaphor – an eddy) is felt. For example, the tidy mother feels annoyed with her untidy children, or the jealous husband goes into a rage when he hears his wife whispering on the 'phone, or the humorously disposed pupil jumps up and down in glee at the success of a practical joke. When one disposition is in direct conflict with another disposition (an eddy brought about by two opposing currents) then emotional arousal, often in the form of anxiety, occurs: a man who wants to be seen as charitable cannot bear to part with his money; or a mother who, while wanting her adolescent daughter to grow up to be independent, is nevertheless apprehensive of the dangers of going out alone at night on her own.

Disposition and emotion may be seen both as distinct and complementary. Both are related to situations, but whereas emotion *occurs* in a situation, disposition *qualifies* that occurrence. The relationship to the situation is that of a verb and an adjective, respectively. For example, two people witness an incident of child bullying. One witness is distressed (verb), being disposed to pity (adjective); another witness feels a mild regret (verb), being disposed to seeing the world as a tough place anyway (adjective). What a person feels is, in part, controlled by the kind of person he is.

As I suggested in my address to the INSEA Conference on the Arts held in Adelaide in 1978[14] ('Emotion in the dramatic process – is it an adjective or a verb?') [see this book, p. 100], participants in drama are often required to qualify their actions by recalling an appropriate dispositional (adjectival) characteristic, so that a child role-playing a craftsman evokes a quality of respect for his materials or role-playing an indian chief evokes a quality of seriousness and dignity, role-playing a gang-member – a quality of toughness, role-playing a jealous husband – a quality of suspicion. That this 'descriptive' attribute is to be found most commonly in the performance mode is obvious, but even in dramatic playing a participant may be dependent on finding the appropriate disposition for achieving credibility i.e. the right action of, say, tapping out the morse code only becomes real when accompanied by an air of determined concentration.

Finding this second dimension may be the only 'way in' to a role available to a child, for he may in fact be more familiar with the disposition than with the role. For instance, the role of Cleopatra may seem formidably complex and remote but being someone who is disposed to having her own way may make Cleopatra seem immediately accessible. Dispositional recall is both personal and universal: the child can recall from past feeling memories that he has in common with others. As Tina Koppel has pointed out, the pursuit of a dispositional dimension does not guarantee any depth of commitment to the role. Adopting a serious attitude of concentration as a craftsman may be just as superficial as simulating the craftsman's actions. Some children can 'switch on' the required emotional overtones as readily as they attach adjectives to nouns in their written essays. Indeed, in the early days of so-called creative drama we used to encourage such glibness. In my INSEA address,[15] I described the typical tambour-controlled story-telling as follows:

> They all came to the entrance of the dark cave; they were s-c-a-r-e-d (the children switch on their 'scared' look). Plucking up courage (their 'courageous' look) they entered the cave slowly, their eyes peering into the dark (some of them are not peering), and then, suddenly (they get ready to be surprised) there is a distant light (they *are* surprised); it is high up in the roof. (Heads raised) they can feel a warm glow on their faces and as they stretch their arms towards it (a good class this) there appears in the middle of the glow a vision. They are transfixed with awe (none too good on awe; must bring that into the next story) and then . . . it has gone . . . and slowly they left the cave. (p. 14)

This is the kind of drama practice that is concerned with describing an event rather than experiencing it. Such adjectival embellishment, even when it is rather more significantly handled than in the above narrative, is static rather than organic. Although the evocation of a disposition is initially effective, it is not *in itself* a potential for development. One of its more flexible features, however, is that a participant is capable of recalling dispositions other than his own. In other words a tidy person could by virtue of role reversal temporarily 'take on' an 'untidy' disposition, drawing on his experience of being at the receiving end of other people's untidiness. One of the satisfactions of doing drama is that it creates opportunities for experimenting with attitudes that are not normally available, so that the most amenable child can enjoy being murderous, bloody-minded, and dictatorial. He *can* enjoy such attributes, but only if he (a) wants to, and (b) can sustain them. Some people, for example, are so afraid of aggression that they have no wish to take on such a disposition, even though they know it is 'only a game'; others find that in the process of playing aggression, the hostile signals in the situation are sufficient to cause them to want to take flight in their normal way. Clearly, what I pointed to as a more flexible feature of taking on a disposition is in fact generative of its own emotional excitement, for the very act of acquiring a disposition that is foreign to one's make-up (or is normally repressed as in the case of aggressive inclinations) is causing a disturbance, pleasurable or otherwise. In Ryle's terms, eddy has been caused by the opposition of two currents. Before we go on to look at emotional disturbance in detail, I would like to draw attention to two fascinating contrasting ways in which dispositions can be simultaneously acknowledged and ignored in theatrical performance and in teacher role-play.

Stanislavski[16] points out that if an actor is playing a 'wicked' character, he does not have to put his acting energies into portraying wickedness, for that particular propensity is assumed by the audience who do their own work in projecting that disposition onto the character. Similarly a teacher-in-role may find it a redundant matter to continue to display a particular attribute, for that is already established in the children's minds. Thus when I was asked by a class of 5–7 year olds to be a witch in their drama (and a frightening one, they insisted) I only need to offer a token sign of my frightening disposition, for they are already projecting this onto my actions. My responsibility is to focus on some particular problem. (I became a witch whose wickedness was thwarted because he had insufficient reading skills to cope with his spell-book. The children are faced with the dilemma of balancing their fear of the wicked outcome of my spells with their frustration in recognising I was misreading the words. So they taught me to read!) Notice that in referring to the children's facing a dilemma, we are again into real emotion. It seems that in drama few currents can be free from eddies! And yet this is what Robert Witkin seems to want to deny. But more of that later. First we have to move away from drama to examine some other relevant views of emotion.

The boulder in the stream is equivalent to a new situation that changes the level or direction of the behaviour. As Lazarus *et al.*[17] point out, the answer to the question, 'Why did he behave as he did?' always has two answers, a dispositional one and a situational one. This is equivalent to Ryle's question, 'Why did the glass break?', the answer being either an explanation of the cause: 'a stone hit it' (situational) or an explanation of the reason: 'glass is brittle' (dispositional), but Ryle's metaphor of current and boulder breaks down in so far as the stream seems passively subjected to currents and eddies, whereas a man at any one moment has active control over, at least, his emotional eddies. And this is where we introduce the notion of a cognitive component of an emotional state. Many writers, as a glance at the publication edited by Magda Arnold[18] on the international symposium on emotion held in Loyola, Maryland will show, see emotion as a response to an act of appraisal. Piaget[19] puts it: 'We do not love without seeking to understand, and we do not even hate without a subtle use of judgement' (p. 207). The implication here is that emotion is mediated or controlled by interpretation of the immediate situation. Jung[20] calls this a 'feeling function' and points out that one can feel appropriately and inappropriately just as one can think appropriately or inappropriately. Reacting emotionally to, say, sarcasm, threat, mystery, seduction, compassion, humour or beauty is the result of a judgement. The disturbance one feels might, respectively, be labelled as humiliation, fear, puzzlement, sexual arousal, gratitude, amusement or awe. It follows that an immature person might well mistakenly read polite interest as enthusiasm or fair criticism as insult. (Indeed I am certain that one of the values of drama in schools is the refining of children's perceptions of other people's feelings and intentions.) Nevertheless, appropriate or not, an emotional response is the result of a 'feeling-about' a situation by the responder, a significant characteristic which Witkin[21] seems to ignore. Emotion – disturbance experienced as sensate impulse – seems to be the passive partner of a stimulus response relationship. The sequence, according to Witkin, seems to be that something causes a disturbance within the organism, subsequently generating energy which has to be expressed. Whereas Jung applies the word feeling to a level of judgement giving feeling value to an emotional response, Witkin chooses to use feeling in respect of outcome, which, to qualify for the designation has to be in a special mode – reflexive rather than reactive. Reactive expression of emotion is to do with discharging, getting rid of, giving vent to one's feelings. Having a good cry, a good laugh, a fit of tantrums seem obvious examples. Witkin's own examples are kicking a door in anger or throwing one's hat in the air in joy. Reflexive expression on the other hand is to do with reciprocation and recall of the disturbance. His examples curiously seem to be drawn from physical sensations such as feeling a pebble or scratching oneself rather than from the expression of emotion. We are left with the clear impression that the arts meet Witkin's requirements of reflexive expression, but I am not clear whether, for example, writing a letter of condolence or having a heated, but controlled, argument with someone would be regarded as reflexive. Certainly both of these examples could be seen as a process of finding a symbolic form recalling the original disturbance. Like Witkin, Ross[22] has a more plentiful supply of illustrative images for reactive response: 'We lash out physically and verbally, we run away, we run amok, we gasp, we groan, we roar with delight or rage, we flash our eyes, raise our voice, wring our hands, hide the face we have lost or are in danger of losing' (p. 41). One could be forgiven for concluding that reflexive expression is merely any kind of behaviour of more moderate proportions than the extreme agitations listed here.

However, when Witkin urges that the creative arts epitomise reflexiveness the search for everyday examples perhaps becomes redundant, for the notion of feelings transformed by a symbolic form into a feeling-idea is one with which we are familiar. Susanne Langer, in her impressive contributions to our understanding of aesthetics, has pursued her theory of art as 'contemplation of feeling' through several volumes. Typically in her third publication[23] on the subject she writes: '. . . what the creative form expresses is the nature of feelings conceived, imaginatively realised, and rendered by a labor of formulation and abstractive vision' (p. 9). Any emotion an artist feels undergoes a sea-change. If he is sad, then his art expresses a sadness, as Ivy Campbell-Fisher[24] puts it, 'released from the entanglement of contingency.'

Witkin[25] uses a Piagetian model. He sees an assimilative-accommodative balance between the sensate impulse and the medium through which it is to be recalled.

The impulse itself has undergone modification (accommodation) as has the medium, and the resultant form is the product of their interaction. The medium and the impulse have both 'changed each other' in the process of building form. This 'changing of each other' and the maintenance of a dynamic equilibrium between impulse and medium is achieved by the oscillation in consciousness that makes possible reflexive control of the medium that is fundamental in all art processes whether in poetry, drama, music, visual art or whatever. (p. 87)

He goes on to discuss the effects of imbalance towards either assimilation or accommodation. 'If it is assimilation that has ascendency then the impulse runs riot in an entirely autistic egocentric manner . . . When accommodation has ascendency then the opposite is the case. The individual accepts the absolute dictatorship of external constraint. He copies slavishly. He seeks to create a pre-determined form; one that has been built on the outside of the self.' (pp. 87–8). Reflexive control, he explains, is only maintained when a proper equilibrium is achieved. It is not clear whether failure constitutes a reactive discharge of the impulse – presumably so.

It is not insignificant that Robert Witkin chose the drama section of his book to discuss the above points about balance and imbalance. I suspect that drama lessons more than any other arts lessons have furnished him with examples of things being *out* of control. Indeed it may be the case that the disservice I claim his book does to drama in schools is a direct result of his having observed inadequate teaching. Certainly he does not include a single example of good drama teaching. One can only conclude that he did not see any!

I shall offer my criticism in respect of three connected aspects of his theory: the nature of an impulse or disturbance; the application of his model to a drama experience, which I shall deal with first; and the relationship between the simulated and the real network within a group.

An important aspect of Witkin's model is its temporal dimension. Likewise, Ross,[26] in applying Witkin's model spells out this stimulus-response sequence clearly:

1 The stimulus encounter arouses a mood indicating an unresolved feeling schema within us.

2 With the mood on us we must first choose between expression and repression and, if we choose expression, between reaction and reflexion.

3 Subjective-reflexive action involves the formulation and the testing of an hypothesis about the deep structure of the schema.

4 We project the impulse through a medium that allows its recipro-

cation, and make a form expressive of and guided by the impulse. (p. 54)

He seems to be ignoring here a danger that Bosanquet in 1915[27] recognised:

> We must not suppose that we first have a disembodied feeling 'and then' set out to find an embodiment adequate to it. In a word, imaginative expression creates the feeling in creating its embodiment, and the feeling so created not merely cannot be otherwise expressed, but cannot otherwise exist, than in and through the embodiment which imagination has found for it. (pp. 33–4)

Witkin, I think, would agree with Bosanquet that the feeling expressed is not the original emotion, for he is very much concerned with the notion of transformation, but transformation that is faithful to the original impulse without allowing for new feelings to enter the experience. He writes,[28] 'To establish reflexive control the pupil requires to use his sensate impulse to initiate a movement or successive approximations to a resolution of that impulse' (pp. 185–6).

One detects that the rigidity of the model Witkin has chosen leads him to hold some peculiar assumptions about the ground rules from which a teacher might operate. He advises for example, 'In the first place it will help if the teacher makes use of different iconic media from that in which the pupil's expressive act is taking place.' (p. 171).[29] This smacks of the well-tried style of lesson planning where the teacher puts on a record inviting the class to write an essay or paint a picture, but if applied to drama this method must not then ignore the potential for stimulation within the dramatic action itself. When a child involves himself in make-believe play in the garden, the original stimulus that motivates him to start is supplemented by or even superseded by the first step he takes into the identification process which may create new 'disturbance' at every stage of the playing. It is not only as Witkin suggests an oscillation between the original impulse and the medium with gradual approximation towards a final form, there is also an oscillation between the recalled modified impulse and newly felt emotional experiences. This second kind of oscillation is especially marked in drama, not merely because it happens to be a characteristic, but *because the identifying process of drama is, by definition, reflexive*. It is the nature of role-playing that an impulse is projected reflexively through the 'as-if' mode of action. Indeed in developmental terms it might be argued that the act of pretence is the first kind of reflexive expression available to the young child. The baby observed by Piaget[30] who between the ages of twelve months and eighteen months used other objects as a pillow and pretended to be asleep (p. 96) is indulging in reflexive action, par excellence.

Witkin[31] also holds a curiously limited view of the characteristics of the disturbance itself:

> In addition to varying the sensate modality of the stimulus forms to distance it from the expressive forms of the pupil, the teacher might find it helpful to use a number of quite different stimulus forms to evoke the same sensate problem. In this way the pupil is able to transcend the particular forms used to set the problem by grasping the resemblance between the different forms, the 'gestalt' they have in common. The 'warm-cool' contrast can be presented in a variety of different forms. Different though the forms would be, they would each possess the same central principle of sensate ordering; the same 'gestalt' (i.e. the warm-cool contrast) and it would be this gestalt that would become embedded in the particularity of the pupil's experience. The setting of the sensate problem is the evoking of a specific gestalt, a sensate ordering in the context of the pupil's experience. The range and variety of different stimulus forms both release the pupil from too great a dependence on any single form, and at the same time encourage him to deepen and widen his exploration of his own experience. 'Sweet-sorrowing' is a sensate experience at quite a high level of complexity. It can be evoked by any number of different stimulus situations apart from the most obvious. Once it has been evoked directly, the elements of sweet-sorrowing are sensate experience. They constitute a sensate problem, transcending the particular forms through which it was evoked. (p. 172)

This passage reveals an important clue to another aspect of Witkin's theory. This is the reference to the use of stimuli like warm-cool contrast or sweet-sour dialectic. It is clear that when he talks of impulse or disturbance he does not have any kind of strong emotional engagement in mind. This is why offering music to listen to or a picture to look at fits his theory. The class are to listen to the *Romeo and Juliet* theme of *West Side Story*; they are to respond to its dialectic; and then, sustaining their feeling response, to find their own dramatic form to express it. He is not interested in their becoming emotionally engaged *in* the theme during the dramatic process. This is where his theory does not, indeed logically cannot, take into account the way in which drama is uniquely different from the other arts. If a child is filled with compassion as he writes his own sad story (as Arnaud Reid puts it, 'enjoying the sadness') the mode of his experiencing (emotional engagement) and the mode of his story-writing are on two different psychological levels, but if a child is thus disturbed during drama, the emotional engagement and the mode of expression belong to the same emotional plane. We need to look at the notion of 'planes' or 'orders' of experiences more closely.

Orders of experience

The basic dimensions of our living are ourselves in time and space. We always exist in the 'now' and 'here'. Through images we can move into the future and the past: we can day-dream and have memories, while our bodies and objects around us remain in the here and now. Through the development of symbolic systems, language and mathematics, we can communicate and build conceptual resources, while our bodies and objects around us remain in the here and now. Bruner[32] has labelled these modes of experience as enactive, iconic and symbolic.

This hierarchy of action, image and symbol Bruner sees as developmental stages in mental growth. Little acknowledgement seems to be given however to the way man applies these mental capacities to the ordering of his life as a social being. Whereas higher animals seem to attend almost entirely to the 'events' of living, a man can, when he chooses, release himself from practicalities (first order experiences) by contriving a detachment from them – he can read a book, paint a picture, play football, sing in a choir, go to a disco, attend a funeral, tell a joke, watch a cookery demonstration. There are thus two kinds of experiencing: the first is direct, functional, circumstantial, with implications for responsibilities and consequences. The second is set aside from the first, an agreed contrivance, relieving the participants temporarily of the burden of exigencies.

The importance to this chapter of the distinction between two kinds of experiencing – the practical and the non-practical – is that it throws light on our understanding of emotion. Because the detachment of the non-practical from the practical is never complete, there occurs what Vygotsky[33] calls 'dual affect'. He writes of child-play, '. . . the child weeps in play as a patient, but revels as a player' (p. 549). Here the author is, of course, referring to a particular kind of second order experiencing, but 'dual affect' belongs to all forms of arts, rituals, games and any other attempts to hold practicalities in abeyance. The importance of such a notion as dual affect was brought home to me when, a few years ago, a friend reported to me that her nine year old grandchild hurried into the room one day, picked up her copy of *Black Beauty*, searched for a particular page she had already read, started to read it and burst into tears. Asked by her grandmother what was the matter she replied, 'This bit is so sad!' The relevance of this anecdote is that the girl had sought out the experience. She could cope with her distress because it gave her satisfaction to do so. There was 'dual affect'. Just as the anger we might feel during a game is tempered by the knowledge that it's 'only a game'. The girl's grandmother could have said, 'It's only a book'.

But there is an assumption behind the concept of dual affect that may well cloud the whole picture. When I use the phrase, 'it's only a game' there is an implication that whereas it is regrettable that someone should get angry, the anger is not as intense as in real life because it is accompanied by an overriding feeling of enjoying the game. Now an alternative way of viewing the anger is to see it as *released* by the knowledge that it is only a game, not regretted, but expected. The nine year old girl could allow herself to weep, *because* it was a book. The tears may roll down my cheeks in the cinema, *because* it is a film. In other words being relieved of the burden of exigencies may be seen as man's way of bringing to the surface his deepest emotions. (I am not suggesting that this is a necessary condition – watching a vacuum-cleaning demonstration is not likely to touch deep wells of awe or even envy!)

The way the emotions are expressed is controlled partly by the forms or rules implicit in the occasion and partly, as Lazarus *et al.*[34] have pointed out, by our culture. For instance societies differ in the way they handle the expression of grief. When I watch a procession of returning heroes, it is permitted for me to cheer, laugh or cry to express whatever feelings of joy, awe or pride I have within me. Thus the rules of the occasion protect the participants, not *from* emotion but, '*into* emotion' a phrase pertinently used by Dorothy Heathcote in respect of her drama work. To summarise, there are two orders of experiencing, one dealing directly with the practical business of living, the other, non-practical, deliberately set apart from the first. In enjoying the second we may in extreme cases seem to have suspended the first, but this is an illusion – our bodies go on attending to the business of living no matter how we are absorbed, for instance, in a good book. The two orders of experiencing stimulate what Vygotsky terms 'dual affect', emotional responses which may contradict each other. We may be sitting in the dark in the cinema silently enjoying our tears or become embarrassed because they have turned to weeping which has got out of hand. On the other hand there may be no contradiction – we may anticipate with relish the comedian's jokes at which we know we are going to laugh. There are two significantly contrasted ways of explaining the emotional accompaniment of the non-practical. One way is to say that when we involve ourselves in games rituals and the arts, we are protected from distressing emotional reactions by the modifying adjustments of the practical world i.e. 'It's not for real', the other way is to say that we are protected into significant emotions that practical living never allows us to express. The explanations may not be as mutually exclusive as they first appear. That we simultaneously hold both worlds in our conciousness does have a modifying influence; that we are released from practical considerations may indeed have a liberating influence. There may well be a two-way pull.

But inherent in my non-practical modes are 'regulating-valves' for channelling emotional expression. Rituals have their public codes, games have their rules of conduct and the arts have their inner forms – which brings us to the point where we can discuss the uniqueness of drama in relation to the other arts.

Drama and emotion

I have suggested that the arts belong to a second order of experiencing. They differ from each other in terms of the degree to which their products occur in time and space. A painting occupies space, not time; a violin solo occurs in time but not in space. Additionally, in each case, the medium of the product (paint on canvas or a musical sound) is different from the actions involved in the process; (dipping a brush into paint and making strokes on the canvas or bowing on a violin). In this sense the product is a projection. Acting and dancing, and to some extent singing, on the other hand, occur in both time and space, and the medium of the product (action) is the same as the actions involved in the process. In this sense there is an absence of projection. The importance of projection in relation to drama was first identified by Peter Slade[35] who based his theory of play on a distinction he liked to draw between 'personal' and 'projected' activity:

> Some child observers would make a distinction between realistic play and imaginative play. But, in fact, play (certainly in the earlier stages)

is so fluid, containing at any moment experiences of everyday outward life and of imaginative inner life, that it is debatable whether
the one should be judged as a different activity from the other. It is
important, of course, that the difference is understood, but the distinction pertains to the intellect rather than to play itself. The child
develops towards reality as it gains experience of life. This is a process
rather than a distinction.

The only true distinction in play is that of personal play and projected play. Personal play is obvious drama; the whole person or self
is used. It is typified by movement and characterisation. We note
the dance entering and the experience of being things or people.

Projected play is drama, too; the whole mind is used, but the body
not so fully. Treasures are used which either take on characters of
the mind or become part of the place ('stage', in a theatre sense)
where drama takes place. During moments of typical projected play
we do not see the whole body being used. The child stands still, sits,
lies prone, or squats, and may use chiefly the hands. The main action
takes place outside the body, and the whole is characterised by extreme mental absorption. Strong mental projection is taking place.
(p. 29–30)

But as we have seen drama is by definition reflexive, that is an impulse is intentionally projected through an 'as if' medium. What is absent from the self (not here and now) is projected through what is
physically present for the self (the here and now). One can understand
of course the distinction that Peter Slade wanted to make between using
one's 'whole self' and 'projecting' oneself, but it seems to me that the
important thing about drama is not that there is no projection but that
there *appears* to be none. In this 'as if' process projection is critical, but
not easily discernable.

The notion of projection is central to our discussion on emotion for
it seems there is an inverse relationship between the emotions that can
be aroused and the degree to which projection is in evidence. To put it
crudely, more people weep in the theatre than in the art gallery. This
comparison between the emotional effect of two such different forms
of projection as painting and drama may seem fatuously obvious, but
the point becomes worth making when we look at drama not as a single
example of projection but as a complex form having varying degrees of
projection within it.

Some dramatic activity appears to be so close to living that no projection is apparent compared with other forms of dramatic activity

where the form of the projection is sharply defined. Children playing being in a haunted house by putting themselves in complete darkness in the room they were playing in might be an extreme example of the former. Children manipulating puppets in a story about a haunted house would be an extreme example of the latter. I have suggested there is an inverse relationship between the degree to which the projection is evident and the emotion aroused. It is tempting to see this relationship solely in terms of proportional intensity, the more clearly defined the projection the less intense the emotional experience, so that our 'haunted house' example could be seen as a hierarchy of intensity:

1 Pretending, in the dark, to be in a haunted house	EXTREME INTENSITY
2 Pretending, in a light room, to be in a haunted house	LESS INTENSE
3 Rehearsing or 'making a play' about being in a haunted house	LESS INTENSE
4 Performing a story about being in a haunted house	LESS INTENSE
5 Using puppets to tell a story about being in a haunted house.	LEAST INTENSE

The logic of such an 'intensity' hierarchy would suit us very well, for we would also be able to point to the fact that even in the most intense dramatic situation the significant 'as if' projection still applies for the children are likely to be far more scared in a real haunted house, a point which in a different form was made earlier when we were discussing second order experiences released from the burdens of practical living. In that discussion the notion of dual affect was introduced and this was further linked with a reference to the possibility of some second order experiences stimulating significantly different qualities of emotion.

It can now be argued however that degrees of discernibility of projection not only affect *intensity* of emotion as in the 'haunted house' list above, but also the *quality* of emotion. That there can be different qualities of emotion (rage, anger and happiness within the same class of emotion (hostility) has been identified by Arieti[36] but few other writers on emotion seem to have taken this seriously. Arieti's point is that level of emotion is dependent upon the degree and kind of symbolic mediation. To rely too heavily here on a particular theory would be to take that theory out of its psycho-analytical context, but it seems not unreasonable to assume that just as the context of an emotional experience will dictate the *kind* of emotion expressed, the medium of projection will affect its quality.

Drama then, combines three characteristics: it is non-practical and as such belongs to all second order experiencing; it is a form of projection which links it with the other arts; its 'as if' characteristic *seems* to deny the previous two, both its non practical nature and its inherent projection. The combination of these three features influences the emotional disturbance experienced during dramatic activity in respect of three factors: the dual affect, intensity and quality.

Thus our 'haunted house' list is not straightforwardly a matter of intensity. It becomes modified and indeed turned upside down by the other two factors. For instance it is possible that the dual affect during the 'haunted house' was such that the fun of being in the dark destroyed any real hold on the make-believe so that the emotional balance could not favour any intensity of feeling. (Incidentally, Witkin in his stated opposition to 'crisis' drama would be nearer the mark if he justified his point in the light of this kind of imbalance rather than from a fear of over-seriousness.) Alternatively, the simple puppet performance of a sad 'haunted house' story might stir a significantly different quality of emotion, intensely felt.

The important point that I have been leading up to is that the teacher is in a strong position to control dual affect, intensity and quality by making a choice from the many different degrees of projection within dramatic activity. We can lengthen our 'haunted house' list:

1 Pretending, in the dark, to be in a haunted house.
2 Pretending, in a light room, to be in a haunted house.
3 Rehearsing or 'making a play' about being in a haunted house.
4 Performing a story about being in a haunted house.
5 Using puppets to tell a story about being in a haunted house.
6 Children reporting what they think will happen when they reach the haunted house.
7 Children enacting what they think will happen when they reach the haunted house.
8 Children meeting a ghost (teacher-in-role).
9 Following a string of coded messages that tell where the house is.
10 Holding a seance.
11 Collating evidence from old letters (in role as historians) that the house was once thought to be haunted.
12 Pictures that are able to speak of all the things they have witnessed.
13 Meeting a past owner (teacher-in-role) who pleads with journalists

(children-in-role) not to disturb the past.

14 Detectives in their office provided with files on missing persons.
15 Scientists writing their reports for the 'National Poltergeist Society'.
16 Performing a 'ghost' incident in stylised mime.
17 A performance where the action is intermittently 'frozen' by a narrator who pieces the story together or invites comments from the audience.
18 Making a sound track capturing the essence of 'hauntedness'.
19 Writing a script.
20 Journalists interviewing people who know the secrets of the house.
21 Holding a ceremony to calm the troubled spirits.
22 Ghosts (children-in-role) scaring away the intruder (teacher-in-role).
23 Interviewing a medium (teacher or child-in-role) about her craft.
24 Drawing a 'ghost' picture.
25 A meeting of neighbours who are worried about the value of their houses being devalued.
26 Writing a letter that is a cry for help.

The degrees of projection are obvious in the above list – indeed they might be roughly graded as:

Being involved in dramatic action 1, 2, 8, 9, 13, 22.
Verbally reporting 6.
Interviewing 20, 23.
Ritual 10, 12, 21.
Various kinds of performance from naturalistic theatre to puppetry 3, 4, 5, 7, 16, 17
Debating 25
Drawing 24
Writing 15, 19, 26
Making a tape 18
Researching evidence 9, 11, 14

There is another kind of classification useful to the teachers – the degree to which the particular form of projection deals directly with whatever emotional import is central to the context. For example 'entering a haunted house to investigate the strange noises' is *direct* compared with 'holding a meeting of rate-payers demanding a rebate because the noises in the near-by haunted house are lowering the value of the property', a dramatic involvement which, however lively, does not require the participants to 'experience' haunted house. In addition to this direct/indirect dimension, a further criterion relevant to the teacher is whether the acting (the 'as if' mode of behaviour) requires merely (at least initially) dispositional recall as in stylised mime or an openness to an emotional disturbance as in 'meeting a ghost' or 'interviewing people who know the secrets of the house' or 'writing a letter that is a cry for help'.

Thus the teacher has control over three dimensions affecting emotional response: degree of projection; direct/indirect; and dispositional/disturbance potential. A point to stress here is that the 'as if' mode removes the disturbance from the 'raw' emotion of first order experiencing. It is not necessarily less intense (indeed we have seen that second order experiencing may release emotion of considerable intensity because it *is* of a second order) but it may be different in kind or quality. In selecting a particular kind of dramatic activity a teacher is obviously concerned with many factors including such crucial matters as learning potential within the material, the cognitive skills of the pupils, the social health of the class and so on, but here we are concentrating on how his judgement about emotional outcome affects his choice.

Although it can be claimed that the spontaneous, 'living-through' interaction can give pupils a powerful experiential reference to reflect upon, there are some circumstances when such a direct, undiluted approach should be avoided. The following examples may serve as useful guidelines:

1 When the topic is currently a 'hot potato' e.g. racism, with a group who have been at the centre of racial violence.
2 When the topic is not emotionally readily accessible, for example death, with a group of pre-adolescents.
3 When the topic is too strong a reminder of a recent painful event, for example family life, when someone in the class has just experienced the break up of a home.
4 Where the action of the drama is likely to reinforce antisocial values actually held by some in the group e.g. mugging, with children who have engaged in the activity.
5 Where there is a danger that the class will abuse their roles in order to perpetuate within the fiction some unhealthy aspect of the existing group dynamics, using the fiction as a pretext for bullying a class scapegoat. (That is not to support Robert Witkin[37] who seems to strike an over-cautious note in respect of permeating the barrier between the real and simulated networks of relationships with the class. (p. 80).
6 Where a class is inclined to be too embarrassed to be in any role other

than that of investigators, commenters or any other distanced intellectual role.

7 Where the topic is of an essentially physical crisis (for example fight-
ing flames or drowning) so that even a token simulation is likely to
strain credibility.

8 Where a class are already in an excitable or anxious state.

9 Where a class too easily indulge in emotional wallowing.

In any of the above instances the dual affect is likely to be overtaken
by first order, 'raw' emotions, for at least some of the members of the
class, unless a high degree of projection, indirectness and/or dispositional requirement distances the participants from the central experience. The various devices at a teacher's disposal can thus be seen to be
protective. For this reason some teachers may wrongly assume that the
direct experiential handling of a poignant or 'crisis' topic should always
be avoided. On the contrary, the distancing devices may only be *pre-
liminary* steps towards the direct experiencing, paving the way for a high
degree of credibility that could not otherwise be achieved. 'But supposing', a teacher might argue, 'that one unwittingly stirs up painful
memories for someone in one's class. Would not the use of distancing
devices have been a safeguard?' Of course they would, but I maintain
it would be professionally inadequate for a teacher continually to work
from such a cautious base-line: only a limited form of dramatic teaching
could ever take place.

But if we examine the reason for using distancing devices, it is that
we are concerned with the break-down of the fiction because first order
experiencing is likely to take over. And the emotion we are most often
dealing with when this happens is more often than not that of *embarrassment* and rarely that of distress. It should further be stated that even
the arousal of painful memories to a point of blocking the fiction *is not
in itself harmful.* Indeed for some individuals the opposite may be true.
The teacher does not seek to cause pain, but if it occurs he should not
assume that tears or tight-lipped silence means either extreme distress
or normal defences broken.

However, although a teacher is not a therapist, when the drama has
caused more pain than can be contained by the fiction (it is incidentally
my experience that the rare times this has happened have been with
adults, not children) then his responsibility is that of any other caring
adult when someone is upset: he must judge the kind of help that is
needed – comforting words, a sympathetic ear, a touch of the hand, a
diversion, privacy or just time to recover.

Summary

I began the chapter by discussing emotional avoidance and the particular responsibility art educators seem to carry as guardians of emotional development. A distinction was drawn between art teacher and therapist.

Using Ryle's metaphor of a stream, one can usefully distinguish between a current which represents an ongoing emotional disposition and an eddy which is an emotional disturbance. These two distinct emotional behaviours can be identified as relevant to drama.

Robert Witkin is interested in emotional disturbance only in so far as it is projected reflexively through a medium of expression. He applies the term 'feeling' to the outcome of an oscillation between impulse and medium. This usage of the term is in marked contrast to other philosophical views of feeling as a cognitive/affective appraisal. For Witkin feeling is a disturbance transformed.

I maintain it is more useful to view emotion in drama as belonging to all second order experiencing of which the arts are only a part. First order experiencing deals directly with the practicalities and responsibilities of living, the emotional content remaining unmediated by distinct forms, rules or frames. The emotion can be said to be 'raw'. Second order experiencing temporarily relieves one from the practicalities and responsibilities, the emotional content being mediated by rules, rituals frames and forms etc. The emotion may be different in kind, quality and intensity from 'raw emotion'. Raw emotion is nevertheless always present to some degree so that 'dual affect' is held in delicate balance. (A hungry man reading about food may upset this balance so that second order experiencing disappears and he sets about the serious business of getting food!)

I prefer to see drama activity as a continual stimulation of second order emotions. In other words, the dramatic medium (the reflexive 'as if') is not only the vehicle through which disturbance is expressed but actively the source of new disturbances. Thus the participant is *experiencing* as opposed merely to finding a means of expression.

Projection is a feature common to all the arts. What gives drama education its richness and variety is the wide range of *degrees* of projection available. It seems to be the case that where projection is minimal the emotional engagement can be more volatile compared with the more contained emotion of a highly projected form.

Degrees of projection, combined with other dimensions such as direct/indirect treatment of subject-matter and the dispositional/disturbance requirement become the parameters from which a teacher may make the basis for selecting a dramatic activity. One of his principal concerns will be to keep the 'dual affect' balance.

I finally discussed the problem when, inadvertently, the drama causes a participant to be upset beyond anything the fiction can contain. Common sense and not over reaction should guide the teacher in what to do.

Emotion in drama. Unpublished, 1981.

References

1 Witkin R 1974 *Intelligence of feeling*. Heinemann.
2 Jones R M 1972 *Fantasy and feeling in education*. Penguin. (First published by N.Y. University Press, 1968.)
3 Bruner J S 1966 *Towards a theory of instruction*. Harvard University Press.
4 Witkin R op. cit.
5 Bloom S, Krathwahl D R, Masia B B 1964 *Taxonomy of educational objectives*, Handbook 2: *Affective domain*. David McKay.
6 MacMurray J 1935 *Reason and emotion*. Faber.
7 Wilson J 1971 *Education in religion and the emotions*. Heinemann.
8 Neill A S 1966 *Times Educational Supplement* (30 Dec.)
9 Ross M 1974 *The creative arts*. Heinemann.
10 Jones R M 1972 op. cit.
11 Witkin R op. cit.
12 Sutherland M 1971 *Everyday imagining in education*. Routledge and Kegan Paul.
13 Ryle G 1949 *The concept of mind*. Hutchinson.
14 Bolton G M 1978 Emotion in drama: is it an adjective or a verb? *National Association for Drama in Education Journal*, **3** (Dec.).
15 Bolton G M ibid.
16 Stanislavski C 1962 *My life in art* trans E Reynolds Hapgood. Bles.
17 Lazarus R S, Averill J R, and Opton E M 1970 *Towards a cognitive theory of emotion*. In Arnold M (ed) *Feelings and emotions*. Academic Press, p. 215.
18 Arnold M (ed) 1970 *Feelings and emotions*. Academic Press.
19 Piaget J 1972 *Play, dreams and imitation in childhood*. Routledge and Kegan Paul. (First published in English by Heinemann, 1951.)

20 Jung C G 1923 *Psychological types*. Harcourt, New York.
21 Witkin R op. cit.
22 Ross M op. cit.
23 Langer S K 1975 *Mind: an essay on human feeling* (vol 1). Johns Hopkins Paperback.
24 Campbell-Fisher I G 1950 Aesthetics and the logic of sense. *Journal of General Psychology*. **XLIII**: 245–73.
25 Witkin R op. cit.
26 Ross M op. cit.
27 Bosanquet B 1915 *Three lectures on aesthetic*. Macmillan.
28 Witkin R op. cit.
29 Witkin R ibid.
30 Piaget J op. cit.
31 Witkin R op. cit.
32 Bruner J op. cit.
33 Vygotsky L S 1976 Play and its role in the mental development of the child. In Bruner J S *et al. Play: its development and evolution*. Penguin.
34 Lazarus R S *et al*. op. cit.
35 Slade P 1954 *Child drama*. University of London Press.
36 Arieti S 1967 *The intrapsychic self*. Basic Books.
37 Witkin R op. cit.

Section three
Implications for drama as an art form

Introduction

Three questions appear to be central to Bolton's thinking about drama as an art form:

(a) What is required of drama to qualify it as art?
(b) By implication what is required of the teacher/participants?
(c) Does 'drama for learning' preclude drama as art?

(a) and (c) are, in essence, questions of form, while (b) is a question of structure.

The third question, (c), is of central concern likewise to Brecht In *Theatre for pleasure or theatre for instruction* he asks:

But what has knowledge got to do with art?

Brecht's thinking here may serve as a useful resonator for Bolton's developing thinking in this section. For Brecht there is a crucial connection between learning and art:

One must have a certain inclination to penetrate deeper into things – a desire to make the world controllable – if one is to be sure of enjoying its poetry.

And, conversely, of art in relation to learning:

Theatre remains theatre even when it is instructive theatre.

The basic 'building block' of such an instructive theatre he describes in his famous example of the eyewitness after a street accident who demonstrates to bystanders what has happened: the actor as demonstrator of meaning.

The first essay in this section contains a strikingly similar example: Bolton has a gardener in a pub demonstrating a problem to a friend. In essence, this is a similar act of demonstration of meaning, but whereas Brecht embraces this concept as central to (his) art, Bolton rejects it. What Bolton appears to mean by art, in the early essays, is an essentially Stanislavskian concept, borne out by the importance given to the process of 'symbolisation' which he appears to equate with art:

Later a powerful 'symbolic' experience, as I would like to call it, took place with more or less the same action. We were now working in an art form.

Symbolisation, as a process, is the accumulation of meanings, and as such can be encouraged but not imposed; as a consequence the structure required is necessarily fluid. Two plays are at work, the 'play for the teacher' and the 'play for the children': the teacher is to seek 'moments of heightened significance', in the flow of what is, for the children, dramatic playing, or 'living-through' experience. One important feature in relation to the art form is the integration of the two, like two spotlights focussing together. This has to happen

if both educational and artistic requirements are to be satisfied.

Another necessary requirement is an *intention* on the part of the participants; but in 'Creative drama as an art form' it is merely an 'intention to create something'.

But the essays in this section reflect a change of direction towards a deepening concern for structure, arriving, in Bolton's second book, at 'game' as the analogy for drama.

By 'Drama as learning, as art and as aesthetic experience' the concept of symbolisation is qualified by two other elements of the art form, focus and tension. Moreover, Bolton appears to be defensive about 'using the word symbol at all'. His example of the 'charge nurse' placing a bib under the chin of one of the invalids encapsulates the change for us. Whereas it would almost certainly have qualified as art in 1977 (it is, like the second 25 dollar bill example in 'The process of symbolisation in improvised drama', a moment of 'heightened significance') in this essay it does not qualify as art. The reason is highly significant: it concerns autonomy within the structure. His requirement for intention on the part of the participants here is that they are conscious that a form is being created, and that the elements of form should be manipulated by the participants themselves:

It is not enough for a teacher, fully alert to formal significance, to structure the dramatic experience so that the pupils are caught unawares in a dramatic form.

This more Brechtian position, whereby he recognises the need for reflection upon action, for understanding and manipulating the medium itself *by the participants* indicates that 'game' is a more appropriate analogy for drama structure for Bolton these days.

But is this move towards Brechtian theory of theatre accompanied by a move towards a Brechtian (i.e. dialectical materialist) theory of knowledge? Like Brecht the relationship of the art form to 'the outside world' is of crucial significance to Bolton, who accuses Ross of ignoring it. However, for Brecht art is a means of understanding 'the great and complicated things that go on in the world' so that participants in art are equipped to 'make the world controllable': Bolton (like Ross) appears to be facing the other way, regarding the outside world, via the art form, conversely as the *means* whereby 'our deepest levels may be touched'. Art for 'personal knowledge' is a phenomenological position.

Creative drama as an art form

This essay serves as a useful introduction to the section because many of the key concepts relevant to the theme of this section are outlined in it, and are worth comparing directly with those to be found in the last essay of this section 'Drama as learning, as art and as aesthetic experience'.

Here Bolton argues for a concept of drama as artistic activity which later he is to reject, namely that the teacher, by involving children, albeit unconsciously, in theatre form, is thereby enabling them to work in the art form. The structure required for this is dramatic playing injected by the teacher with 'a sense of time, a quality of meaning, and a quality of feeling'. The educational purpose is described ambiguously as being that the 'participants should undergo some change'; 'that there must be some growth in the artist' akin to the concept of teaching as cultivation of plants. Autonomy is a low priority: 'Rarely can they do this for themselves.'

'The process of symbolisation in improvised drama', 'Imagery in drama in education' and 'Drama as concrete action'

Although 'Drama as concrete action' was in fact written after 'Drama in education and TIE – a comparison', it is included here because of its thematic relationship to the other two essays.

'The process of symbolisation' develops the concept of symbolisation introduced in the opening essay, identifying the *dialectical* nature of the relationship between drama and the concrete: 'Drama is/is not doing'. Two levels of abstraction in drama are described as (1) problem solving/decision making, and (2) value laden concepts. Later, in 'Drama and meaning', he identifies, as well as unconscious 'personal knowledge', plot, context and theme, relating drama consciously with other art forms, notably literature. Here drama is seen very much as an end in itself: the '"symbolic" experience' *equals* the art form.

In 'Imagery in drama in education' he amplifies these concerns further, and identifies a new problem, that of teaching context: 'How do you *really* convey, for example, Dickensian poverty to the children in western cultures today?' Where Dorothy Heathcote has developed 'mantle of the expert' as a mode of teaching enabling authentic exploration of context, Bolton has always seemed uneasy about the relationship of drama to context. In this essay he recognises the limits of *objects* used in a 'living through' mode of drama to answer this question; later he gives the responsibility for teaching context to theatre-in-education, regarding the context, in drama in education, merely as an excuse for teaching other things, an answer which is equally unconvincing.

'Drama as concrete action', a collection of teaching examples modifies the concept of symbolisation by developing the concept of focus, particularly as a 'concentration away from the self' (to be compared with Heathcote's 'the Other'). 'Action' is distinguished from 'activity' in terms of significance, as is 'focal objects' from 'stage props'.

Drama as learning, as art, and as aesthetic experience

With the concept 'aesthetic experience' developed here for the first time, Bolton is able to classify some drama experiences, while falling short of art, as having a *tendency towards* art. Many examples of his practice hitherto regarded as art would appear to fall into this category, because of his new evaluation of the concept of autonomy. Whereas in 'Drama in education and TIE – a comparison' he equates 'working in the art form' with participation in the teacher-in-role experience, here this is not enough.

Now he requires both a consciousness on the part of the group as a whole to use form (focus, tension, symbolisation) and a manipulation of it. A different concept of structure is therefore apparently called for with a tendency towards 'game' as developed in his latest thinking. He develops on from 'Drama and meaning' the theme of focal and subsidiary awareness: however, a contradiction in his position with regard to Ross's views becomes apparent. While warning Ross of falling into the trap of subjectivity, his evaluation of drama for 'personal knowledge', and his concept of the outside world as being the *means* whereby 'our deepest levels may be touched', appears to lead him into the same trap.

'Theatre form in drama teaching', 'Drama in education and TIE – a comparison'

It is interesting to compare these two essays. Written within a short time of each other soon after the Riverside Conference, which set out to explore differences/similarities between Drama and Theatre, they each focus upon opposite ends of the Drama/Theatre spectrum from the other.

'By drama do I still mean *not* theatre?' Bolton asks. His contradictory 'No' and 'Yes' indicate a rejection of the theory of mutual exclusion in favour of a theory of dialectics, mutual inclusion (each within the other). This is likewise reflected in his revaluing of 'Emotion as an adjective', and marks a shift away from purely 'living through' experience.

'Theatre form in drama teaching' is highly subjective, with an air of a diary about events which receive more rigorous analysis in *Towards a theory of drama in education*. However, it contains an interesting and curiously un-Boltonian feature – the outline of 'a perfect lesson', which invites speculation on what changes to this model he would now envisage.

In 'Drama in education and TIE – a comparison' the question of autonomy, hitherto neglected, becomes crucial. Theatre in education appears to remove it, while also requiring participation in what Bolton assumes is a 'living through' experience. Teacher-in-role, of which TIE is an extension, appears to resolve this contradiction; once more he argues that the teacher can involve the participants in the art form in this way.

Emphasis on the context, Bolton argues, distinguishes the two forms; whereas TIE has a duty to make the context significant, in DIE the context is often 'but a pretext for opening up the theme'. Later thinking appears to move him from this position, however.

Creative drama as an art form

It is sometimes suggested that with the emphasis drama teachers now place on creative activity as problem-solving and as a way of learning about life, drama as an art experience gets lost, left out or even abused in the zealous search for educational objectives. I shall argue in this paper that the opposite in fact is true, that great depth of learning is likely to take place when the experience is structured in a way that simultaneously meets the requirements of the educational objectives and of the art form.

The first half of this paper will be taken up with an attempt to isolate the principal features that appear to characterise drama, but before we can do that we need to look at dramatic activity in general terms as a behavioural phenomenon. A definition, or rather a description, must be found that distinguishes it from other forms of behaviour. Consider the following kinds of child play:

(a) A boy throws a long stick.
(b) He repeats this action many times.
(c) He repeats this action many times explaining that he is Robin Hood and this is his spear.

Most people would agree, I think, that dramatic activity can be said to have begun at (c). They may label it pretence, or make-believe or symbolic play. Vygotsky,[1] however, draws our attention to a functional significance. He points out that the essential difference between (c) and the other two forms is that in (c) the child has separated meaning from the action and object. Whereas in (a) and (b) the meaning is to do with throwing a stick which is exactly what is presently occurring, in (c) the meaning is to do with Robin Hood and his spear, neither of which is actually present in the environment. The action and objects of the physical world (in this case the stick-throwing and the stick) he calls a pivot, an aid to the creation of new meaning.

A description of dramatic activity may therefore run as follows:

dramatic activity is the creation of meaning that is independent of the environment by using actions and objects present in the environment.

The reader may think this has been a protracted way of arriving at a definition of behaviour we already recognised as make-believe play and therefore as dramatic activity, but the advantages of this perspective are that it immediately draws attention to the independent/dependent relationship with the environment, a key factor we shall be turning to later, and it also anticipates a view of art held by Arnaud Reid,[2] which I shall be adopting in this essay, that art is 'embodiment of meaning'.

But is a child playing at Robin Hood art? I have called it dramatic activity because its medium is that which drama employs, but I cannot claim that the child has created 'drama'. Indeed the following illustration will show only too clearly how far removed from an artistic experience the use of a dramatic form can be:

A professional landscape gardener, sitting in a pub, gives advice to his friend on how to set about turning a rubbish tip into a rockery. Not content with *telling* he switches to *showing* what to do by piling up tables and chairs with the liberal use of beer mugs to represent clumps or plants.

Although this illustration fits the above definition of dramatic behaviour, its very ordinariness throws up sharply the three criteria that play a significant part in judging dramatic activity as artistic activity. These are (1) a sense of time (not timing!), (2) a quality of meaning, and (3) a quality of feeling.

A sense of time

The most obvious distinction between the child playing Robin Hood and the gardener is that the child is saying 'I *am* Robin Hood throwing a spear'. The gardener is not saying 'I am landscaping'. Whereas the latter is operating in some kind of conditioned future tense, 'If I were solving this problem, I would etc. . . .', the child is operating in the present tense, a characteristic of make-believe play that seems to match an accepted view of drama as an art form related to the 'here and now'.

And yet this appears to be an oversimplification. It seems to me that although the action is in the present, that present is loaded with a sense of what has gone on before. It carries a significant accumulation of events. Susanne Langer[3] extends the concept further: 'Theatre . . . moves not towards the present as narrative does but towards something beyond; it deals eventually with commitments and consequences.' She goes on, 'It has been said repeatedly that theatre creates a perpetual moment; but it is only a present filled with its own future that is really dramatic'.

It can be argued then that one of the characteristics of the art form is a sense of time that does not rest in the present but is continually looking backwards and forwards, that carries a tension of 'commitments and consequences'. Not only have we with this criterion removed our gardener but also our child enjoying being Robin Hood.

Quality of meaning

It is easier to indicate the quality of meaning that an art form is *not* concerned with. Bullough[4] in his article on Psychical Distancing writes of clearing the art object of 'the practical concrete nature of its appeal'. Our 'gardener' illustration, therefore, with its single practical meaning is finally dispensed with as art. The Robin Hood illustration, however, may not necessarily be confined to the practical. If the child in his play was concerned with more than just the skill of throwing a sword, if he was exploring other levels of meaning to do with, for example, 'being a hero', 'growing up', 'having power', or 'a show of physical prowess' then the playing, at least in this respect, meets the requirements of the art form. It is at a level of 'symbolic abstraction', as Witkin[5] calls it, a crystallisation of all the child has felt about a particular concept.

Even as I give the symbolic meaning a name-tag like 'being a hero', I am doing a disservice to the very process I am attempting to describe, for in fact the essential nature of the aesthetic symbol is that the meaning is not accessible to discursive description. Mary Warnock[6] in summarising Kant's view of imagination says that 'what we appreciate or create in the highest art, is a symbol of something which is forever beyond it'. All we can do then is to indicate the area, quality or level of meaning. We cannot make it explicit.

Let us not be misled into assuming that an awareness of several layers of meaning is confined to artistic behaviour. An adolescent's view of his own bedroom is likely to include the practical one of a place to sleep in, but it may also represent a refuge, an escape, a sanctuary or an identity. These deeper levels are not prerequisites of practical living but they appear to be a *raison-d'etre* of art.

In examining now how levels of meaning are reached in drama, we find a fascinating paradox. We have established already that art requires a release from the concrete and practical and yet dramatic activity can only be expressed by action and object (actual or simulated). This brings us back to our earlier attempt at a description of dramatic behaviour when we noted the independent/dependent relationship with the environment. It is not in fact a *release* from the concrete that creates the meaning but an interaction between the concrete and the abstract. So that if the child creating Robin Hood is working at an artistic level, the practical starting point of handling a sword gradually changes through a process of symbolisation so that the sword and the throwing take on other more universal meanings and yet the concrete object and action continue to anchor those meanings in actuality.

Quality of feeling

It seems logical to suggest that the feeling quality must reflect at all times the level or (more correctly) the mixture of levels of meaning. Reid[7] writes 'if the understanding of art presupposes, as it does, the exercise of general intelligence in the ordinary sense, it also requires a

141

special *aesthetic* intelligence which might be called the intelligence of (aesthetic) feeling'.

Dramatic activity is not a normal stimulus-response behaviour; 'raw emotion' (as Witkin calls it) only pertains in so far as the meaning is sought in actual events and objects. As objects and actions take on symbolic overtones different qualities of feeling that have little to do with the immediate sense experience are tapped.

Drama and education

I have suggested that dramatic activity is concerned with creating meaning that is both dependent on and independent of the physical environment. I have also suggested that when dramatic activity becomes Drama as an art form it is characterised by three significant features: a special sense of time; a special quality of meaning; a special quality of feeling. The reader may have already decided that our poor child playing Robin Hood has little chance of ever reaching the art form. Indeed there are two more features to be taken into account which reduce the playing child's chances!

For Reid[8] the *intention* to create an art form is a factor so that what the child does in his playing may be aesthetically satisfying but it is not art unless he deliberately makes it so. This is why a group of children 'doing a play' together appears to have greater artistic potential.

Another feature which is achievable in some forms of child play and should be central by definition to *educational* drama is that the participants should undergo some change. It seems to me that an act or process of creativity must bring about some growth in the artist. I maintain that rarely can children do this for themselves. Herein lies the major responsibility of the teacher.

Which brings us to educational objectives. There are two kinds in drama: those that are achieved independently of the drama experience (extrinsic) and those that are reached within the drama itself (intrinsic). An example of the former would be the occasion when in order to achieve the objective of social co-operation a teacher structured a dramatic sequence portraying a day in the life of a farmer. The drama itself was of no higher level than our landscape gardener in the pub (even lower for his motivation was genuine) but the educational goal was achieved as the children had to co-operate in order to give coherence to their presentation. Quite obviously extrinsic objectives are not going to very much affect the dramatic activity itself. My claim in the first paragraph linking educational goals and the art form related in fact to intrinsic objectives.

Let us take an example of a class of 10–11 year old primary school children who have chosen *outlaws* as their topic. Now as Gillham[9] points out in educational drama there are always two plays: the play for the children and the play for the teacher. The former provides the equivalent of child play plus the intention to create something; the latter is the teacher's opportunity to structure a learning experience. My hypothesis is that he achieves this by incorporating the principal features that characterise an art form.

A teacher cannot ignore the children's play: it provides immediate satisfaction, a plot and a way in to the teacher's play. In this particular 'outlaw' illustration it was about being clever enough to escape capture. The 'play for the teacher' was to do with the nature of freedom, the consequences of losing it and the implications of buying it back again. A sense of time was cultivated that was loaded with the guilt of the past and apprehension for the future. The meaning deepened as objects and actions took on symbolic connotations: a piece of paper with a house drawn on it became a symbol of past life and a recognition of identity; the box the gold was kept in became both a treasure and a burden; taking away the sheriff's horse became the way of reducing the sheriff's status; ceremoniously pricking one's finger became an oath of loyalty. The key word in this account is '*became*'! A symbol is not something that a teacher imposes all ready-made; objects and actions that logically belong to the 'play for the children' gradually take on meanings at a deeper level of abstraction with a corresponding change in the quality of feeling. Dramatic activity has moved into 'drama' and subsequently a change of understanding may take place,

Of course, I have made this sound absurdly simple. The integrity of the experience is dependent on the way the two plays dovetail together. But 'dovetail' is the wrong metaphor, for the situation is fluid: there is a continual alternation between the 'play for the teacher' and 'the play for the children'. Resting too long with one to the exclusion of the other renders the drama ineffective. In this 'outlaw' illustration, for example, the teacher in the third lesson checked the flow of the drama experience by deliberately promoting the action at the plot level ('the play for the children'). He did this, as the new objective – to raise the status of the girls in the class – had no relevance to the symbolic meanings emerging within the drama. The only way the girls could be seen to be indispensable was from within the plot. Here then is an example of the 'social' educational objective having priority (at least temporarily) over other forms of learning at the expense of the drama experience.

Normally the difference between the two levels of operation is not as clear-cut as in this example; the movement between them is often too fast for observation. Indeed it might be true to say that at those times when the two levels remain apart the activity, however educational, does not belong to the art form.

In summary, it appears that drama and learning objectives can be mutually supportive. The features that appertain to an art form appear to promote learning but the feature that distinguishes children's drama from all other dramatic activity is that two sets of objectives, the children's and the teacher's, have to be integrated with each other if both educational and artistic requirements are to be satisfied.

Creative drama as an art form. *London Drama*, April 1977. (*London Drama*, Drama and Tape Centre, Princeton Street, London.)

References

1 Vygotsky L S 1976 Play and its role in the mental development of the child. In Bruner J S *et al, Play: its development and evolution*. Penguin Educational.

2 Reid L A 1969 *Meaning in the arts*. Allen and Unwin.

3 Langer S K 1953 *Feeling and form: a theory of art*. Routledge and Kegan Paul.

4 Bullough E 1912 Psychical distance as a factor in art and as an aesthetic principle. *British Journal of Psychology*, 5, part 2: 87–118.

5 Witkin R W 1974 *Intelligence of feeling*. Heinemann, p 177.

6 Warnock M 1976 *Imagination*. Faber, p 63.

7 Reid L A op. cit., p 311.

8 Reid L A op. cit., p 279.

9 Gillham G 1974 Report on Condercum School Project by Live Theatre. Unpublished.

The process of symbolisation in improvised drama

At a recent drama in education conference in Ottowa, I puzzled and perhaps shocked the audience by giving my keynote address the title 'Drama is not doing'. This seemed almost blasphemous to teachers and educationists who for years have pinned their faith and philosophy to the very notion that drama essentially is doing. In case my readers at this point are too offended to continue let me hasten to say that the title of my Canadian address presents but a half-truth, a qualification which, this paper will argue, should also be applied to 'Drama is doing'.

I would like to invite readers to accept a paradox, a paradox that is the central component of good drama generally and of good improvised drama in particular. It is this: that when an action in drama achieves a moment of heightened significance it does so because the meaning created is largely released from its dependence on that action. Let me begin to illustrate what I mean.

A few months ago I had the pleasure of working in a sustained piece of improvised play-making with some Austrian teachers; the following action took place:

A man in the role of Austrian emigrant in 1910 took a piece of paper representing a 25 dollar (American) bill out of his inside pocket and, with everyone watching, placed it on the table. It was to buy land in New England.

Another action had taken place earlier in the improvisation.

In the role of American immigration officer, I gave a man in each immigrant family four simulated 25 dollar bills; they represented an American government grant to emigrants. Each man placed the bills in his inside pocket in silence.

Both actions took place in the same improvisation. Only one of these actions had reached a drama experience. If you examine them, they are virtually indistinguishable, each to do with the same kind of event – an exchange of money. What then was the difference between them and which one was inside and which outside the art form?

When I in role gave the money, I was attempting to use dramatic art form (indeed making quite a ceremony of giving out the grant to inject significance into the experience). In turn they responded by trying to do the meaningful thing – putting the money in an inside pocket, for example. In other words: consciously behaving as if they were concerned. But this was not drama; it was an exploratory searching for drama. The only real meaning that was established was the practical one to do with the exchange of money.

But in the hour that followed the participants moved to a different quality of experience; they became concerned and everything they did gained new levels of meaning related to the theme. The plot was that in 1910 some poor Austrian farmers were forced by circumstances to emigrate to America. They were proud and suffered humiliation. They had never been outside their own villages; America was just a myth. Their roots were deep; to cut off these roots was to lose identity.

The teacher's function in drama is as a playwright's, to help the group find a focus that can reflect as many connotations as possible. So I had built into my role of immigration officer the suspicion that I was a con man. Thus all the fears of trusting the unknown situation could be filtered through the single focus of not trusting the man in charge of the operation. The feeling of insecurity was considerable, for none of the normal 'checking for trust' criteria were available in this new context where it was impossible to know what normally was.

It is important to distinguish two levels of meaning here:

1 There is a problem of trust: a decision has to be made. The feeling of distrust may or may not be verbalised. 'Shall we trust this man?' the dialogue may overtly reflect, but on the other hand the verbalisation may ostensibly be about something else, with a strong 'non-trusting' subtext. The drama, however, is not about whether the immigration officer should be trusted. That provides but the filter through which less easily articulated meanings can be experienced.
2 Humiliation, insecurity, loss of identity are the qualities that characterise enforced emigration. Unless these meanings become available to the participants, the drama cannot be said to be working. It is not likely that the dialogue will directly articulate these feelings, but its form and content will nevertheless be controlled by them.

Both levels (1) and (2) are levels of abstraction, and the important point to be made here is that the significant aspect of a drama experience lies in one or more levels of abstraction. But it is the concrete action that makes the abstraction available.

This brings us back to the actions described earlier. The action of handing over a 25 dollar bill is not of itself significant. When I handed out the 'grant' earlier in the session I tried, unsuccessfully, to inject implications into the action but the action did little more than extend the storyline, i.e., 'We've reached the point where the immigration officer gives us the grant.' The meaning is here bound to the action and is no more than what the action says it is. But the later action of putting a 25 dollar bill on the table represented at one level an enormous decision to do with trust (it is not the purpose of this article to go into how this was achieved), and at a more universal level, all the feelings of impotence, frustration, insecurity and loss of identity related to emigration. It can be argued then that there are at least three levels of meaning operating interdependently:

CONCRETE: the practical meaning of the action (in this case an exchange of money)

problem solving/decision making (in this case, do we trust this man?)

ABSTRACT: value-laden concepts (in this case, insecurity, loss of identity etc.)

The abstract meanings are both dependent on the concrete in so far as they are expressed through the action and independent of the concrete in so far as they are released from the contingencies of the action. This is the paradox that is drama.

I claim therefore that simply to say 'Drama is doing' is to miss its essential nature. In the same way I am not happy at the blanket usage of symbolisation to all make-believe action. That drama is doing is linguistically correct, that make-believe action (say using a piece of paper to represent a 25 dollar bill) is symbolic is as logical as saying all words are symbols. But such broad usage of terms invites merely a denotative interpretation of the action, where there is a one-to-one relationship between the action and the symbol, e.g. a miming action symbolises digging. The art form, it seems to me, must be concerned with the connotative, where the miming action of digging accrues other meanings to do with status, past history, expectations, etc.

I prefer, therefore, to think of the dynamics of an improvised play-making experience as a shared process of searching for symbolic action (or objects), a moving towards those moments when meaning can be released from the action and objects. In the emigration illustration symbolisation in my terms was not present in the initial exchange of money – the teacher cannot force it – the action simply denoted an exchange of money. Later a powerful 'symbolic' experience, as I would like to call it, took place with more or less the same kind of action. We were now working in an art form.

I happen to have used an example from work with adults but a fairly recent example from children's drama will help to reiterate the point I am making. In a mixed age group of 8–12 year olds who chose to make up a play about a desert, the use of bandages as sweat-bands (denotation) gradually changed from the functional to the symbolic. We were supposed to be a primitive tribe lost in the desert. We each had responsibilities (the keeper of the water, the handler of our only knife, etc.) so we marked in colour on our sweat-bands the signs of our responsibilities: a pitcher, a cave door, etc. I chose for myself the setting sun – I was in role as the eldest, the most incompetent and most scared member of the group! Then events as the week went on took various turns and gradually people became identified by the sweat-bands. We slept in a cave, the sweat-bands marking our personal territory. Two men went on an expedition for food and did not return. Their sweat-bands were mysteriously 'found' (in fact the two boys were absent from school that day). They (the sweat-bands) were ceremoniously carried back to the cave, and were placed, signs upward, on the cave floor. We sat round them and pondered helplessly on the terrible things that might have occurred, and then deciding our fellow tribesman had met their death, we buried their bands.

A succession of meanings had accumulated round the few bandages so they became, in the artistic sense, symbolic objects. The operative word is perhaps 'became' because as teacher I am not in a position to predecide, 'Let's use some bandages as sweat-bands so that later they can represent the dead bodies of their owners'. The meanings must accrue for the children, not for the teacher. The teacher, however, by seeing all kinds of possibilities in things and actions will anticipate and structure sensitively so that symbolic opportunities are made available to the children.

The process of symbolisation in improvised drama. *Young Drama*, **6** (1), 1978.

Imagery in drama in education

In a drama with junior school age children about the nature of slavery, the children playing the slaves were thrown some real chicken bones, bones which they had just witnessed actually being gnawed clean of their meat by their Roman masters – the other children in the class.

The effectiveness of any imagery in drama can be tested by the degree to which it combines three important functions:

1) it provides a focus in action that encapsulates a thematic meaning of the topic,
2) it features the context in some way, and
3) it engages the feelings of the participants.

The 'chicken-bone' image meets the first requirement satisfactorily – having to eat others' left-overs does indeed capture the notion of sub-servience and dependence in a slave/master relationship. Whereas there is nothing about the action that particularly represents the *Roman* context, the image of a Roman elite sitting in a sunny arbour leisurely nibbling chicken flesh is not inappropriate. The third requirement, however, is met with unmistakeable force – the sense of injustice would be felt very strongly by those children who were thrown the scraps. Similarly, in a lesson about the mid-west farmers leaving their dust bowl in the 1930s, I, in role as a rich Californian who refused to admit the newcomers onto my territory, ate an orange to symbolise the difference between the 'haves' and the 'have nots' to represent the rich groves of California and to stir the children's wrath as I dropped the orange peel at their feet.

These two examples, though effective, are crude in two respects: they are dependent not on dramatic simulation or fiction but on gross actuality; and also on actuality that promotes the extreme emotions in the children of anger or frustration at a real injustice. This dependence on actuality to promote gross emotion does not in itself invalidate the method, but it is not one that a teacher could use with any regularity.

Compare this kind of deliberate provocation with the much more subtle promotion of feeling in a drama about a dangerous monster with infants where I, as teacher in role, started the experience by taking up a shawl, turned into a curled 'baby' shape and with anxious expression approached the group saying that there was a strange deep scratch on the baby's face – what should I do? The emotional engagement here has to be *worked for* by the children themselves: only if they make the mental effort to see the shawl as a baby, only if they make the effort to tap whatever wells of concern they might have for a baby's scratched face, only if they further can make the connections between teacher's chosen focus and the dangerous monster they want their drama to be about, does this selected imagery become effective. Similarly, I recall a class of six year olds 'planting' flowers outside the entrance to their primitive huts as a ritual preceding their departure on a journey into the African bush from which they may never return. 'Will the flowers still be alive when we get back?' is the question that voices unspoken meanings to do with time, returning, death and home – for those children who have allowed themselves to turn the simple miming action into a symbol rather than just a sign of planting flowers.

It is interesting that imagery initially used functionally merely to represent the environment or some feature of the environment can gradually accrue symbolic meanings during the process of the drama, thus becoming a central focus. The following description is an example of what I mean:[1]

In a mixed age group of 8–12 year olds who chose to make up a play about a desert, the use of bandages as sweat-bands gradually changed from the functional to the symbolic. We were supposed to be a primitive tribe lost in the desert. We each had responsibilities (e.g. the keeper of the water; the handler of our only knife, etc.) so we marked in colour on our sweat-bands the signs of our responsibilities – a pitcher, a cave-door, etc. I chose for myself the setting sun – I was in role as the eldest, the most incompetent and most scared member of the group! Then events as the week went on took various turns and gradually people became identified by the sweat-bands. We slept in a cave; the sweat-bands marking our personal territory. Two men went on an expedition for food and did not return. Their sweat-bands were mysteriously 'found' (in fact the two boys were absent from school that day). They (the sweat-bands) were ceremoniously carried back to the cave. They were placed, signs upward, on the cave floor; we sat around them and pondered helplessly on the terrible things that might have occurred, and then deciding our fellow tribesmen had met their death, we buried their bands. A succession of meanings had accumulated round a few bandages so they became in the artistic sense, symbolic objects. The operative word is perhaps 'became' because as teacher I am not in a position to predecide, 'Let's use some bandages as sweat-bands so that later they can represent the dead bodies of their owners'. The meanings must accrue for the children, not for the teacher. The teacher, however, by seeing all kinds of possibilities in things and actions will anticipate and structure sensitively so that symbolic opportunities are *made available* to the children.

Of course, there are objects and actions that already have symbolic significance outside the drama. Whereas there is nothing immediately significant about a chicken bone, an orange or a sweat-band, the use by teacher of such things as a cross, a begging-bowl, a gun, a skull, a dagger, a Bible or a white flag may well already carry overtones that effectively meet the requirements listed above: encapsulating a thematic meaning of the drama; representing a feature of the context; engaging the feelings of the group.

A teacher of drama learns quickly and often uncomfortably that one group's stimulus is another group's sedative – a wedding ring will obviously have a different effect on fourteen year old girls from fourteen year old boys! A good teacher will sense the 'rightness' of a particular symbol. I recall Dorothy Heathcote working in an approved school where the adolescent boys were doing their drama about the death of a President At a point where interest in the project was flagging she introduced into their 'prison cell' a bucket and a mop. Each 'prisoner' lying on his bunk with eyes closed heard the swishing of a mop on the floor – the very sound that was symbolically loaded for these youths because in their approved school situation the daily routine of washing floors was a painful instance of drudgery in captivity.[2]

But the interesting point to make here is that the 'bucket' imagery might well have left another group of adolescents – say, a group of uniformed socially conforming grammar school pupils – feeling quite indifferent or even amused. The barber's scissors or the censor's stamp on personal letters might be nearer to the mark in this case. Indeed there are some themes that *seem* almost impossible to teach because the distance between the experience of the children we teach is so far removed from the reality implied in the fiction. What sort of imagery do you choose if the very secure well-fed class in front of you are supposed to be doing their drama about hunger in the third world? – when it isn't even much of a reality for the teacher either! How do you *really* convey, for example, Dickensian poverty to the children in Western cultures today? The imagery necessary here may be tactile rather than visual – replacing shoes and socks with torn strips of bandage round the feet or wearing coats that are the wrong fit etc.

In all this discussion on imagery in drama in education the teacher's sensitivity to both the potential meanings within a topic and the likely personal response of a group to those meanings is very much in evidence.

There seems to be a message for teacher-training here I think!

Imagery in drama in education. *SCYPT Journal*, No. 5, May 1980. (c/o SCYPT Journal Committee, Cockpit Theatre, Gateforth Street, London.)

References

1 Bolton G M 1978 The process of symbolisation in improvised drama. *Young Drama* **6** (1).
2 Bolton G M 1979 *Towards a theory of drama in education.* Longman. (Also discusses this illustration.)

Drama as concrete action

It has been emphasised in recent years that drama is a mental activity. Many of us have adopted this view as a reaction against all the mindless 'doing' of drama that has been encouraged in the past. Indeed, in an address to a Canadian conference a few years ago I announced (with tongue in cheek, admittedly) the title as 'Drama is *not* doing'. But drama *is* to do with the use of the concrete, not however for the limited purpose of expressing the particular, which in itself is rarely important, but as a means of building belief, protecting from self-consciousness, giving identification to a role, focussing group energy or symbolising meanings beyond the particular.

In this article I propose to reflect on a selection of lessons I have taught during the last twelve months and to examine them in terms of the use of concrete actions or objects. It is interesting that sometimes the use of an object functions in the particularisation process just as effectively or even more effectively than the use of action. The crumpled blazer 'left behind' by the boy who has taken his own life was a more powerful image to the sixteen year olds taking part than any of the actions they were actually involved in. On the other hand, the first year secondary children's silent wait for a signal and their furtive descent below deck, one by one and in the dark, symbolised a secret meeting, danger and a decision taken.

Sometimes the actions are merely insignificant activity. Working with a class of 10–12 year old ESN children, we 'played at' feeding animals in a zoo. But in the second half of the lesson the *activity* became significant *action* for the children were now feeding the animals because the irresponsible zoo-keeper (teacher in role) was neglecting them.

Activity in moments of 'crisis' is often empty of important meaning. In a drama with six year olds on the topic of the sinking of the *Titanic*, the rush from one end of the hall (the ship) to the other end of the hall (the sea) in order to drown was as crude and casual as it sounds, but the stylised speaking that followed by each 'spirit of the dead' recalling his drowning was awesome.

There was nothing crude or casual about the miming of a game of football by a group of top junior boys, who, in a drama about Victorian England, valiantly tried to retrieve some pretty ham-fisted handling of their drama by me. Here, the clutching at a chance for aesthetic action by these outer London children could not mask the inadequacy of the experience I was offering them. I just hope the children were more forgiving of their teacher than the teachers watching!

It is fairly common that when a lesson goes badly one of the first solutions found in assessing the experience is that *activity* would have given meaning to the drama. 'Why did you not get the footballers to mime getting their football gear ready?' challenged a disappointed observer. And indeed it is often the case that the concrete identification with a role elicits belief in the fiction. But sometimes the weakness may also lie in more subtle directions. I did nothing for those children by way of object or action to symbolise either Victorian England in general or class hierarchy in particular, which is what I tried to make it about. In other words what was being represented thematically remained *in our minds* and was never made concrete until the last few minutes of the lesson when the physical arrangements of a court scene symbolised to some degree the injustice of one law for the rich and one for the poor.

There are times when even the most careful miming is not enough; at others precision of action does not matter. An example of the former occurred in a lesson with top juniors about the nature of education. Each child was to teach a 'human-like' robot (a college student) to feed itself and then later to educate it by teaching it whatever knowledge was felt by the children (they were in role as professors of education!) to be the most important. Clearly the meaning of the first task resided in the action itself for which a real spoon and tin dish were essential. The experience had to be more concrete than simulation would have achieved. On the other hand, that there was no food was not a regrettable compromise, for whereas the implements effectively signalled 'teaching a skill', the presence of food would have had too many overtones of 'actuality' – to do with the intimacy of contact in feeding someone and the potential messiness of having food around. The tin spoons and plates developed another usage at the end of the lesson when (as planned) the robots started to resent their lessons! As they banged their spoons on their dishes in deafening protest one disappointed 'professor' explained to the others: 'They seem to have feelings'. On the other hand the action of feeding by the ESN children at the zoo did not have to be precise in its imitation. For the meaning was to do with their self-righteousness which their token gestures adequately signalled.

Another different use of the concrete by the teacher occurred in the work with top infants. I was requested by their teacher to do drama about the *Titanic* as the children had been so impressed with the story that very morning. Now drowning is a gross dramatic activity more likely to be hilarious than serious, so I had to find a focus that could be coped with. I had a clue from the teacher who said that one of the things that had struck these children on hearing the story was that when the catastrophe fell children were separated from their parents. So, as Captain, I welcomed the parents of newly-christened babies aboard, each child simulating having a baby-in-arms, to join us on a 'christening' voyage of the ship. Each child was required to write his baby's name on a *label* which was then attached to the *little mat* representing the baby's cot area in the ship's creche. We also used half-sized *screens* to delineate the ship from the sea beyond. Thus I attempted to direct attention away from themselves to the babies for whom they were responsible and who had to be left sleeping while we had our party to cut the ship's birthday cake (not real!) The focus of the disaster was not on the simulation of drowning but on whether you had time to grab your baby from its cot. Thus the particularisation of the label and the mat were not so much to do with building belief, or finding an identity or symbolising a theme (they were all these to a degree) as much as creating a focus for concentration away from the self, as though who you were in the play became projected onto your baby in the cot. Incidentally, for those readers who are worried by the apparent trauma that might be attached to being 'drowned souls', let me add that we finished the lesson replaying the voyage as it would have happened if only the foolhardy captain had listened to his sensible passengers.

In this brief account, I have tried to emphasise the importance of concrete action and objects, while distinguishing the action from merely *doing* as an end in itself. A distinction also needs to be made in respect of using objects as part of the drama, as I realised when, recently, in commenting on a teacher's lesson I suggested that if the drama was about looking for hidden treasure, then some kind of representation of a map would be more effective than vaguely holding out one's arms holding nothing, another teacher (not the teacher of the lesson who understood the point very well) remarked, 'Oh, he means we're back to using stage-props again'. I hope this article has reinforced the crucial point that the use of objects and stage-props involves two quite different principles, even though, in practice, they often appear to coincide.

Drama as concrete action. *London Drama*, **6** (4), Spring 1981.

Drama as learning, as art and as aesthetic experience

A few months ago I met for just one drama lesson a class of very bright fourteen year old Manchester boys who, when asked by me what they would like the drama to be about, after some considerable deliberation, chose 'A city preparing for a nuclear holocaust'. Eagerly they chose roles from a range of expertise: army experts; scientists; doctors and city councillors. In separate groups they discussed the task: 'From the point of view of your expert knowledge list the priorities you intend to put later to a joint meeting'. They tackled this task energetically and with some imagination, one or two groups improvising charts and diagrams in order effectively to communicate the points they wanted to make. The joint meeting (chaired by the 'city councillors' whose main concern was to build shelters on the cheap!) raised issues to do with such matters as the number of minutes between the warning signal and the nuclear blast; the depth of the shelters and the best material for building them; and the effect of radiation on animal, plant and human life. It was in connection with the latter that the 'doctors' observed it would be necessary to furnish each shelter with a supply of suicide pills so that (to use the doctors' own words) 'they could be offered by the respective families to those family members who were still alive but too mutilated to be looked after'. This piece of horror did not stand out as I have singled it out here; it was just dropped in among a list of requirements for a first-aid kit. The discussion achieved a level of liveliness, purposefulness and articulateness that can be expected from a group of intelligent, well-informed and highly motivated young people.

This anecdote may worry those of you who are interested in the arts because however valid it may seem to have been as an educational exercise, it does not fit your conception of an art form. Its purpose seems to be a clarification of issues, some real and some hypothetical, related to the objective world of events and objects. It required the pupils to draw on prior knowledge and to apply it through rational discourse to the logistics of a problem. In other words, dramatic role-play was being used to stimulate a high degree of focussed attention at that imaginative and intellectual level necessary for most good subject-learning. You may feel, as Witkin[1] does, that this should not be regarded as drama. He writes: 'The role play becomes the central exercise for many drama teachers. There is no doubt that drama has a lot to contribute to role simulation and furthermore that role simulation is one important form of drama. It is not synonymous with drama, however, and a great many of the role-play situations improvised in drama sessions in schools have nothing whatever to do with drama although there is no doubt they are a good basis for practical sociology' (p. 92). My own view is that, limited as this learning experience may be in terms of an art form, it would be perverse for a drama teacher to exclude it on these grounds. It does, after all, give practice in the skill that is basic to all kinds of acting, which is: *an ability to engage with something outside oneself using an 'as if' mental set to activate, sustain or intensify that engagement.* I am using the word 'engagement' as a central feature because it implies a relationship at an affective level between a person and the world outside him. The dramatic 'as if' mode implies release from contingencies of the present into the logical rules of a hypothetical present. These two characteristics combined suggest a mental activity that is both dynamic and rational. Such a description is not far away from Warnock's[2] view of imagination:

> For the imagination is the power to see possibilities beyond the immediate; to perceive and feel the boundlessness of what is before one,

the intricacies of a problem, the complications or subtleties of something previously scarcely noticed. To work at something to begin to find it interesting, this is to begin to let the imagination play on it. To begin to see it stretching out into *un*explored paths, whose ends are not in sight. (p. 155)

One way of activating the imagination is to use the dramatic mode. It is a pity that all teachers do not recognise this. But we are discussing drama teachers and although I have given strong support to the notion of using this dynamic, rational activity towards intellectual ends, as in the Manchester pupils' illustration where they were required to make propositional statements about the world of facts, I also acknowledge (as Witkin suggests) that this is to deny drama as an art form.

Let us now look at the second half of the Manchester lesson. The discussion finished with an air of self-satisfaction among the pupils – they had displayed considerable competence in sustaining their 'expert' roles, in engaging in rigorous debate and in bringing some sense of order to their understanding of the subject matter. I suddenly switched roles and addressed them as if I were a charge-nurse of an institution for people 'mutilated' by radiation and they were the patients. The shock of the switch and their awareness of what demands were now going to be made on them was almost too much for some of them. They giggled in embarrassment. But these mature boys only needed a little help from me to regain their concentration. The result was spellbinding. When I as nurse started to 'feed' one of them with a spoon, first carefully placing a bib under his chin and somewhat patronisingly complimenting him on how well he was managing today as I removed some 'gravy' from the side of his mouth, most individuals could be observed adjusting to the situation. By the time I role-played a journalist trying to get an inside story on that day five years ago when Manchester had been within 50 miles of a nuclear disaster, they responded with a poignancy that, remarkable in itself, was further enhanced by the memory of the recent demonstration of their natural debating skills, which they now sensitively held in abeyance. They stammered out their words, failing to make sense, trying with their eyes to say what their lips could not formulate. They were no longer the decision makers; they were the passive victims.

So what is happening here? The basic skill has not of course changed. What has changed is their perspective on the subject matter. One could describe it as 'experiencing' as opposed to making observation; they were 'within' the subject matter rather than outside it; they were involved in 'knowing this' instead of 'knowing that'; their understanding remained implicit rather than propositionally explicit; they were speaking from their guts rather than from their minds. Are they then just as concerned with 'something outside themselves'? Yes indeed they are identifying with a cripple in an institution. The direction of the engagement is the same – it is, to use Dewey's[3] phrase 'an active and alert commerce with the world' (p. 19), but I would suggest that the quality of *investment* has changed. They can no longer rely solely on their prior knowledge of a factual kind and on their verbal skill. To be effective they may have to recall feeling memories and motor memories and to acknowledge, adapt and submit to the rules of the new context. Although there was engagement with the material when they were 'experts', their very form of discursive expression simultaneously detached them from that engagement. This notion of submission to the experience suggests a more personal and more sustained attachment. What is the nature of the learning? This is difficult to answer because if we are prepared to recognise any learning at all it is not the kind that educationists are used to talking about. Fleming[4] in a thesis on drama and education in his chapter on Drama and Learning points out that to acknowledge this kind of dramatic activity as having learning potential we have to accept that 'Not all learning is necessarily preceded by attempts to learn'. He quotes from Dunlop[5] 'The passive side of learning is itself highly important since a great deal of what is ever learnt is unspecifiable and hence has to be picked up or acquired at a less than fully conscious level' (p. 246). This brings us to an important feature of dramatic activity in relation to learning. It seems that if learning at this experiential level is to take place the participants must be both passive in the sense of holding in abeyance any intention to learn, and active in the sense of focussing attention on creating an 'as if' context. In the Manchester illustration the teacher also has a hand in focussing attention by deliberately imposing a structure. Indeed I unashamedly manipulated the situation so that learning might take place. But I could not be specific in terms of what was to be learnt – my intervention changed the mode of experiencing and thinking, an act of faith that the switch from the pupils' being outside the subject matter to inside it had some kind of learning potential. The nature of the learning process is akin to one's attention being engaged by a poem. It is to do with experiencing the poem rather than learning about it. It is perhaps not unlike the experience of interacting with another person – coming to know another in a way that requires a degree of personal investment. In neither case could one define precisely what one had learnt.

I am convinced that dramatic activity used for personal knowledge of this kind is educationally significant and is consequently more central to my work than the drama for intellectual stimulation described earlier. But does this particular usage also deny drama as an art form? Given that one accepts the educational potency then one might answer, 'who cares?'

Well this conference cares. And it may be that you do not really want to hear about this kind of dramatic activity for it may not fit in at all with a developmental theory of aesthetic education you have in mind. For here I am spelling out a usage that is directly concerned with understanding the objective world, its facts and its values, a function which when placed against, for example, music as an example of the arts, makes it very difficult for one to conceive of arts subjects as one discipline.

I think if I am pressed into answering the question was this example of a drama lesson also an example of drama as an art form, I have to say no. The experience was no more than an episode of dramatic playing with sufficient sophistication of structure and poignancy of subject matter to guarantee an engagement by the pupils of some depth and concentration. I do not want to undervalue the experience in any way but to say that it was an instance of dramatic art would be to give the impression that the art form is something that can be created by a few deft strokes of teacher-structuring and an obliging commitment on the part of the class. Let me reiterate however that the basic skill of drama as I have described it also applies to the participants in an art form, so that although we may not want to give even the second half of the Manchester drama lesson that superior label, at least we can recognise that the kind of personal engagement required was dispositionally right for a dramatic art experience. If we had the opportunity to develop the 'nuclear disaster' work we would have found that a great deal of the psychological spade-work had been done.

But drama as an art, although incipiently present in the Manchester episode is on a different plane of experience to do with *consciousness of form*. However let us leave the psychological perspective and switch to drama as a product. Let us look at 'the thing created'. Some of you may have been expecting me to say that drama does not operate as an art form until there is an audience. This is not the case. Most drama in schools in this country is enacted without an audience in mind. The history of drama in education had polarised between the two camps, between what was called 'creative' or 'child' drama and 'performance', the teachers of the former camp stressing the importance of play, free expression, sensitivity, spontaneity and social health; the latter teachers stressing acting skills and theatre crafts. It seems to me that these factions, in emphasising difference at a rather peripheral or surface level of skills, are failing to recognise the common ground between them. Indeed I would like to argue that most drama teachers of whatever persuasion are at a fundamental level using the same dramatic form. The 'clay' of drama is the same for the teacher, the pupil, the playwright, the director and the actor. It's just that they handle it differently. Regrettably we do not train our teachers to know the basic feel of that clay and yet this is what they should be passing on to their pupils – the essence of dramatic form.

The principal elements of dramatic form are focus, symbolisation and tension. I will briefly consider each in turn. Focus is the particularisation of a theme or topic. Themes and topics are abstract ideas. Drama is concrete action operating in time and space. For the action to occur in the here and now focussing has to go through two stages: (a) the selection of an angle (in the Manchester drama lesson the topic was nuclear holocaust – it was focussed down to anticipations of the 'experts' and the experience of the 'mutilated') and (b) the selection of a moment in time and/or a particular action (for example the 'experts' beginning their meeting with the 'city councillors'; and the 'charge-nurse' placing a bib under the chin of one of the invalids). Dramatic action is a particular instance of a more general idea. The test of focussing is whether the instance conveys the meaning intended by the idea.

Which brings us to symbolisation. I am well aware of the dangers of using the word symbol at all. I do not want to be trapped by the academic discussions that have been pursued in the name of clarification. I am using the term here in a special way. By symbolisation I am referring to a process whereby certain actions or objects accrue meanings for the audience or for the participants (in a non-performance mode) during the playing out of the drama, a process of evolution of meanings rather than 'given' meanings. The action of putting a bib under a man's chin is evocative. Pupils sensitive to such meanings in drama could build on this so that the bib becomes a symbol of helplessness, humiliation, subservience, loss of individuality or a symbol of institutional life. A drama could proceed that centres round a patient's attempt to refuse the bib. Thus, the original focus initially acknowledged as an adequate concrete instance of hospitalisation gains in significance because of its symbolic potential. A playwright is of course also concerned with the selection of evocative images through language as well as through objects and action. 'Put out the light, and then put out the light' whispers Othello. And we, the audience, see Desdemona asleep in her bed, a symbol of her refuge, her innocence, her sexuality, her trust and her vulnerability and we yield to a sense of inevitability as we witness a candle snuffed out.

Tension is the third essential element of drama which at its crudest is displayed as conflict between protagonists. At its most fundamental it is a tension between virtual and actual time and between virtual and actual space. Langer[6] identifies tension between the present and the future, a present loaded with 'commitments and consequences'. O'Neill[7] noted the tension in the rhythmic rise and fall of a scene or episode. A group of Durham School of Education's Drama Diploma students[8] recently published a hand-out for inexperienced drama teachers which classified fourteen different kinds of tension. Such tension, however, must be integral to the drama itself. There was certainly tension in the Manchester exercise but it had more to do with the psychological tension related to the reaction to the subject-matter and to the responsibility of creating the difficult 'patient' role than to anything inherent within the fiction.

I now would like to suggest that for dramatic action to qualify as an art form not only should these three basic elements of focus, tension and symbolisation inhere within the form, there should also be a consciousness on the part of the group that a form is being created. It seems there should be two kinds of significance involved: (a) the participants must be engaged by the subject-matter (b) there must be a sense of responsibility towards the form itself. It is not enough for *individuals* to be conscious of the 'form' of their acting for the basic elements of focus, symbolisation and tension are related to *group* product. It is not enough for a teacher, fully alert to formal significance, to structure the dramatic experience so that the pupils are caught unawares in a dramatic form: when I worked recently with a class of six year old children on the theme of a wicked witch, I consciously used all three elements to give them an exciting experience. But the responsibility was mine. This latter is a fairly typical example of certain contemporary drama teaching with young children[9] where the teacher-in-role is using the very clay of the art form in order to promote engagement and learning. In my view this can be fine education but not art. That (with some qualification I shall make later) is how I also see the Manchester drama lesson.

You must be thinking that I am spending an unconscionable amount of time on something that turns out to be *not* an art form! There are two reasons for this. One is that dramatic method is potentially so educationally rich that experience falling short of art can still be hugely beneficial. And secondly, linked with the first, it is possible that pupils even at secondary level may not acquire the necessary skills to create a group artistic product and yet still have a worthwhile course. Some teachers, in directing their pupils in productions of classical or contemporary scripts, delude themselves into thinking their pupils are necessarily experiencing the art form. Unless the pupils are consciously manipulating focus, symbolisation and tension in their interpretation of the playwright, they will merely be puppets operating within the teacher's sense of theatre. Teacher and pupils may mistakenly conclude that practice in acting to an audience leads to insight into the essential nature of the dramatic clay. There *are* exciting ways of handling the performance mode so that pupils gain that insight, but emphasis on the acting techniques required of naturalistic theatre, still so popular in schools, often inhibits progress.

But how then do pupils develop an understanding of the art form so that they might achieve it? There are one or two clues to the answer in what I have already described. I pointed out that in the second half of the Manchester experience the degree and quality of personal investment with the subject-matter was dispositionally appropriate. Certainly children need to have practice in engaging themselves in this uninhibited way throughout their schooling. But this in itself does not account for development of insight into dramatic form.

It is here I have to rely on the term 'aesthetic'. I am using it to mean *'a sense of form'*. Now I have already made the point that a good teacher of young children working in drama will be conscious of form and will be harnessing focus/tension/symbolisation to that end. The children are experiencing their drama within a formal structure. Their concentration is on substance (the drama is about a wicked witch) but *their aesthetic sense* may help them to feel in their bones that somehow the incident is heightened, sharpened, condensed, etc. Although the latter part of the Manchester lesson could not justify the term art form, it was nevertheless an aesthetic experience. I am suggesting therefore that children can 'absorb' form. Gradually, as and when they are ready, some aspects may be made explicit, so that they consciously inject, say, the tension of contrast into their work. They can learn it is form that makes the simple action significant. This is the nature of aesthetic understanding. In the past teachers have often misdirected their pupils' attention towards climax to a story or a surprise ending to a plot, confusing form and outer shape.

The conscious creation of an art form is a sophisticated group responsibility that requires tacit or explicit agreement on choice of focus, injection of tension, and sensitivity to shared meanings that may resonate from the continual focus on a particular object or action or language image. We want children to acquire those very skills previously used by their teacher on their behalf. This is what CSE or GCE Drama Courses should be about so that within both the dramatic playing *and* the performing mode of drama, pupils, in engaging with the content, also work with a sense of form to create a dramatic experience.

Within the context of this conference however, I suspect that what I have said lies somewhat uneasily. It is true that the notion of 'aesthetic' sense may be the common link among all the arts, but I cannot yet find a place in my theory and practice of drama education, for the arts as 'education of the senses', as 'self-expression', or for 'gaining access to the drama each carries within him'.[10] All these are present to some extent but I prefer to heed Murdoch's[11] warning against subjectivity:

> The chief enemy of excellence (in art) is personal fantasy: the tissue of self-aggrandizing and consoling wishes and dreams which prevents one from seeing what is there outside one.

It is this emphasis on the world outside that provides the logical connection between the different forms of drama work in school. At its most profound, through the art form, our deepest levels may be touched as we engage with what is outside ourselves.

Drama as learning, as art and as aesthetic experience. In Ross M (ed) *The development of aesthetic experience*, 1982 Pergamon Press. (Headington Hill Hall, Oxford, OX3 OBW.)

References

1 Witkin R 1974 *Intelligence of feeling*. Heinemann.

2 Warnock M 1977 *Schools of thought*. Faber.

3 Dewey J 1958 *Art as experience*. Capricorn Books, New York.

4 Fleming M 1982 A philosophical investigation into drama in education. PhD thesis, University of Durham.

5 Dunlop F 1977 Human nature, learning and ideology. *British Journal of Educational Studies*, **XXV** (3).

6 Langer S K 1953 *Feeling and form*. Routledge and Kegan Paul.

7 O'Neill C 1978 Drama and the web of form. MA (Ed) dissertation, University of Durham.

8 Durham University School of Education Diploma Students 1981
Tension. *Newcastle Drama*, **3** (Winter 1980–81).
9 Bolton G M 1979 *Towards a theory of drama in education*.
Longman.
10 Ross M 1978 *The creative arts*. Heinemann.
11 Murdoch I 1970 *The sovereignty of good*. Routledge and Kegan
Paul.

Theatre form in drama teaching

Ten years earlier the Bristol conference brought together educationalists and theatre-in-education representatives. At the Riverside conference the issues were much broader for the personnel were different – actors and directors from straight theatre were now being invited to consider whether their work had anything in common with what goes on in schools. Interestingly, theatre-in-education people were not even invited!

When I talk about my work in schools I call it drama. What I mean by the word has altered for me over the years. By drama do I still mean not theatre? Sometimes I insist on the term drama in education, for I am conscious that undergraduates in University Drama Departments refer to dramatic literature as drama, and I know that in schools I am not so much concerned with the study of drama as the experience of it.

The content of drama lessons, to use educational jargon, is interdisciplinary, for experience cuts across the subject disciplines. Through this experience, five year olds, fifteen year olds, twenty-five year olds and sixty-five year olds may have their understanding of themselves in relation to the world they live in reinforced, clarified or modified and secondly they may gain skills in social interaction which include the ability to communicate their understanding and feelings.

But does this experiencing of drama imply not experiencing theatre? The answer is 'No' and 'Yes'. I put 'No' first for only if we accept a distinction between the two which can never be ignored can we usefully pursue the common ground.

It is not easy to find the words to describe the experiencing of drama. The quality is perhaps best suggested by saying the process is a mixture of 'it is happening to me now; and I am making it happen now'. There are at least three features here, (1) a spontaneity, (2) a 'nowness' that is tied to the future and, most importantly, (3) ME in the experience: 'It is happening to ME; I am making it happen. I am climbing Everest; I am being imprisoned; I am attending an enquiry about Windscale; I am to be brought out of hospital today; I am hiding from the Round-heads.'

In another sense, of course, it is not happening at all. It is a piece of fiction. The potential for learning lies in this very ambivalence that it is happening and yet not happening. So it is a metaphorical experience which still retains the spontaneity, the now-ness and the me-ness of an actual experience. It is because it retains such a close resemblance to living that teachers can harness this 'dramatic playing' to help children find and reflect upon all kinds of meanings that may not be available to them in their daily living.

Now if we move into theatre, the actors are in a very different order of experiencing, a difference that is crucial. The degree to which the actors can say 'it is happening to me now; and I am making it happen' is significantly reduced or overshadowed by an orientation towards interpretation, repeatability, projection and sharing with an audience. The reinforcement or clarification or modification not to mention the entertainment must ultimately be enjoyed by the audience.

I watched a child recently hiding from the Roundheads by getting behind the school piano. He was actually hiding not really knowing whether or not he would be discovered. Deep in belief he held his knuckles tight to his mouth. In theatre the actor may or may not use that gesture, but it is the audience who must, at least emotionally, hold their knuckles tight to their mouths. It seems to me that the art of acting is the drawing out of both an emotional response and, more important, a reflective response in an audience. For the child in drama the skill lies in behaving with integrity and spontaneity in a fictitious situation, not acting in the sense just described, but being.

But such dramatic playing can be superficial. Unless the living through is experienced with a sharpened consciousness, its value will be, at best, cathartic. It is the teacher's responsibility to help the children to find significance in their work. And this is where, paradoxically, we find a common ground between drama and theatre, for the teacher uses the very elements of theatre that are normally the tools of the play-wright. As the playwright focusses the meaning for the audience, so the teacher helps to focus meaning for the children; as the playwright builds tension for the audience; the teacher builds tension for the children; as the playwright and the director and the actors highlight meaning for the audience by the use of contrast in sound, light and movement, so does the teacher – for the children; as the playwright chooses with great care the symbolic actions and objects that will operate at many levels of meaning for the audience, so will the teacher help the children find symbols in their work. The mode of the children's experience must continue as 'I am making it happen; it is happening to me'. I claim that when the teacher 'folds into' this mode a structure that would be valid for the playwright, then there is a greater chance of learning taking place.

To the question what have drama and theatre in common, my answer is that whereas there is no useful comparison between what the child does and what the actor is required to do, the two forms share the same basic structure.

The teacher's function

The principal function of a drama teacher, then, is to use theatrical form in order to enhance the meaning of the participants' experience: by using the theatrical elements of tension, focus, contrast and symbolisation, actions and objects in the drama become significant. I have suggested that this theatrical structuring is combined with the spontaneous existential mode of the participants. A useful parallel for comparison can be found in formal games. Such games as football, Monopoly, and tick'n hit are good examples of participants experiencing within a highly structured framework.

Both games and drama require commitment. Making a start with a game seems to be relatively easy, although one can imagine a group of adolescents, unquestionably committed to football, feeling rather unsure of tennis, and although intensely and secretly intrigued, nevertheless distrustful of the party game of 'consequences'.

Whether it be a game or a drama, to start requires commitment; and drama is further complicated by requiring emotional engagement with the subject-matter. Another function of the drama teacher, therefore, is to work for commitment to drama and, more importantly, delicately to adjust the quality, degree and intensity of emotional engagement the topic arouses, so that the participants may with integrity, spontaneity and a sharpened consciousness enter the fictitious context. If some of the class are not interested in the topic, he may have to 'capture' their interest; if they are interested but inhibited by it, he may have to work to make it safe; if they are over-excited, he may have to contain their excitement.

Thus another purpose to teacher-structuring is emerging. Often a teacher cannot use theatrical form to enhance meaning, that is to bring about some change in the participants' understanding of a topic, until steps are taken to modify the emotional loading that topic carries for a particular class. He often finds himself structuring the dramatic activity in order to change the 'emotional temperature' as it were. The three lessons at the Riverside Studios are good examples of a teacher working towards this end.

Before I describe them I would like to share with you the 'luggage' I take with me into a classroom.

A perfect drama lesson

I suppose every drama teacher has at the back of his mind some notion of a model educational drama experience. It is unlikely to be of the kind that I was once taught – if you have exercised all five senses you have had a good lesson! It may not have any particular shape or content or steps. It may be just a vague sense of direction, or a series of hunches about inner experiences. However unfettered with plans a teacher may be, he must walk into the classroom with some kind of expectations.

In my dreams the perfect school drama experience round the corner will look something like this:

Expectations of class

1 They know that drama is for understanding.
2 They know it requires patient, reflective, hard work both in and out of the activity.
3 They know it only works if they contribute with an openness and critical awareness.
4 They know it is an art form in process not product.

Trust

1 They trust the situation; trust the teacher; trust each other; trust drama – indeed they are committed to it.

167

Implications for drama as an art form

Selection

1 They agree (this perfect class are bound to I suppose!) on a topic that is important to them.
2 Through discussion it emerges in what way it is important. They are neither over- nor under-stimulated by the subject-matter.

The drama

1 They or their teacher select (this is the playwright's function) a focus for starting the action, an action that carries some kind of tension, an action (and any properties used) that is susceptible or potentially susceptible to symbolic meanings.
2 They work with commitment in five directions: (i) they work in anticipation that something is going to be learnt from the situation; (ii) they work for credibility; (iii) they find a feeling quality that is appropriate to the fictitious context; (iv) they work towards form; (v) they take risks so they can experience.

The teaching

1 Teacher introduces some theatre strategy to help extend, deepen, change the perspective or simply make explicit their understanding of the chosen theme.
2 If selected with care (and in this model lesson everything is done with care!) the strategy meets other important objectives such as language development, increase in social responsibility etc.
3 The theatrical form is such that actions and objects resonate meanings of both personal and group significance.

The outcome

1 The satisfaction they found in the experience leads them to want to reflect upon it in a way that is productive.
2 It becomes a significant future reference point for them in their own lives.

It would be nice, just once, to experience this perfect model in practice just to find out whether it really is – perfect, that is!

What gives it unifying direction is the assumption that the main target of the drama work is some change in understanding. This does not imply that if you don't get there, you have failed. It is rather like intending to go on a journey. You may find out that you are not ready to reach the destination you have in mind, but you looked at maps and packed as if you were going to get there. The map work and the packing turn out to be worthwhile experiences in themselves because they were carried out purposefully.

The point that I am making is that the assumption behind all drama must be that it will lead to some change of understanding – of oneself in relation to the world one lives in, an assumption that a playwright might not unreasonably have about the effect of his play on an audience. It is this assumption that gives any use of drama its dynamic: whatever limitations there may be, whatever immediate problems one finds oneself dealing with, whatever temporary goal one finds oneself pursuing, this overall purpose characterises all the variety of activities that can go under the name of a drama lesson. This is an assumption that is not always shared by the children themselves. Very often one meets children for whom drama has no overall purpose, children who have had drama too sporadically for them to have grasped anything about it, or who have been implicitly taught that drama means 'fun', or 'getting rid of surplus energy', or 'learning acting tricks', or 'an escape from reality'. In other words, children too bring luggage to the classroom, a factor again well illustrated at the Riverside Studios. Let me now begin to describe as fully as is useful in terms of the above discussion, what happened during the three weekend sessions.

Three lessons

The Riverside Studios teaching was a very happy experience for me – apart from the second of the three lessons which I handled ineptly. But the pleasure I derived did not stem from a destination reached in terms of changing those pupils' level of thinking and understanding, although I would claim that the potential for doing so, given a third and fourth lesson, was there. (I can hear some readers at this point either muttering 'The arrogance of the man!' or, as one commentator said during Sunday turkey luncheon – 'You have spent three long lessons[1] achieving nothing'!)

'Change in understanding' implies an affective/cognitive shift in the topic. This class of lower band twelve year olds chose: 'Violence in schools'. As it turned out, the intellectual learning, although providing the dynamic, was peripheral to the real learning that appeared to be going on. It seemed to me that for most of the three lessons we were finding an appropriate level of emotion and, in this respect I believe important things were happening. But first let me give you the bare-bones, the external features of the lesson sequences.

Lesson one

1 The class are invited to choose a topic. The most popular two topics from the class's four suggestions were 'Violence' and 'School'. They put the two together so that topic for the drama became 'Violence in school'.
2 A 'school staff-meeting' is held with me in role as headmaster, to discuss the outrageous behaviour of a particular class – a fifth year as it turned out.
3 Out of role, in small groups, they discuss the kind of outrageous behaviour they want it to be and select, 'throwing food about in the dining-room'.
4 A further staff-meeting to discuss punishment to fit the crime.
5 Role-play in pairs – as adolescents reporting to each other 'what happened in the school dining-room today!'

Lesson two

1 On a long roll of paper, they draw or describe all the public places like clubs and X film cinemas that are open to sixteen year olds, but not twelve year olds.
2 I then role play a journalist trying to get some gossip for my paper from the 'notorious' adolescents about the dining-room incident.
3 Out of role, we select the class 'ring-leaders' and look at their attitude to school.
4 In role, just using two or three children at a time, with the rest of the class watching, we explore attitudes of their parents to school.
5 They all move into small groups of 'ring-leader' families to rehearse the moment when the parents first hear about the 'incident'.

Lesson three

1 They 'show' in each family how each ring-leader is received when he gets home from school (the parents just having heard the school's version first).
2 They become the troublesome fifth year class, after having indicated to me what kind of class teacher (in role) they want me to play.
3 They become staff again – except for the ring-leaders – holding a

staff-meeting to make final decisions about punishment, now that they are better informed of the various attitudes to the incident.

I now propose, using the above three outlines as reference points, to discuss teacher structuring in terms of commitment and emotional adjustment.

Trust

From the very start the children at Riverside found themselves in a situation they could not trust, not simply because of the place and the milling throng of adults, but because of the expectations of drama that they brought with them. Apart from the covert hints during the first lesson, their assumptions about drama were made clear to me in the lunch break. They made but three comments about the experience so far:

'We were told we would play games.'
'When are we going to get into our groups to act something for them (the audience)?'
'We don't have to carry on with the same thing next lesson do we – we don't at school?'

Already the first section of my model lesson is scrubbed! So here we have a class and teacher with two different sets of luggage as it were. Everything he does says 'process'; everything they do says 'product'. They say short-term; he says long-term. He says 'learning'; they say 'games'. Could anything be more threatening to a group of twelve-year-olds especially in physical surroundings with banked rows of 'short stay' spectators, a context clearly signalling to the children that product, games and short term would be more appropriate.

Now I know that given these special circumstances, it is very tempting to reduce the feeling of threat by letting them play games etc. This would seem the right step to many teachers and, possibly, to theatre people. But I know with my whole rational and irrational self that that is exactly what I must not do. The most important thing I have to teach is that an art form is for understanding. So from the outset, I am going to make a painful situation more painful by pulling in the opposite direction from the one in which they want to go. But of course I will do all I can as a person to build trust in other ways: for example, to signal to them that I understand what they are going through and protect them during the journey as much as possible.

Once this dynamic of a purposeful destination is established, however, I can use their luggage, often luggage they did not know they had brought with them. For instance, on this particular occasion, as you can see from above, they were entirely responsible for the choice of topic; in choosing violent behaviour, they were free to indicate what they wanted that behaviour to be; towards the end of the second lesson they had the chance they seemed to want to rehearse in small groups.

But these freedoms were heavily countered by restrictions imposed by me: my insistence that most of the time we worked as a whole group; the slowness of pace; a good deal of sitting and talking. These represent the external features of a slow, thoughtful process that is nearly always necessary if pulling in the opposite direction (I say nearly always – sometimes sudden shock tactics switch the direction at one stroke!). There are risks of course. Teaching is about weighing up risks. You may bore them to death, a natural reaction from a class who feel that they ought to be 'getting on'. Signs of this emerged strongly in the second lesson. It is when they begin to see glimmers of compensation that they begin to trust the teacher and the situation: their hearts may sink when they find themselves gathered round a blackboard but may lift again when it is their thinking that goes up on the board. And what they learn eventually of course, true of all creative work, is that the apparently endless troughs lead to richer peaks – as they discovered in the third lesson. But if they have been taught by 'Let's-get-up-and-go-for-drama-is-doing' teachers they will be unlikely to know this pain/joy of creativity.

One restriction I imposed is a significant one which leads us into a discussion of the central feature of the experience: emotional engagement with the subject-matter. The topic the class unanimously chose was a combination of 'violence' and 'classroom'. Hearing this decision some members of the audience of actors and teachers assumed that the proper thing to do would be for me to let the class dramatically have their 'violent' experience. This would give a useful reference point for extending their thinking and also be a means of letting them 'let off steam' in a controlled way. I think they assumed that because I did not let this happen, I was protecting myself by dodging the experience. Now this point of view, well articulated after the lesson was over and subsequently repeated by my Sunday lunch critic, is opposite to my own and is worth examining in some detail, in the next section.

Protecting

Whether you are a professional actor in an improvisation or a child in symbolic play the integrity of the experience will depend upon the quality of feeling you bring to the activity. The feeling must be appropriate to the context. If the child or actor, for example, bursts into a fit of giggles or passes some witticism as he is being chased by a killer shark, unless the pre-decided form is comedy, we could reasonably agree that feeling and context were incompatible. Getting into the action of drama is an approximating process of finding a quality of feeling that matches one's understanding of the theme and context. It is often very difficult in fact for children, however well-intentioned and however genuine their interest in the topic, to evoke appropriate feeling quality. Grief and ecstasy, for example, cannot be easily tapped. Much depends of course on the mood the pupils are in before the drama starts. If they are particularly happy and excited about something, it might be comparatively easy to transfer that mood to a drama about ecstasy. Equally, a child with a recent bereavement, will perhaps only too readily call upon a feeling of grief.

Thus the emotional starting point for dramatic action is initially dependent upon where a class is emotionally, at the actual level. It seems to me that there are two broad bands of emotion – the introverting and the extroverting, i.e. closing and opening, or momentum-reducing and action-impelling. For instance, compare shyness and boldness, or quiet amusement and ecstasy, or riveted with fear and fleeing in fear, or (more relevant here) feeling threatened and being threatening. If a group of children or adults choose a topic that happens immediately to demand an expression of feeling that is poles apart from their actual feelings then the starting point for the fiction must somehow legitimately cater for their actual feelings: an oblique way into the theme must be found. It is no use expecting a class of sullen, reluctant fourteen year olds to act out a cheerful birthday party ('Come on now, how would you feel?', one might find oneself asking hopefully!). Nor would you, faced with an eager, fun-seeking class of twelve year olds saying, 'Let's do a play where we get frightened by ghosts', start the drama with the ghosts' arrival!

Now a 'violence in school' theme requires a release of aggressive, hostile or angry feelings or some extrovert feeling of that order, in marked contrast to what was actually felt by that Riverside Studio class of children, who were clearly threatened and wracked with self-consciousness. One quite popular way round this problem is to turn to 'acting'. In many schools we have trained children to 'switch on' imitative emotional display, so that they give a demonstration of anger and hostility in a way that has little to do with real feeling. We sometimes mistakenly think that this is what a professional actor does. Our theatre schools know only too well the effort that some of their students have to put into unlearning these glib techniques. Unfortunately many children, given a taste for superficiality, resist working at finding an appropriate feeling quality. At Riverside it was my responsibility to show the class an alternative way of working.

So the only way it seems to me is to 'protect' them into a context that does not expose, a context that naturally permits them to indulge an 'introverting' emotion while gradually opening up the topic. It is also flexible enough to allow, as some of the class break from their self-consciousness, a change in feeling quality. Thus it was we became a staff meeting with me as headmaster (again they must be allowed to lean – another example of my giving support after having threatened). As they gained in confidence some of them began the next key move – working for credibility; picking up the rules of the game and beginning to use them creatively.

Negotiating meaning

This phrase, coined by the Schools Council Secondary Drama Project,[2] is a useful way of describing the delicate, uncovering process that follows. The 'staff-room' structure for the 'protecting' purpose as discussed above, also fulfils this vitally important function of negotiating meaning.

The class has chosen violence in schools. This could mean anything, depending so much on their backgrounds, attitudes to school and to violence, etc. As teacher I need to find out what they mean or I cannot do anything about extending that meaning. So often as a teacher I find myself with even the best of intentions working at what I mean by violence or some such topic. Now by initially placing the children in a school situation, but as a staff not as pupils, I am giving them a chance at more than one remove, to indicate what the 'kicks' are to be for them. For as staff they can let imaginations work in any direction that is most satisfying. Getting in touch with one's private desires and dreams and wishes is a thought process that can often only be made public in a form that is indirect, so that shifting to an off-centre activity is a fairly typical piece of structuring for emotionally charged topics. It was not insignificant that very early in the 'staff meeting' when asked by me what form in school was creating the most trouble, they seized the chance to distance it further by saying 'a fifth year'.*

My expectation of what they would offer when given the chance to describe the violence of this fictitious fifth year verged, I suspect, on something sensational, but what we actually got was:

'Being caught climbing through a window'.
'Taking your trousers down in front of the girls in the classroom'.
'Mixing mud into the food in the dining room'.
'Throwing food at the cooks'.

They chose the last two. So they are not really after violence as such but some form of school illegality. It was interesting that some of the fantasy imagery that later arose from one or two of the children in the 'ring leaders' homes' came nearer to a concept of violence and the macabre. We proceeded from there to look at the reported 'terrible incident in the dining room' from the point of view of teachers, parents and ring-leaders – all after the event. I know that they must not be trapped into experiencing that fifth year class of anti-social pupils until they are really ready for it. But there is something about this particular topic that is in itself unique and consequently creates a set of special emotional circumstances that are both an opportunity and a problem for all the participants – including teacher!

Before we move into this, however, there is an important point that I want to take up to do with what I understand by acting in drama as a process. One of the adult spectators (I do not know whether it was an actor or a teacher – it would have been interesting to find out) commented dismissively during the lesson to a neighbour: 'How can he expect twelve-year olds to act sixteen year olds?' Now to ask this question shows in my view a total misunderstanding of the educational function. Drama provides an opportunity for the participant to find out about himself in any context. The valuable metaphorical experience lies in a juxtaposition between the child and the role he has selected. As I said above, 'It is happening to me now'. It is not that he has become someone else nor is it that if he is role-playing a sixteen year old there is some standard recognisable performance that has to be reached. The only objective criteria that must be met are those that he needs to make his role credible to himself and to his classmates. This point is made even

---

* It is interesting that at the time I did not interpret this as a distancing technique but as a direct clue that they were interested in finding out what it was like to be fifth years. This misinterpretation led to some inappropriate questioning by me later on.

more effectively where, as it turned out in this case, the children were not interested in sixteen year olds as such but only as a mask behind which they could indulge their fantasies. The role is merely a reference point for something more important.

Containing and harnessing emotion

The peculiarity of the topic they happen to have chosen – illegal behaviour in school – is that its personal and group reference points are equally strong, in that the topic not only offers personal excitement but is also very near to their actual situation. They are a school class role-playing a school class – a context that is ripe for both individual and group fantasy trips. This could be emotional dynamite! Robert Witkin in his book *Intelligence of feeling* has written about this kind of situation and its dangers: 'Sometimes teachers do operate with dramatic situations that threaten to permeate the barrier between the simulated network (the relationship among pupils and between teachers and pupils)'.[3] He then goes on to describe a particularly unhealthy instance of a third year secondary group enacting head teacher/pupils roles as a way of dealing with a set of real problems with their own head teacher – a direct use of dramatic role play that, if it must be used, requires more expert handling than most teachers are trained for.

But the Riverside instance, although different in kind from Witkin's example, is not without its hazards.

These three lessons presented an extraordinary emotional sequence for once the class were protected and led from their own introverting emotion, with this particular context group extroversion could be released like a thunder storm!

What are the possible safeguards* in such a situation? One of them is that the role play is nominally at one remove – they are sixteen year olds; it is the formidable, fictitious 5Q that is the centre of concern. Indeed during the first lesson when they labelled the class 5D – a real class in their own school – I insisted that we were in some other school – and with a class with an unfamiliar title. Another safeguard lies in the tightness of teacher structuring. The third lesson was planned in three

---

* One very useful form of safeguard which I did not use on this occasion is to work by analogy, ie placing the subject-matter in a different and therefore safer context. The centre remains the same but the fiction is different. 'Violence in School' might become symbolised by threats of mutiny from the crew of Columbus' ship or Tom Brown's Schooldays or even the Tolpuddle Martyrs.

clearly defined phases which were explained to the class at the beginning of the lesson: (1) small group 'showing' of how different sets of parents received their 5Q child after the event had been reported; (2) a 5Q classroom episode; (3) a staff meeting. The third safeguard is teacher's planning for affective/cognitive change. I intended to use the double experience of their being the 'terrible 5Q' with me as their 'teacher', followed by a final staff meeting in which they, now as staff, would be required to counter their own arguments expressed earlier in their role as 5Q. That the potential for such learning is there and that teacher is constantly looking for an opportunity to promote it, is a crucial feature of the structuring. But the class denied themselves this opportunity by hardening their position as a badly behaved class into a class with power over their 5Q teacher!

Now I know this alarmed many of the spectators, but in fact as long as they are required to work symbolically within the theatre form, far from being dangerous, it requires the most disciplined behaviour. In other words it becomes a fourth safeguard. Dramatically the experience of being 5Q gives them enormous freedom (I was told afterwards by one of the spectators, one of their own teachers, that it was the quietest girls in the class who 'threatened me with a knife' during the scene), but psychologically that freedom is taken away, for they are bound by the rules of working symbolically: they are released into self-discipline. During that classroom scene the teacher's bag was stolen, the blackboard overturned and he was physically threatened, all of which, I am sure, sounds alarming, but every action was a symbol of power, not a raw expression of power. The question undoubtedly arises and indeed was hurriedly discussed after the lesson whether such an experience gives children a taste for power. Some people felt these children might now return to their school with the intention of challenging authority. I have not done any follow-up on this, but I would be very surprised if this was so. I have not developed a rationale to support it, but my hunch is that this kind of drama experience has the opposite effect and is really no more alarming than a four year old saying to his mother: 'I'll be your mummy and you be my child' and then setting out to symbolise all sorts of extreme 'mummy behaviours'. The danger comes of course when the children are not working within an art form at all, as in the instance described by Robert Witkin, when their actions are no longer symbolic.[4]

Another safeguard in this kind of fantasy trip is that teacher continues to hold firmly on the reins in two directions. Having noted the implied consensus of agreement by the class on the degree to which objective reality must be met in order for their fantasy context to have credibility, the teacher will then insist that they either keep to that degree or increase it: he will not tolerate a further slide away from objectivity. Connected with this is that whatever reality is found within the fiction it will have its own logic, its own rules: again it is a teacher's responsibility to insist that the class keep to that logic. Sometimes an over-excited or particularly egocentric child will break the implied rules and distort the fantasy beyond the class's intentions, again challenging credibility. The teacher must step in on these occasions – as indeed I had to during the staffroom scene.

Another safeguard is that I have no qualms whatsoever at stopping the progress of the drama. Indeed I establish with most classes that I shall often hold up the drama for us to examine what we are creating. I often use the device that 'When I move to this chair we are no longer in role'. So I constantly put a brake on the dramatic flow, not to hold some intellectual discussion, but to check on the integrity of the experience.

It was a pleasurable experience for me to work with that class as we searched together for a viable dramatic form. By lesson three they were struggling as a group to discipline their release of energy – and they succeeded – just! One commentator had remarked, 'All that surplus energy – why doesn't he let them play games?' I hope he would share with me the satisfaction of this degree of energy purposefully and dramatically harnessed: I don't want to get rid of it; I want to use it – but it takes time. I saw this as a satisfying, important step forward that the class and I had taken together. We smiled at each other in our farewells – a sharing of a new understanding that was full of promise should we meet and do drama again.

And then, over my plate piled with turkey: 'These children are at the same level of thinking they were at when you started and you have had far longer than most teachers ever get.' I returned my plate (still piled with turkey!) and pondered. Here was someone using the very criteria I use myself: 'Has the drama broken these children's stereotyped thinking?' The answer must be that my critic is unreservedly right. Then why was I so pleased with myself? What do I think they had learned?

The answer lies in the headings of this chapter: trust; protecting; negotiating meaning; and containing. I claim that each of these is a worthwhile experience for me and the class to share. But more than that I would be satisfied if I could guarantee that they have learned three vitally important things:

1 a new sensing of dramatic form and a glimmer of what works in the dramatic process
2 at least a tentative grasp that drama is for understanding – this is its purpose
3 that this understanding is reached through finding an integrity of feeling.

I would not expect that the children themselves could articulate these points. If indeed I have planted these seeds then that class and I are ready to move forward with leaps and bounds. I may have achieved in three lessons (three long consecutive lessons) what it takes teachers with their one hour a week six months to achieve – and what those confined to thirty-five minutes periods have little chance of achieving.

Conclusion

In this chapter I have attempted to discuss two teacher functions that are critical to the drama teacher's work. The peculiarity of the choice of topic by the Riverside children, their own expectations of what drama is and the circumstances in which they found themselves, stressed the first of these functions: working for commitment, for an experimental as opposed to an 'acting' mode of behaviour and towards stimulating or tempering emotional engagement with the theme. The second function is to move in the direction of change of understanding. The structures that are available to a teacher in carrying out both functions are often the structures employed by the playwright. A drama teacher is consistently working in theatre form.

Theatre form in drama teaching. In Robinson K (ed) *Exploring theatre and education*, 1980 Heinemann.

References

1 Bolton G 1980 *Towards a theory of drama in education*. Longman. (For a detailed analysis of the three lessons.)
2 MacGregor *et al.* 1977 *Learning through drama*. Heinemann. (A report on the project.)
3 Witkin R W 1974 *The Intelligence of feeling*. Heinemann, p. 80.

4 Vygotsky L S 1976 Play and its role in the mental development of the child. In Bruner J S *et al. Play: its development and evolution.* Penguin Educational. (For a discussion on child symbolic play as self-imposed discipline.)

Drama in education and TIE – a comparison

In this chapter I will put forward a theoretical framework and terminology for 'drama in education' (DIE) and then proceed to apply the same framework and terminology to 'theatre in education' in an attempt to outline similarities and differences between the two.

I have never worked professionally in TIE, but I have, since its inception, found myself caught up in its development. I have sought to understand it for two reasons. One is the obvious one that it has significant educational value. The other, much less obvious, is also an explanation of why I am now writing this particular chapter. I have always been impressed with the pioneers I have met in TIE as educational thinkers. At a time when as drama teachers we were content to be cosily imprecise about what we were doing in schools – 'developing personalities'; 'building confidence'; 'training in sensitivity' were the kind of high sounding platitudes we offered, if challenged (fortunately for us we were rarely challenged!) – it was both refreshing and threatening to find that teams of actors coming into our schools were not only asking fundamental questions about education and the part that theatre might have to play in it, but were also very capable of articulating their answers. I thus found myself learning about my own job from people who came from outside the normal drama teaching system. I have called them pioneers and have put the last sentence in the past tense, but in fact if newcomers to the TIE scene are anything to go by we in DIE can continue to look to the TIE world for hard thinking about drama in education.

In his excellent survey and analysis of TIE, John O'Toole discussed many issues common to both TIE and DIE.[1] It is some of the connections between the two that I wish to pursue further here. I shall confine my discussion to those aspects of TIE work that require the pupils to participate. I shall not be concerned of course, with external differences between the two like organisational characteristics or conditions of employment, or timetabling, or staffing. I shall examine the nature of the experience itself. With this in mind I shall look at DIE under the following headings: (1) Mode; (2) Structure; (3) Purpose; and (4) Content.

1 Mode

An examination of drama in schools will reveal there are three basic kinds: (a) process-orientated – derived from 'child play'; (b) performance-orientated – derived from theatre; and (c) skill-orientated. The first is characterised by its spontaneous, existential qualities of experiencing; the second by communicability, repeatability and demonstration of experiencing. The third tends to be concerned with short-term activities that give practice either in theatre (e.g. acting exercises), or in living (e.g. trust exercises).

Neither the emphasis on the presentation of experience inherent in the second nor the goal-orientation of personal skills implied in the third has any relevance for a TIE team. TIE does not require pupils to perform or to practise something. (I am referring here to practising skills as an end in itself – not to short-term practice which immediately feeds back into the drama experience, as for instance, the 'weaving' practice in 'Poverty knocks' [a TIE programme for top-junior and first-year schoolchildren].) It requires them to 'Be'. The only DIE mode therefore that is likely to be harnessed by a TIE team in promoting participation is the first, where the emphasis is on experiencing. It is the nature of this process in DIE that I shall now examine in some detail.

When children are in make-believe, playing on their own, they are, for the most part, in this particular 'living-through' mode. Let us suppose they are playing 'cowboys and Indians'. They are experiencing, but in a special way that is different from the normal tenor of living in that they have agreed to contrive a fictitious situation. They are the agents as well as the recipients of the experience. They can say 'we are making it happen, so that it can happen to us'. In 'making it happen' they are also acknowledging and defining for themselves the rules, in this case, of the cowboy and Indian context. Thus there are three components to the process of dramatic playing: the agent, the recipient and the rules.

The highest degree of autonomy is available to the child playing cowboys and Indians on his own – he is the agent, the contriver of his own experiences and indeed he may manipulate the rules to suit himself. If another child joins him the rules have to be agreed upon and freedom is thus constrained. They are both agents but only in so far as they abide by the agreed rules and respond to each other's contriving. The subsequent experiencing is the result of a subtle balancing of these complex factors. Many drama teachers seek for their pupils the comparative freedom of this dramatic playing mode as an important educational experience in itself. It becomes a feature of their drama lessons and is regarded as something rather precious to remain untampered and protected from teacher 'interference'.

We are describing then a form of dramatic activity that depends upon a high degree of autonomy for releasing an experiential mode. And yet TIE work which appears, to a large extent, to remove autonomy from the pupils, nevertheless requires them to participate by 'living through' the experience (the team certainly do not want the participants to act the experience!). Put like this it happens that TIE's position is somewhat paradoxical. However there is already a precedent for resolving the paradox in a certain kind of drama teaching – the use of teacher in role.

2 Structure – teacher-in-role[2]

When a teacher takes on a role as part of his class drama he is at a fictitious level joining in with them, but at an educational or psychological level he is working ahead of them. It is, as Geoff Gillham has pointed out,[3] as if there are two plays going on at the same time – the play for the child and the play for the teacher. They are different in respect of (a) intention, and (b) structure. Difference in intentions can be illustrated as follows. In their drama about cowboys and Indians the children's intentions are, say, to have fun doing a cowboy and Indian adventure, whereas the teacher's objectives may be to do with responsibility or loyalty or territorial rights or law or prejudice or minority groups. In other words the teacher is operating at a different level of meaning from the children. His problem is to find a right balance. If the experience stays entirely as a play for them, he might as well have stayed out of it; if, on the other hand, he imposes his play to the extent of sacrificing theirs, only he will be having the experience. Drama orientated around a teacher-in-role is then a partnership between teacher and children as agents, a 'folding in' of teacher's intentions with the children's intentions.

There is also an interesting interleaving of structures. Left to themselves children will structure for sequence, for the 'what-happens-next' of a story; the teacher will structure for situation. They will manipulate the contextual rules (e.g. cowboys and Indians rules) to suit their wants; the teacher will manipulate the rules to meet what he sees as their needs. They are using the fictitious context to release themselves into experiencing; he is sharpening and deepening that experiential mode by structuring the fictitious context towards a theatre form.

By theatre form I mean those basic elements of theatre that a playwright employs and a director builds upon: focus; tension; contrast; and symbolisation. A teacher-in-role, therefore, in a very special way, is working in theatre. Just as a playwright and director will consciously create tension etc. so that an audience might experience, so a teacher-in-role uses tension so that the participants might experience. The relationship of teacher to class is equivalent to the relationship of playwright to audience.

When a TIE team work with pupils their function can be usefully seen as an extension of teacher-in-role. The team is not just offering the children a play, as in traditional children's theatre: they are anticipating 'a play for the children' where the participants, at their own level of meaning, can discover and retain their own dynamic within the action. Where the type of subject matter embodies a great deal of factual information, as in 'Poverty knocks', there is a danger that the children may remain submissive 'passengers' within the complicated experience, unless the team find a way of bringing in an opportunity for enactive or emotional engagement. For example, in this particular programme, the 'factory workers' find themselves having to take the initiative of distracting Bash from the Round Robin; they elect their own Chartist Committee; the handloom weavers are under pressure to give in to an offer of only 5 shillings for the cloth; they can choose to side with Eleanor or Jack; they design their own Chartist banners, etc. Thus the team can then use their roles to structure for theatre in a way that both stimulates and extends a 'play for the children'. It seems to me that unless the quality, intensity and purpose of the participation is similar to that of a drama experience, the notion of participation becomes relegated to the old-fashioned 'Let's all help to blow the giant away' kind of audience support, where the participation is 'embroidered' on to the real action. In the initial stages of a programme participation of this superficial kind is often unavoidable. In 'Poverty knocks' one group of children obligingly and, no doubt, enthusiastically mime a handweaving process for a variety of reasons other than belief in their roles.

The test is whether later on in the TIE experience, the quality of the miming of weaving has changed because the play is now theirs as well as the actors'. It is interesting that in DIE work a similarly shallow phase is often an inevitable part of the process, before the right balance between teacher's and children's play is found.

3 Purpose

As I mentioned earlier in this chapter, objectives in DIE were something we used to be smugly vague about, as though, because we were working in an art form, the normal requirements of justifying what one was doing did not apply.

It is possible to list many objectives for drama teaching which vary in importance according to circumstances but, it seems to me, there is one objective which more than any other has permanent place in a teacher's planning. If drama is to be included in a school curriculum, then its principal purpose must be to do with change in understanding. Change in understanding what? 'Whatever the drama is about' is the answer, i.e. the content of the drama which is something we shall be looking at closely in the final section of this chapter. All other objectives of teaching drama are incidental to this one. A table of teacher objectives might look like this.

Objectives in teaching drama
A Change in understanding
B Others
    1 Social skills, including sensitivity, empathy and listening skills
    2 Language skills, including speech, thinking, writing and reading skills
    3 Movement skills
    4 Skill in doing drama, including working with selectivity, economy and a sense of form

Although 'change in understanding' has priority over the others as an objective, in practice one or more of the skills could, for particular drama lessons, take prior place. Indeed there are one or two prerequisites for drama such as trust and reasonable behaviour which may become a teacher's immediate goal, leaving 'change in understanding' in abeyance, as it were. The important point to be made in this discussion however is that DIE and TIE share the same goals. Both have 'change in understanding' as their principal objective. Indeed it seems to me that for TIE there can be no other. It is not the place of a TIE team to attempt to teach a variety of skills. If the educational purpose is shared by DIE and TIE, does it follow that there may be common ground in the material they both handle? This is a more complex question than may first appear.

4 Content

Let us get the easiest part of the answer out of the way first. It obviously is relatively simple for a drama teacher to choose material appropriate for the class. An infant teacher may wisely set up some drama to teach the children not to accept sweets from strangers. Her choice of topic would be based on the particular class's needs and level of readiness to learn from the material. Now no TIE team is in a position to make such a judgement, so such a team has to make enormous assumptions about needs and readiness and will necessarily avoid strongly personal topics for that reason. Thus a TIE team cannot tailor the drama to a particular class as a teacher can.

If the team are to be involved in an extension of the teacher-in-role function where they will be required to accommodate what they have to teach to a 'potential play for the children', it is a huge disadvantage that they do not personally know the children. They have to make wise guesses based on their own experience of advice from teachers as to what might generally be appropriate for, say, particular age groups.

The more difficult part of the answer to the question whether TIE and DIE handle the same material is complex because it is concerned with levels of meaning. 'Change in understanding' as an objective implies that some modification of (or awareness of, perception of, insight into or knowledge about) something takes place. Now in drama in schools there tend to be two interpretations of this objective. One is a simple straightforward use of a dramatic medium to represent some absent context so that the context might be better understood by the pupils. Such a use would be where the drama sets out to simulate 'a day in the life of a farmer' as an approach to studying farming or where mock interviews are set up in order to give the pupils interview practice. In other words this use of drama is functional: it provides a useful way of teaching about the objective world. The meaning is contextual.

The other orientation is artistic, where the purpose is not to represent an absent objective context but to select some universal aspect within that objective context and to explore that aspect for personal, subjective, as well as objective meanings. Thus the drama might be about (a) outlaws, at a contextual level but the meaning of the experience, or more accurately, the many layers of meaning of the experience are to do with (b) what it is like when you cannot return home (a universal concept that extends both into and beyond the outlaw situation) and (c) whatever personal, subjective identification each participant draws from the experience. The complexity of meanings in this artistic use of drama derives from the ambivalent relationship (b) and (c) have with (a): they are both simultaneously dependent upon and independent of (a), the contextual meaning.

The three levels of meaning can perhaps be best tabulated as follows:

(a) concrete, 'surface' level of meaning	Objective facts about outlaws: e.g. they are people who have been banned for committing a crime
(b) a universal level of meaning that is abstracted and shared by the class	universal concepts that go beyond the outlaw context and could apply to many other situations: e.g. not daring to return home; always on the move; always looking over one's shoulder
(c) each individual's personal level of meaning	each child will draw differently on past 'feeling' experiences in order to identify, say, 'not daring to go home'

In contextual drama the 'surface' meaning is the drama. For instance, if the objective was to show the participants how trade unions work, the action of the drama would be a simulation of trade union procedures; that is, the relationship between the participants and the fictitious (trade union) context would be representational. The nearer the children got to imitating trade union procedures, the more likely is the objective to be reached. It might be shown diagramatically like this:

Participants' actions ——————— represent ———————→ Trade Unionists' actions

But in artistic drama (going back to our 'outlaw' example) the interrelationship is complicated because there are necessarily at least three levels of meaning. Diagrammatically it might look like this:

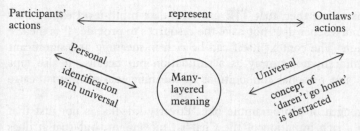

The above diagram is an attempt to show the both circular and two-way relationship between the three interdependent levels, a relationship that is dialectical rather than representational. Now where does TIE stand in relation to these distinct uses of drama in schools? It seems to me that for a team to confine itself to contextual meaning would to impose an unnecessary limitation on its skill and talents, although one does find some teams who simply set up nothing more than a simulation exercise.

I have suggested that the power of drama used as an art-form in schools derives from the ambivalent dependent and independent relationship the personal and universal meanings have with the objective context. Indeed in some drama in schools significant meanings may emerge from the most casually-handled contexts: for example the context may be 'robbing a bank' but the experience is to do with 'trusting one's mates', not really about robbing a bank at all. Now a principal expertise of a TIE team lies in its ability to create highly credible exciting contexts. So whatever universal meanings the team may intend to tap, they must additionally focus on the context as an important end in itself. That there is this major difference in emphasis was brought home to me sharply and uncomfortably when at the opening of a SCYPT conference in Aberystwyth a few years ago I demonstrated a way of working in drama that included teacher-in-role and an underlying universal theme of what it is like to face apparently unresolvable problems. I chose for a context a story I had just been given by some eight year olds in California that had a Jason and the Golden Fleece kind of flavour to do with going on a quest at the behest of a king, a context that I regarded as arbitrary but quite useful for the underlying experience. I should have known better! When my demonstration lesson was over (I had asked actors to be my class of eight year olds) my expectations of a discussion on what I regarded as the real content were abruptly halted, for the meaning the TIE actors and directors watching were interested in was the contextual one, and as far as they were concerned, I was just another establishment voice from the educational past attempting to resurrect values to do with obeying kings!

It seems to me then that TIE can stimulate multi-level experiences that a drama teacher does not have the resources to provide. It is theatre in education. The context itself can be rich in meaning and significant for the children, not simply as a simulation but because it also taps universals and personal connotations of meaning that all good theatre provides.

The strength of a programme like 'Poverty knocks' is not just that it sets up a rich imitation of the Chartist movement, but that it does so within a true theatre experience where many universals are tapped. (Being paid to spy on one's mates and the treacherous capitulation by Eleanor when she denies having been a marcher are examples of gut-level experiences for the children that go deeper than Chartism.) DIE can sometimes achieve the latter; it can rarely achieve the former; and has little chance of ever achieving both.

Summary

In this chapter I have outlined a theoretical framework for a particular kind of drama in schools where 'teacher-in-role' is employed as a principal device. Such a device permits the integration of two modes that are normally thought of as incompatible: an existential, living through mode where the participants have some degree of autonomy over their experiencing and a theatrical mode that through use of tension, context, focus and symbolisation heightens, sharpens and intensifies that experiencing.

Theatre in education, I claim, can be seen as an extension of this teacher-in-role device; TIE work also can be seen as offering a highly structured 'living through' experience (I have confined the discussion to those aspects of TIE work concerned with participation).

I make the point that whereas a drama teacher may have a range of objectives including social health, trust, skills, etc., DIE and TIE share the same principal objective, that of bringing about a change in understanding. An important difference between the two, however, is that whereas the learning area in drama may centre on the theme of the subject-matter, the context becoming but a pretext for opening up the theme, a TIE team must bring a different emphasis to the subject-matter. Their very skills as actors allow them to offer a rich context not normally available to the drama teacher, so that this work must be both contextually and thematically significant.

Drama in education and TIE – a comparison. In Jackson Tony (ed) *Learning through theatre: essays and casebooks on theatre in education*, 1980. Manchester University Press (Oxford Road, Manchester, M13 9PL).

References

1 O'Toole J 1967 *Theatre in education*. Hodder and Stoughton.
2 Bolton G M 1980 *Towards a theory of drama in education*. Longman. (For a detailed description of teacher-in-role.)
3 Gillham G 1974 Report on Condercum School Project by Live Theatre. Unpublished.

Section Four
Drama and teaching/learning

Introduction

Drama and knowing

It is perhaps in this area of teaching/learning that Gavin Bolton has changed least. He has always (at least since the earliest writings in this collection) advocated the responsibility of the teacher to bring about learning in the drama process and this learning has always been to do with cognitive development. This cognitive development involves conceptual change: modifying (developing or challenging) existing concepts or introducing new concepts into the child's conceptual framework. This emphasis has always meant that he takes as his central concern the development of the way the child knows the world. This marks him out from all those educators who are concerned to bring about unconscious change in a behaviourist tradition. But more importantly he also marks himself out from the dominant tradition in English education, even though this tradition (at least in theory) is concerned with cognitive development. Unlike in North America, there has been strong resistance to any encroachment of behaviourist approaches in English education, a resistance led by Hirst, Peters and Dearden.* But it is a cognitive development Gavin Bolton is unhappy with. He sees it as involving the formal transmission of knowledge. The teacher inculcates the child into the culture by pouring knowledge into him (as water into a pitcher, which is the frequent Dickensian image he uses). So, although he is concerned with the development of knowledge he diverts from this dominant tradition in two important respects.

In the first place Bolton rejects this more passive view of the child as a receiver and insists that the child is active in the learning process. In this aspect he adopts a progressive approach more in keeping with Bruner's who sees learning as 'the active pursuit of knowledge'. Gavin Bolton insists that children take responsibility for their learning, not complete responsibility, for this would negate the teacher's role, but an equally active and responsible part in the joint teaching/learning process.

In the second place Bolton disagrees with the concept of knowledge promoted by Hirst etc. This school of thought influenced by the heritage of logical positivism in this country, sees knowledge as that which can be propositionally stated. Paul Hirst, the leading philosopher of education who has been most influential in this tradition defines knowledge as follows:

* For an example of their writings, see Dearden R F, Hirst P H, Peters R S 1972 *Education and the development of reason*. Routledge and Kegan Paul.

. . . the domain of knowledge I take to be centrally the domain of true propositions or statements . . . Certainly we speak not only of knowing truths but also of knowing people and places and knowing how to do things. Detailed analysis suggests, however, that there are in fact only two distinct types of knowledge here, that in which the objects of knowledge are true propositions and that in which the objects are practical performances of some kind, knowledge of people and places being reducible to complexes of knowledge of these two types based on specific forms of experience.[1]

These two types of knowledge are commonly referred to as 'knowing that . . .' and 'knowing how . . .'.

Gavin Bolton prefers to add to these two types of knowing a third type, which is for him the most important one. He follows Reid's expression of it as 'knowing this'. This is the personal experience of knowing something which modifies the whole person rather than seeing the person/child as a blank receptacle of knowledge. Reid, in another context to do with teacher education, describes the process of 'knowing this' in the following way, and if we substitute child for teacher I think we have a reasonable picture of the sort of knowing which interests Gavin Bolton. The child (through the drama process) 'has to think through . . . his principles of value, and with his feeling and will and imagination as well as his intellect. If he does so, then through time these principles becomes so assimilated into his personality that all his dispositions are subtly changed, and his outlook illuminated so that he *sees* situations differently, notices new aspects and relations, and (with some reinforcement of deliberately willed effort) acts differently.'[2]

This has two important implications for the way Gavin Bolton sees knowledge. It colours the sorts of concepts he most often chooses to explore and his concern with personal knowing leads him to a phenomenological position in relation to knowledge.

To take the former implication first, it means that his learning areas are most often to do with values, with moral issues. Drama 'is seen as a vehicle for cognitive development giving significance to the learning of those kinds of concepts which . . . are of central importance to living,' is how he expresses it in 'Philosophical perspectives on drama and the curriculum'. This echoes throughout his work from early writings onwards, 'Our aims are helping children . . . so that they develop a set of principles, a set of consistent principles, by which they are going to live.'[3] This emphasis leads him to regard other sorts of conceptualising or knowing, to be of second order importance, such as knowing about dramatic form or knowing how to work positively in a group. This does not mean he regards other areas of knowledge as unimportant, on the contrary they may even have pride of place on occasions, but this is the general ordering of his priorities.

It is in relation to the second implication noted above that Gavin Bolton has made the most obvious development in his position over the years from advocating the importance of personal knowing, to now openly embracing a phenomenological position in relation to a theory of knowledge. He sees there being objective knowledge (e.g. that some people are more privileged than others) but is concerned with the subjective/objective relationship of the knower to this knowledge. That is to say the way that which the knower already knows relates to the new knowing. . This gives a personal investment to the knowledge. It creates a personal meaning mediated by the group process.

In Curtis and Mays[4] they set out the three areas phenomenologists agree on in broad terms. The first two of these are stated as

1 a belief in the importance, and in a sense the primacy, of
   subjective consciousness
2 an understanding of consciousness as active, as meaning bestowing
   (p. xiii)

This inter-subjectively negotiated meaning is the classic position of those who see knowledge as socially constructed.

In the drama experience a personal knowing is created in relation to the objective world and this personal knowing is mediated for each other by the class and predominantly by the teacher.

The dialectic set up is between personal knowledge and social objectivity but perhaps the dialectical relationship that would merit investigation would be the inner dialectic of what is meant when Gavin Bolton talks about knowledge as 'uniquely his knowledge'. Perhaps the dialectic needs to be found that mediates the 'unique'.

Papers in Section Four

Leading this section of writings is an early piece interestingly called 'In search of aims and objectives'. It is interesting for the way it highlights an unchanging concern of Gavin Bolton's that the teacher is constantly in a living experience with children, sweeping them continually with teacher's radar antennae, to search out what the children's needs are from their moment-to-moment interactions and to respond as teacher, to set up learning situations. Here we have the notion of 'play for class, play for teacher' before this classic wording had been invented.

In 'Creative drama and learning' he classifies the major types of learning possible in drama and the modes of dramatic activity that can be promoted in a drama lesson. It has the feel of a first draft of those categories that were shortly to be developed in *Towards a theory of drama in education*.

'An evaluation of the schools council drama teaching project (10–16)' is a delicately handled devastating critique of the team's three years' work. He criticises them for only selecting or noticing or knowing about one type of dramatic activity i.e. 'acting-out' to make a statement and for leaving out the 'living-through' experience for learning in drama. They have ignored the fundamental differences in orientation of dramatic activity; to practise a skill, to experience and to demonstrate. In relation to this he charges them with ignoring the importance of feeling in drama, that is drama for a felt change in value. He has more recently described this sort of feeling as a verb rather than an adjective (see p. 100). Central to his critique is that they do not pay enough attention to the symbolisation process in drama. He also berates them for virtually ignoring Dorothy Heathcote 'the world's greatest thinker and practitioner of the seventies in drama in education'.

'Assessment of practical drama' again highlights that what needs to be assessed is the extent to which participants in the drama are engaged with the content/theme/meanings. But again nothing is said about the role of the teacher in the drama process. Bolton is apparently concerned here with drama where no teacher is involved which would mean the pupils being focally aware of form and yet assessed on the extent to which they had become involved with the meanings and some of this involvement in a living-through mode.

In 'Drama in the curriculum' Gavin Bolton sets out an argument for drama to be at the core of the curriculum for both its poetic and functional uses.

'Philosophical perspectives on drama and the curriculum' gives the most precise account so far in this collection of writings of how Bolton views the knowledge to be gained through drama. There is a factual level relating to knowledge of the actual world and more importantly one's responsibility to the objective world. It is interesting to note that the other major area of learning in drama, learning about aesthetic form, he argues cannot be 'taught' but it needs to be 'acquired' through experiencing creating it.

In 'Drama and meaning' Bolton argues against a phrase of Dorothy Heathcote's that to get the action right means concentrating on meaning. (It is doubtful if she would want to be held to this statement: her actual work with young people belies it.)

He argues that for the appropriate feeling content to develop for the not the theme. In this paper can be noted the greater emphasis he is placing on the uniqueness of individual learning and his growing reluctance to specify *exactly* what the children might learn. He is much less certain that they will all be learning the same thing and his image of teacher casting a net for learning appears.

The article which completes this section 'Drama in education – a reappraisal' is chronologically slightly out of order but is useful as a last article to summarise major areas to which Gavin Bolton has contributed. His section on the myth that drama is anti theatre captures the essence of his new position and is perhaps the clearest early exposition of what is fully developed in *Drama as education*.[5]

References

1 Hirst P 1974 *Knowledge and the curriculum.* Routledge and Kegan Paul, p 85.
2 Reid L A 1962 *Philosophy and education.* Heinemann, p 96.
3 Bolton G 1971 Drama and theatre in education – a survey. In Dodd D, Hickson W (eds) *Drama and theatre in education.* Heinemann, pp 12–13.
4 Curtis B, Mays W (eds) 1978 *Phenomenology and education.* Methuen.
5 Bolton G M 1984 *Drama as education.* Longman.

In search of aims and objectives

I am interested in the wide range of strategies teachers employ in order to help children in a variety of learning situations. I suppose it is impossible to record the number of quick decisions a teacher makes almost unconsciously, within the space of a drama lesson. His professional skill is exhibited in his ability to interpret the multitude of signals emitted by a class of children, to use his interpretation to define the needs of the individuals and of the class as a whole, and then to structure a learning experience most appropriate to those needs.

Before a teacher can decide which particular device, exercise or experience is likely to be most effective at any one time he must be clear as to what goals need to be reached. In this article I shall concern myself with drawing attention to the constantly changing pattern of objectives that may fairly typically emerge during a short series of drama lessons. I shall use some of my own teaching to illustrate my theme. Please do not assume that in describing my own work I am recommending a way of teaching drama. Indeed, the reader's view of what the work was actually like will be seriously distorted because I shall deliberately limit myself to describing it in terms of the kind of thinking that went on in my mind at each point where I found I had to redefine objectives. I am not concerned here with whether the decisions I came to were the right ones; I am merely hoping that in attempting to indicate the educational principles and aspirations that guided me, I may interest the reader in attempting to analyse the processes by which he reaches his own conclusions, when, as a teacher, he is confronted with this often difficult but essential task of clarifying aims and objectives.

A few weeks ago I asked a primary school headmaster if I could take a class of children for a few sessions of drama (and any activity stemming from the drama) in order to demonstrate the value of this particular educational medium to our Primary Diploma Course Students. The headmaster kindly offered me a class (unstreamed) of top juniors.

Faced with this kind of teaching situation where I am a visitor taking a class of children what kind of aims should I have in mind? My top priority was:

To *establish* that the children are required to make decisions in the organisation of their own learning.

My second broad aim was:

To *introduce* drama as a useful way of exploring living.

My immediate objective was:

To *ensure* that something should happen during the first lesson that would give the children enjoyment, satisfaction and a sense of achievement.

Bearing in mind my principal aim, my first lesson began with 'What shall we make up a play about?' From a number of suggestions which ranged from Richard the Lion Heart to Key-Stone Cops a majority vote landed us with Florence Nightingale (hereafter referred to in this article as 'FN').

My thoughts race along a number of dimension at this point of the lesson: i) How do *I* see the FN situation? (Answer: Women in a Men's World), ii) How do the children see it? (Answer: Can't tell from what they say; better let them have the chance of showing me). Thus my immediate objectives now became:

To *give* the class a chance of working freely, in their own way, at their own level.

So the school hall was turned into a hospital ward. They were about to use all the available rostra and apparatus when I restricted them to a certain number of boxes. New objective:

To *establish* that this new teacher makes rules, that freedom has bounds.

The children started their 'Crimean hospital make-believe', leaving me to observe. To the girls FN apparently meant simply 'playing' at nurses among themselves. To the boys FN meant rolling on the floor or on top of each other as patients, giggling away uncontrollably. A rush of new objectives!:

TO ESTABLISH that the greatest satisfaction in drama comes from working seriously.

TO HELP the boys and girls to work together (they had either totally ignored each other or nurses had tentatively tickled their patients – and *vice versa!*).

Exercises in seriousness, related to the nature of pain, employing boys and girls in pairs (mother and son with cut finger, etc.) followed, so that the lesson ended with something of a working atmosphere. 'Can we do FN again?' they said as they left.

The second lesson was a couple of days later. My thinking in preparation, went along these lines: What are the possible developments within the FN situation that are worth pursuing and will take the class beyond a level of 'playing at hospitals'.

1 Biographical dramatic sequence of FN story.
2 Portrayal of hospital conditions – then and now.
3 Dramatic portrayal of battles.
4 Drama of war, suffering and death.
5 Drama of conflict between the authority of FN and the authority of the doctors.

I decided that number (5), the theme of authority was the most appropriate for this group; the other elements like nursing conditions for example, would probably emerge in incidental support of the drama.

When I came to the second lesson, therefore, I had crystallised a new principal aim:

To *help* the children understand the concept of authority.

My principal objective now became:

To *use* the FN situation to illumine certain aspects of authority and to relate this situation to authority situations in the children's own lives.

But the teacher cannot happily press on with his own objectives without taking into account the children's own objectives. During the second lesson, although boys and girls were now prepared to tolerate working together there was a marked divergence of interests: the girls were fascinated by the problem of living conditions at Scutari Hospital; the boys zealously threw themselves into being ill and wounded. For some reason or other they found this totally absorbing. I had to structure the drama, therefore, to give both boys and girls the immediate satisfaction they needed and to introduce gradually the authority theme. Having read the Woodham-Smith biography of FN, the dramatic situation that appeared to be the most powerful vehicle for achieving those particular objectives, theirs and mine, arose from the fact that the doctors at Scutari refused to let the nurses, newly arrived from England, have anything to do with the patients. For the remaining lessons we proceeded to examine this situation from many different viewpoints, revealing various shades of authority relationships – doctors/chief doctor; FN/chief doctor; doctors/patients; FN/nurses; nurses/patients, etc. – each time transferring, in order to consolidate or refine what we had learnt, to the enactment of contemporary scenes – father/child; mother/child; teacher/child; parent/headmaster; policeman/child, etc.

From the second lesson onwards a different kind of class need appeared: the boys lacked any inclination to verbalise either inside or outside their drama and whereas the girls enjoyed talking they tended not to listen to each other. Thus, another objective emerged:

The *drama* must provide an opportunity for talking and listening skills.

None of these 'teacher objectives' could have been achieved if the class as a whole had not been motivated by their overall aim of *creating a play about FN*. So to the children the play was an end in itself, but it was noticeable that as individuals they also pursued minor objectives such as getting historical facts right; making a nurse's uniform; drawing a map of the Crimea; collecting pictures; studying weapons; visiting the local Durham Light Infantry museum; experimenting with paint to contrive a blood effect on bandages; writing poems and personal accounts as a patient or a nurse. For some children these pursuits became major, totally absorbing activities.

I still returned throughout the remaining two or three sessions to my original plan to let the children have some responsibility for their own learning; I constantly sought their advice on how we should organise the morning's work or on whether we should use the hall or the classroom (it is significant that these children for whom drama had meant using the large space of the hall finished up advising me that their classroom provided the best working area) or on what means we should employ to evaluate our work.

In terms of objectives therefore we moved forward on several fronts (social skill; verbal skill; individual goals; the boys' means of satisfaction; the girls' very different means of satisfaction; responsibility for learning dimension; and understanding of the authority concept) all the time seeking for those dramatic moments that embraced all the objectives simultaneously.

It is difficult to assess with any precision to what extent any one of these objectives was achieved. Indeed the intellectual one, the grasp of the many shades of meaning within the concept of authority, although apparently fully understood by many of the children, can really only be tested when children meet a real authority situation. One hopes that when they do so, their approach will be more enlightened, more readily aware of the likely range of viewpoints, motivational factors and tensions within it. If this happens, then drama has served in the way we do often claim for it; it has helped to broaden and deepen a child's understanding of the world he lives in.

May I suggest there is a greater chance of achieving this when a teacher consciously clarifies for himself his own objectives and his children's objectives; he is likely to employ the most effective strategies if the goals to be reached are regularly defined and checked as the needs of the children are revealed.

In search of aims and objectives. *Creative Drama*, 4 (2), Spring 1969. (c/o 1 Hawthorndene Road, Hayes, Bromley, Kent, BR2 7OZ.)

Creative drama and learning

This article will attempt to classify the major kinds of learning that appear to take place when children participate in creative drama activities, confining the discussion to areas of learning inherent in the activity rather than to any indirect development (e.g. reading skills). A distinction will be made between the internal and external features of the activity. The hypothesis will be made that the latter (external) are a potential source of learning of facts and certain skills and that the former (internal) are a potential source of learning about value-laden concepts. *Feeling* as a prerequisite for learning will be discussed. Two major influences, the contribution of more than one participant and the function of the teacher, will also be considered. Indeed, the main purpose of the paper is an attempt to define which kinds of learning the teacher is likely to be most helpful in promoting.

Let us begin as simply as possible by concentrating on the play activity of one child, say a three year old boy pretending to cook as his mother does or involving himself in dressing and undressing a doll. In drama terms, these two play episodes would be described as follows:

As drama behaviour (A)		Behaviour (B)
Title	Cooking	Dolls
Plot	A sequence of simulated actions	Dressing/Undressing actions
Setting	Kitchen/Utensils (simulated or real)	Bedroom/Bathroom Doll's clothes

If asked what he has been playing, the boy might well answer from the Title; if pressed for further information he might well draw upon the Plot or the Setting. These aspects of the activity shall be referred to as the 'external action'. Such action appears to offer learning at the skills and factual level – three kinds of skills in fact:

(a) motor skills (especially where the action is real, not simulated);
(b) memory skills and facts (e.g. getting the sequence in the right order);
(c) make-believe skill (e.g. simulating cooking without the proper ingredients or utensils).

201

The activity might so far be set out as follows:

As drama	As behaviour		As potential learning
Title	Sequence of actions in		Skills
Plot	a simulated or actual	External action	Facts
Setting	environment		

The above presents an inadequate picture. Just as in dramatic terms Title, Plot and Setting are incomplete without Theme, which supplies the underlying meaning of the play, so the activity of the child has an 'Internal' aspect which controls the meaning of the behaviour. The answers of our child playing at cooking and with dolls are only partially correct. The more significant answer (the 'thematic' answer) might have been, 'I am creating the experience of being in charge of things.' The energy for starting to play stemmed from a desire to be in control of his own environment, and/or to find out what it is like to be Mother, etc. So our model now looks like this:

As drama	As behaviour	As potential learning
Title	External action	Skills and facts
Plot		
Setting		
Theme	Internal action (To be in charge)	?

If the internal action is the principal source of meaning, it seems logical that it should also carry the most significant potential for learning. 'To be in charge' is an abstract concept. It also represents an attitude in that the meaning cannot be neutral. The child must inevitably express that it is either pleasant or unpleasant (or any other kind of feeling/judgement within this range). In other words it is within this value-laden concept that a potential for learning lies.

Another kind of skill emerges. Whatever the internal action, its meaning can only be expressed through external action. Theme and Plot are interdependent, the crucial factor being the quality and intensity of feeling that characterises the activity. Let us call this combining of internal action with the external action the 'aesthetic skill'. Our model now reads:

As drama	As behaviour		As potential learning
Title/Plot	External action		Facts and skills
Setting	Dressing/Undressing doll	Aesthetic skill	
Theme	Internal action It is fun to be in control		Value-laden concept

The third column may be called potential learning as there is no guarantee that learning takes place. Supposing a child knows all the facts about dressing a doll; supposing he can manipulate the garments with consummate motor agility; supposing he puts himself in this 'it's fun being in charge' situation over and over again. What is he learning? He is doing nothing more than reinforcing what he already knows (in facts, skills and feelings). One of the points I shall later want to make is that much weak drama work is confined to this kind of reinforcement.

But supposing another child comes along, an objectionable little child who knows even better how to dress dolls and who firmly 'takes over'!

As drama	New child	First child
Plot	Refined sequence of actions	Observes refined sequence of actions and tries to join in
Theme	It's fun to be in charge	It's horrible to be controlled when you want to be in control

The possible learning potential here is clear – a new set of facts and, more importantly, an understanding that competition for control is a matter of negotiation, capitulation or retirement!

Let us change the game. Supposing a group of children are playing 'shipwrecks'. The model might read like this:

Drama and teaching/learning

As drama	As behaviour			As potential learning
Title	Shipwrecks			*Facts –* about boats, etc.
Plot	Spying danger: signalling distress manning life-boats; nearly drowning	External Action		*Skills –* minimum of action is simulated
			Aesthetic Skill	
Theme	It's exciting to escape drowning	Internal Action		*Value-laden concept –* attitude toward drowning

At the factual level some learning from each other might take place if, for example, one child passes on his knowledge of Morse code to the others. At a thematic level nothing much is likely to be learned, as the feeling-appraisal (It's exciting to escape drowning) is a glib one. For the same reason no aesthetic skill can be developed. After a time no new facts are available for learning: the position is reached wherein a group of children enjoying their dramatic playing are not even at a level of reinforcing what they know because the feeling quality is inappropriate to the context. Could the activity still be satisfying? Yes, in two directions. First it might be important for these children to escape from harsh reality and have a 'fun' adventure or, second, it might be important for these children to share an experience, any experience, irrespective of its merit as dramatic play. In the latter case the dramatic play simply becomes the pretext for being together. The learning, therefore, is purely social.

Let us now list all the kinds of learning that seem to be possible:

A Acquiring or refining *facts*
B Acquiring or refining *skills* related to external action:
  i motor
  ii memory
  iii simulation
C Acquiring or refining *skill*, related to the combining of internal/external action – the aesthetic skill. (**Note**: Practice in this skill can lead to development of communication skills.)
D Acquiring or refining value-laden **Concepts**

E Acquiring or refining **Social skills** sometimes independent of artistic activity. (**Note**: Practice in this skill can also lead to development of communication skills.)

It is theoretically possible that there could be no learning or every kind of learning. In moving now to discuss dramatic activity in schools we have to ask in which of these areas a teacher can be most helpful. One tendency among teachers in England, is to be very satisfied if an improvement is made in category E, social skills, irrespective of the quality of the drama itself. A skill within the drama that has interested teachers for a long time is Biii – simulation. It has been thought that the closer the child can get to an imitation of actuality, in both action and setting, the better the drama will be. This, it is maintained, is to mistake the function of an artistic activity, which is to explore meanings beyond the practicalities of living.* It is the skill in category C with which children really need help, the combining of a child's feeling about a situation with the external action. Finding the child's true feeling about a theme may not be easy. Often drama never really starts because the thinking involved stems from disguised, withheld, or 'pretend' feelings or just generalised excitement. In the 'Shipwreck' playing, no matter how accurately the child sends out a Morse code, the make-believe will not have integrity until he discovers in himself a feeling that matches what he already understands of 'danger' situations and then allows that feeling to interact with the action of signalling.

Notice the emphasis is placed on discovering a feeling that matches what is already understood. It cannot be otherwise. In educational terms the crucial question is whether, in the subsequent dramatic process, there is any change in feeling and therefore change in understanding. I am not implying that if there has been no change in understanding the experience has necessarily been insignificant. Often the drama process can put a child in touch with his feelings about something with the result that his understanding is clarified. If there is to be a change, however, something must happen to bring it about, that 'something' being a source outside the child. In the case of our doll-playing boy, the change of understanding was brought about by the second child's different perspective of the situation (and the learning in this case was painful!) This was a chance experience. In drama in schools it need not be left to chance, for this, it seems to me, is the major role of the

---

* For further discussion by Gavin Bolton on drama and meaning, see 'Drama as metaphor' (p. 42, this book) and 'Emotion and meaning in creative drama'. *Canadian Child Drama Association Journal*, February 1976, pp 13–19.

teacher. His top priority must be to function in category D, toward deepening and broadening the understanding of his pupils in these value-laden conceptual areas.

It seems possible in a fairly crude but nevertheless useful way, to describe dramatic activities in an order of potential significance.

1 Make-believe action where the feeling is artificial.
2 Make-believe action where the process simply reinforces what the children already feel and understand about something.
3 Make-believe action where the process clarifies what the children already feel and understand about something.
4 Make-believe action where the process modifies what the children already feel and understand about something.

Although this list is hierarchial it cannot be assumed that the best teachers are at (4) and the weakest teachers at (1). For a variety of reasons an excellent teacher may find himself working in (1) and staying there (for example, a group of adolescents may not yet trust the situation enough to be emotionally honest or, as mentioned earlier, the sole objective has to be a 'socialising' one), but because he is a good teacher he will not delude himself into thinking he is really operating at (2), (3), or (4). The opportunity to move to the later stages will always be at the back of his mind. Indeed, if what the children are reinforcing is antisocial, for example, then the teacher must work very hard at moving them to (4). But this raises one of the problems related to the responsibility of the drama teacher to his pupils and to society. Such an enormous question cannot be tackled here.

Two more points need to be made. First, the above list is not just four categories of drama; it can usefully be regarded as four possible stages inherent in each new piece of work. The search for the right initial feeling may include one or two false starts (the 'artificial' stage); the process may then include reinforcement and clarification before any modification can take place. The second point is that the two most important processes, clarification and modification, cannot take place without yet another, perhaps the more crucial skill: the ability and the predisposition to reflect on experience.

Creative drama and learning, *Children's Theatre Review*, Feb. 1977. (American Theatre Association, 1000 Vermont Avenue N.W., Washington DC 20005, USA.)

An evaluation of the Schools Council Drama Teaching Project (10–16)

It is my purpose to evaluate the conceptual framework. Many people have been involved directly and indirectly in its evolvement, which for the team members has been a polarising process of reward and frustration, of learning and unlearning, of unfavourable criticism and approbation; and which for the many teachers, advisers and lecturers caught-up in the project has provided what the team members intended, an opportunity to have the practice of drama publicly examined. Many people, not least the evaluators, who have been lucky enough to have had contact with Lynn, Maggie and Ken during the last three years will recall the Schools Council Drama Teaching Project with some considerable warmth. The team's personal growth during that period would make its own story, which they may one day attempt to write. Riches offered to other people in the form of courses, conferences and personal contact must also be left largely unrecorded. The Project must finally stand or fall by what it appears to offer the majority of teachers whose only contact will be through the document the team has spent three years creating, *Learning through drama*.[1]

The task of observing

Few people will realise what a sophisticated, complex, delicate, threatening, exhausting and time-consuming task the three team members took on when they chose to observe teaching in seventeen schools. It was just not possible for them to anticipate how the schools might receive them. Teachers could be apprehensive, eager to please, or suspicious. Headteachers could be sceptical, supportive or indifferent. Both tended, even before the team member arrived at the school, to project on him their own feelings about being chosen for the project, so he found himself endowed with a role that varied from super-teacher to inexperienced upstart, from detective to inspector, from theoretician to sage.

The team member did not see himself as any of these. He had to gain respect as a sympathiser, a listener, a questioner, a commentator. To do this when other roles were being thrust upon him required a formidable degree of sensitivity, tact and firmness, qualities which each of the three members demonstrated impressively. They not only succeeded in building a mutual trust with each teacher, they additionally brought a professionalism to their role, so that when, in exceptional cases, that trust could not be achieved (one or two schools failed to adapt to the project) a potentially inflammatory or potentially intractable situation was skilfully contained. Similarly, where the team were faced with inadequate teaching (one or two teachers had little to contribute to the project) that professionalism ensured that respect for the teacher concerned characterised subsequent dialogue or reporting.

One role that the members found very difficult to resist, especially when mutual trust was built, was the role of adviser. Many teachers sought their advice and indeed modified their teaching during the year as a direct result. The team were uncertain at first whether their purpose should be a neutral recording of drama teaching from which they would then abstract a theoretical framework or a much more dynamic interacting with the teachers towards mutual development. They ultimately decided on the latter. They evolved a useful principle which has held for their one to one relationship with teachers in schools, their working relationship with teachers on the many dissemination courses and in their publication: the team determined to be prescriptive only in so far as they directed their recommendations towards challenging teachers to examine their own practice. The first of their aims became:

> To give teachers who use drama in the classroom some starting points for reflecting on the nature and value *of their own work in drama* and to suggest ways in which they might be able to tackle the problems of assessment and evaluation (p. 3)

The team have determinedly resisted being seen as mentors who know better that anyone else, which works fine in the exposing classroom and course situation, but could be the death of a book! There is a tentativeness, a blandness, a self-effacement in the above aim which seem uninviting if not discouraging. Fortunately, the publication is written with more authority than the aims suggest but they may imply a limited readership target. The emphasis appears to be on beginners and beginning, 'We hope that individual teachers will find enough starting points here to continue the enquiry in their own terms and according to their own specific interests' (p. 8), and on experienced teachers who do not 'reflect on the nature and value of their own work'. This puts a limitation on the scope of the book which may well seem right at this moment in time, especially as it is also aimed at headmasters and administrators, who it assumes are in the early stages of thinking about the place of drama in the curriculum, but which in ten years' time will seem short-sighted. This point will be returned to later.

The members of the team gained in authoritative stature in two ways. One was through the rigorous intellectual grasp of the concepts with which they were dealing; the other was in the unusually high degree of skill they each brought to the observation work itself. One evaluator, at least, was deeply sceptical of the ability of three such inexperienced observers to perceive what was really taking place in a lesson, but he soon had his mind changed for him! During the year the team developed techniques of recording and analysing teacher/pupil behaviour and interaction that were appropriately impersonal, detailed and intelligently selective. The examples shown in chapter 5 are but a token of a vast amount of material covering some 159 lessons. These records should be very useful to anyone wishing to do further research.

The conceptual framework

Using the six months of observation as a basis for their theorising the team evolved a conceptual framework that placed *Learning through drama* as one of the most significant major publications on drama in education to have come onto the market. Just as in the 1950's Peter Slade offered a new concept of drama in schools that pleaded for recognition of drama as a form of expression that was 'natural' to the child, so, twenty years later the Schools Council are shifting our perspective to drama as a medium for learning. This is a fundamental philosophical change that could have enormous repercussions on the status of drama both in terms of teacher training and its place in the school curriculum. Teachers in the past have not had expectations of *learning* in their drama work. That the learning may be conceptual as well as social and aesthetic may cause headteachers to see new possibilities in the subject.

For years teachers have floundered in their self-defeating attempts to find criteria of assessment in terms of skills or personality attributes, but never in terms of the thing being created, as though that did not matter. But now it is pointed out that drama is concerned with a continuous process of negotiating meaning. The teacher is not concerned with how well a child acts, but how well a child works at finding meaning in his symbolic interaction with the others.

They have introduced too the concept of 'acting-out' which they distinguish as an activity involving interaction at two levels, the real and the symbolic. This concept is significant in two respects. Firstly it removes at one fell stroke all the confusing forms of activity – improvisation, scripted work, movement, mime, etc. They all have the same basic currency – a process of identifying meaning using 'the medium of the whole person'. Secondly, the teacher must be aware of what is happening at both levels of operation. The meaning created emerges from a dialectic set up between the real and the symbolic.

This perspective on drama is bound to affect the teacher's thinking, his objectives, his plans, choice of strategies, forms of assessment. All these are well illustrated. In that well-written chapter 3 the wide range and subtleties of teacher intervention are discussed with a thoroughness that cannot be found in other publications. In the same chapter the reader is given insight through the 'tramp' example into the enormous potential to be found in the most apparently simple and clichéd material.

But there do appear to be some conceptual inadequacies in the framework which I now propose to discuss under the heading 'Drama orientations', 'Thinking and feeling' and 'Symbolisation'.

Drama orientations

For reasons that are understandable the team have been anxious to emphasise similarities rather than differences within the wide range of activities that go under the name of drama. Unless they found what the activities have in common they felt that they were unlikely to evolve any kind of coherent theory. It seems to me, however, that they ignore differences to a point that is unhelpful to teachers. They say of theatre and drama, for instance, 'Both essentially rest on the ability to adopt and develop roles and characters within 'as if' situations; they rely on the body and the voice as the main media of expression, and make the same symbolic use of space and time. Here again it may be more useful to look for similarities rather than differences in trying to pin down a relationship.' It is surely nearer the truth that one of the major differences between drama and theatre lies in their contrasting use of space and time. And there is surely an enormous difference in experience for the participants. One only has to picture the contrast between a child 'hiding from the Roundheads' by literally disappearing behind the curtain as part of dramatic playing, and a child having to *show* that he is hiding for the sake of an audience. The common ground between drama and theatre is structural not psychological.

Having usefully established for us that good drama is dependent on quality of meaning, the authors do not discuss what distinctive features of 'acting-out' are likely to enhance or reduce that quality. No mention is made of that cliché form of acting that runs through many of our schools like a disease, where this very point we are discussing, the distinction between teachers and drama, leads to the acceptance by children and teachers alike of an uncreative convention: children who are in improvised drama without an audience unconsciously adopt a style of acting as if there were an audience. They are not being; they are *demonstrating*. So a child does not hide; he demonstrates hiding. He does not pour out the words he is driven to say; he demonstrates what would be right for that character. He does not feel frustration; he demonstrates the frustration that character would feel.*

This hybrid style of 'acting-out', a common feature of much inadequate drama work in schools, is not even referred to by our team. Indeed one wonders whether they do not recognise it or whether they perhaps even support it. The following quotations certainly describe a kind of drama that might well trap the participants into demonstrating.

'Children should become increasingly able to translate attitudes and ideas about various issues into dramatic statements which reflect their understanding' (p. 144)

In acting-out children are often given an idea and asked to go away and make something of it, perhaps to arrive at a dramatic statement which encapsulates their feelings and ideas about a particular topic or issue (p. 32)

Acting-out then is the exploration and representation of meaning – . . . (p. 16)

Problems of shaping may arise because some children find difficulties in organising ideas. They may also arise because at a particular time children have not clarified their ideas enough to devise a statement about them (p. 13)

Explore and express (p. 30)

Exploring and representing meaning (p. 31)

* 'Being' and 'demonstrating' are best thought of, not as distinct alternatives, but as extremes of a continuum. Even in 'being' there can be an element of demonstrating, and *vice versa*. It is the degree that is significant. On some rare occasions, it is appropriate for the pupils to adopt a 'demonstrating' style. The point to be emphasised here is that the teacher needs to be aware of these different kinds of 'acting-out' and to understand their respective validity.

211

In all these conditions there are two significant assumptions, (1) that there is some kind of sequence in the activity, first an exploratory and then a final phase, and (2) the final phase makes some kind of statement. Further examination reveals that the majority of the lesson illustrations quoted in the book have a structure that require children to 'get something ready' based on a given or not given theme. Now this in itself is just one kind of drama, in my view often a very limited kind, and yet it is, on balance, this kind of drama that the book appears to be about. Could it be that the Schools Council team have been given from the seventeen schools a diet overbiased in this direction or that their own background of teaching has tended to have this particular structure? Is it this narrowness of perspective that causes them to write a very weak chapter 2 where 'learning to use the process' and 'shaping' seem to be concepts very shallowly thought through?

A search among the illustrations reveals very few that exemplify children learning during the very activity of 'living-through'. Below is a quotation from one of them:

> Wrapping the paper round the wand he picked it up and carried it triumphantly back to the other villagers. There was a momentary pause and everyone weighed up the effects of Graham's action. Then several rushed forward . . . . etc. (p. 64).

The above epitomises what educational drama means to a great many teachers. With its clarity of theme, its use of significant symbol, its single focus, its power to arrest attention, its isolation of a single significant moment in time, everything is structured for learning to take place. In the moment of the child's action and in the 'momentary pause' that followed, there are the seeds for new learning. The children from then on have a shared reference point that they can then and later reflect upon. It is shared not because they all saw it, and certainly not because they all 'expressed' it, but because they *lived* it. (Lived here is used in its fullest sense of 'being' and 'reflecting on being'). It was existential, not to be repeated or reshaped (the wand was taken: how can you pretend it wasn't?) but examined as an irretrievable act.

This existential orientation in drama needs most careful structuring or otherwise it deteriorates into a 'playing' level as in the illustration on 'landing on an island' (pp. 26, 27). Does the book guide the teacher towards good quality 'living through' drama or does it really steer him towards a small group 'making a statement' kind of activity? The latter sadly appears to be the case. (Fortunately in the film *Take 3* the balance is somewhat redressed by the work of that fine teacher from Leeds, Eric Prince.)

Interestingly there is an orientation in drama which many previous 'how to teach drama' publications follow almost exclusively, but which the Schools Council team seem to eschew – the use of exercise. Wisely they advise the reader, 'The decision to include them (exercises) must depend on how appropriate they are to the teacher's intention, and the pupils' state of development'. It would have been useful to have been given a few examples of well chosen exercises, well chosen in that they also serve to enhance meaning and sometimes do so more economically and effectively than either the theatre or the 'living through' orientations. Again, advice on what kinds of exercise and, above all, when to use them would have been helpful to teachers rather than relegating their use, as they seem to do, to 'getting to know a class or trying to establish a working relationship in readiness for drama' (p. 56).

It is my view that the team's attempt to find common ground in all drama teaching has rightly ignored barriers between the traditional categories of activities – speech, movement, improvisation, mime, etc., has rightly ignored the huge variety of individual teaching methods, but that they have made a basic mistake in ignoring the three fundamental differences in orientations or intentions.

1 The intention to isolate a skill (exercise)
2 The intention to experience (living through)
3 The intention to demonstrate experience (theatre)

It seems to me that when a drama teacher understands the essential differences between these three orientations, he is then in a position both to value the educational potential in each and also to distinguish between those exciting, subtle moments when a resonance is set up between those orientations which is productive and those times when an unproductive compromise becomes the conventional currency.

Thinking and feeling

It is indeed this close inter-relationship of knowing and feeling and the way in which they are combined, not separated, which opens up so many opportunities for drama in the education of all children (p. 23).

This is an admirable statement placing as it does the emphasis on the relationship between knowing and feeling. The reader might justifiably expect that he will learn more about that relationship as the book proceeds. Certainly from time to time feelings are described: 'They were embarrassed' one reads. But these are feelings within the real situation, outside the drama. If drama is the art form they claim ('A primary function of the arts is to make sense of the life of feeling . . .') (pp. 15–16) then surely the teacher needs to know what part feeling does play. Discussion with supportive illustration would have been useful along the dimensions of appropriateness or intensity or (perhaps especially) safety. Many teachers feel that in using drama they are handling dynamite. A discussion of possible dangers stemming from over-stimulation of feeling, trivialisation of feeling and avoidance of feeling might well have been very helpful.

The subject is closely linked with assessing the quality of the experience and brings us back to the importance of knowing which orientation is operating, as the integrity of feeling is very much bound up with whether or not the level of the experience is existential, audience directed or the selective practising of a skill.

During the 150 lessons the team will have seen some very poor drama (one can understand their reluctance in not publicly saying so). One of the principal reasons for bad work will have been that the quality of feeling appropriate to the make-believe has not been achieved.

Unless the quality of feeling brought to the 'acting-out' is appropriate, there is no chance of learning taking place, for the feeling a child evokes must be his honest appraisal of the context. Let us look at a hypothetical case of 'acting-out'. If an adolescent honestly understands that most old people are feeble-minded then a feeling in respect of this handicap will provide his starting point in acting-out, and the learning must be his subsequent re-appraisal, a breaking of his stereotype view. If he deliberately selects a particular case of feeble-mindedness, knowing full well that other old people have other characteristics but this happens to be interesting to him at the moment, then the feeling quality that he starts with will be similar to the first instance, but the area of learning will be different: not an adjustment and broadening of his understanding about old people, but greater insight into the nature of feebleness, perhaps its consequences for oneself and for other people. In each case the modification to understanding develops from the feeling quality that is initiated. But if the adolescent chooses to trivialise or avoid the feeling quality that he could have brought to his role and replaces it with say, a clever piece of entertainment for his peers, then virtually no learning can take place, *at least not from within the drama itself*, for it may, inadequate as it is, have still provided a stimulus for further discussion. In a book that purports to answer the question, 'Does drama have a distinct and unique function?' (p. 7) one might have expected to have found outlined in it this crucial connection between feeling/appraisal and modification of understanding. Learning in drama is a *felt change in value*, felt because it is lived through, in a use of space and time that is not available to the other arts, and is different from ordinary living because it is contrived.

Instead of just telling us in the brief section on p. 22 what feeling in drama is *not*, not catharsis, not therapy, not something separately to be developed, the authors might have given the subject the positive and significant attention it deserves.

Symbolisation

It is unlikely that anyone will want to argue with the explanation of 'meaning and symbolising' given on pp. 13–16, but the reader may be disappointed that there is little there that helps the teacher to know in what way being conscious that drama functions symbolically is likely to affect his teaching.

Again, in practice, the way a teacher views symbols will depend on how he views drama. In 'making a statement' drama the teacher and children are bound, as in the example on privilege given on p. 11, to see the symbol as the thing created and as something that then they can do something about to 'make it better'. If, on the other hand, a teacher is working in existential drama, a symbol is seen as something that develops and gradually accrues meaning. It *becomes* significant. Just as a shopping basket might begin in the drama simply as a *sign* of shopping activity, so as the work develops it might gather meanings to do with family responsibility, or sexism, or starvation, or 'mother's left us' or shop-lifting, or possessions, *or any other meaning that goes beyond the initial practical meaning of the object.*

It is in this respect that symbolisation is significant for the teacher. It links again with the quality of the 'acting-out'. Although drama operates at a concrete level, it is only worth while in terms both of art and of learning if the meaning that accrues becomes independent of the immediate concrete and practical meanings. A teacher may observe a child posting a letter as part of his drama; his miming of the action may be excellent – he gives an impressive imitation of posting a letter. The teacher needs to know that this action is not in itself an important achievement; it is only when the letter posting takes on for the child a meaning that goes beyond the action itself and beyond (so many teachers stop at this level of meaning) the meaning of the plot to more universal implications of commitment, irretrievability, or self-exposure, etc., that a letter posted may have. It is within the teacher's power not to dictate the form or meanings of a symbolic object or action, but to keep open avenues that are more likely to generate meanings in a way that the whole group can share. It is this collective hearing of resonances that is unique to drama. It is a pity the book does not contain more examples of these significant moments, and, more important, an account of how they were achieved.

Summary and conclusion

I have suggested that many drama teachers have had a rich experience through the privileged contact with the three team members of the project during the last three years, but that ultimately the project must be judged by the final publication *Learning through drama*, which for many teachers will be the only available resource.

From masses of material, the team have abstracted lesson samples that have provided the basis for a highly readable and significant conceptual framework, which in many ways is a considerable advance on previous major publications. I have wholeheartedly commended the team for their skill in making those observations.

For many teachers the concept of drama as negotiation of meaning will be a huge step forward in their understanding of teaching the subject. For them the project will have done all it set out to do.

My concern, however, is for those teachers who were already in the habit of examining their own practice, who already knew that drama was concerned with (although perhaps not phrased as such) negotiation of meaning. Does the book give them enough or anything to bite on? Here I have grave doubts. Perhaps because of the narrow range of work observed (I am not here referring to teaching styles or methods) or because the team members were too inexperienced to back up their own new thinking, the implications for the teacher of such matters, central to the team's own framework, as drama orientations, the place of feeling in relation to thinking and symbolisation have not been satisfactorily explored.

And what will better trained teachers in the future think of a book that virtually ignores the world's greatest thinker and practitioner of the seventies in drama in education, Mrs Dorothy Heathcote? It may seem odd to them that the authors find a place for themselves in the bibliography but Dorothy Heathcote does not even get a mention. It may seem odder that forms of drama which she has promoted, such as drama as analogy, or drama as 'mantle of the expert', have no place in the publication. More important than that however, is that a Schools Council Project should be so far behind the most advanced thinking in a subject.

Is this in the nature of Schools Council work, that it cannot look forward with the most competent but must set its target at raising the level of the average? If this has to be the target then *Learning through drama* is well aimed. There is no doubt that it will give a sense of purpose to a teaching population that has, for a long time, badly needed this kind of direction. The book will be well received. They will understand its clearly expressed theory, respond to its advice, respect its honesty and enjoy its warmth.

An evaluation of the Schools Council Drama Teaching Project (10–16). *Speech and Drama*, **28** (3), 1979. (*Speech and Drama*, 211B Old Dover Road, Canterbury, Kent.)

Reference

1 McGregor L, Tate M, Robinson K 1977 *Learning through drama*, Schools Council Drama Teaching Project (10–16). Heinemann.

Assessment of practical drama

In this paper I shall raise what I consider to be fundamental issues affecting assessment of practical drama. I do not elaborate upon them nor do I attempt to supply methods of procedure. I attempt to direct our attention to the nature of dramatic activity, posing the question, not of 'how' or 'why' but *'what'* we are assessing.

Assessment of practical drama has behind it a tradition from the amateur drama movement of speech and drama festivals where monologues, duologues and play productions are adjudicated and from speech and drama examinations where solo acting performances are graded. These well-tried procedures have been challenged in schools by a child-centred movement emphasising personal growth through drama. Whereas the former tends to employ criteria of achievement in stage-crafts, acting skills, speech and movement, achievement in the latter relates to less identifiable skills and attributes such as creativity, sensitivity, spontaneity, decision-making and self-esteem. Such a challenge is not merely less amenable to assessment, but, with its emphasis on the uniqueness of the individual, is philosophically incompatible with the notion of comparing one person's achievement with another.

Drama syllabuses often reflect these contrary movements, dividing a syllabus into drama and theatre, implying that the one is concerned with process, the other with product; one with personal satisfactions, the other with artistry. Sometimes the dichotomy is further stressed by drawing a distinction in teacher function between a drama teacher as a mere catalyst or facilitator offering a variety of stimuli to which pupils may respond and a theatre teacher as a trainer in skills or as a director of play-productions.

I suggest that the divisions are false, that although there are significant educational and artistic differences among, for example, (1) a public performance of Wesker's *Chips with everything*, (2) the use of an excerpt from that play as part of a dramatic collage on War, (3)·the presentation of improvised material on the theme of war, (4) the structuring of a drama to give the participants an 'experience' of war, and (5) an improvisational 'romp' on the same subject, but that the division of such a range of activities into drama and theatre, and into process and product etc. does not reflect usefully or even accurately the real nature of the dramatic medium and its place in education.

Process/product

Looking more closely at the process/product dichotomy, one can understand the educationalists' point of view that the experiences the pupil gains from the activity of creating are more important than what is created, but this should not be interpreted (in my view) as a denial of the critical part played by what is created. It seems to me there is always a product; even in the most loosely structured improvisational dramatic activity there is some kind of contrived, self-contained entity that can be observed as 'a thing created'. It may be perceived differently by pupils and teacher. To give an extreme illustration, the pupils may see their spontaneous drama product as a portrayal of strife in Northern Ireland, but the teacher may recognise they are merely using the topic as a vehicle for their own aggression. A 'product' extremist will only too readily point out that the pupils failed to reach any kind of objective reality; a 'process' devotee might firstly challenge with 'whose reality?' and secondly claim that the real value for the participant lay in the controlled way in which they handled their aggression. To hold beyond a temporary position either of these views, that drama is an imitation of reality or a vehicle for cathartic release is doing a disservice to both drama and education. The greater educational value is attained when the pupils' aggression (or joy or wonder or concern or sympathy or intolerance or tenderness or shame or pride or whatever light or dark feelings they have about anything) becomes channelled by their understanding and respect for the topic and harnessed to a chosen, dramatic form. In other words doing drama is bringing something inside oneself into a formal relationship with something outside oneself. Although a teacher may be justifiably pleased with his pupils' 'Northern Ireland' drama because they are twelve year old maladjusted boys who normally cannot co-operate in their dramatic playing, he must be aware that if only their aggression could have been directed towards identifying some objective aspect of the Northern Ireland context within their intellectual grasp, the potential in terms of 'satisfactions', artistic achievement and learning would have been greater. Because of the peculiar circumstances he may withhold this latter kind of judgement, but as we are here mostly concerned with adolescents entering examinations in drama we can expect to identify a product and make a judgement relating to the participants' engagement with the topic within a dramatic form. Drama is, in my view, not so much concerned with the uniqueness of the individual as with the meaning created when a participant aligns his individuality with whatever is universal in the subject matter, topic or theme. Drama perhaps more than any other art form celebrates what man has in common with man.

The subject-matter

The subject-matter or topic therefore is critical to the drama experience. It may seem odd that this has to be stressed but it is my experience that many examiners are prone to isolating what they see as basic skills such as speech and movement as if the meaning of the drama were but a vehicle for expressing these skills. An examiner of practical drama must in my view be concerned above all else with the quality of meanings the participants sought and found in the material. The Schools Council Drama Project (Secondary) 1977, usefully coined the phrase 'negotiation of meaning' in describing drama's principal function. This applies to both unscripted and scripted drama and the same question can be asked in each case: 'How sophisticated is these pupils' understanding of the meanings they have been handling?' The teacher/assessor has three sources – the pupils' thinking processes during the work, the product itself and the way they reflect upon the work in retrospect.

The art form

Having asked about their understanding of the topic, the examiner can now proceed to the second question: 'How effectively did they use dramatic form in order to explore and create meanings?' An examiner who adheres to the drama/theatre dichotomy may too readily rush to apply contrasted sets of well-tried criteria to what he sees as the differences between two kinds of activity. I would like to offer a different perspective on what is meant by dramatic form. I shall initially concede that a polarisation does exist within an aspect of the drama/theatre concept, but I will further argue that as the essential components of theatre form can be found in all kinds of dramatic activity there is little value in attempting to keep drama and theatre as separate categories.

If we look again at my illustration of five kinds of 'War' dramas, one dimension distinguishing them could be the degree to which the participants are aware* of an audience. Only in the case of (4) (the structuring of drama to give the participants an experience of war) could one categorically claim that an audience did not figure in the bias of the work. Even in (5) (an improvisational 'romp' on war) the emphasis could be on what *would* be entertaining *if* an audience were present. Along this dimension of audience stimulating/communicating/ignoring/denying one can determine two significantly contrasted behaviour orientations. One tends to be characterised by an existential quality of 'living-through' or 'experiencing' (in the sense that

---

* Some of the degrees of 'awareness' might be seen as steps going *from* setting out to give an audience an experience, *through* acknowledging that an audience is there but not doing much about it, *to* doing the drama entirely for themselves with no-one else present.

when one enters a game of football one *experiences* the game. The other tends to be characterised by a demonstrating, communicating, entertaining or stimulating quality of sharing or showing a situation (i.e. not experiencing the game of football but, as it were, *presenting* it). Distinct as these two modes of acting behaviour are they are rarely seen in a pure form – even a child absorbed in his own play can be observed to some degree to be 'demonstrating' something to himself and even the most rigid theatrical presentation can retain a degree of spontaneity. Different dramatic styles require different blendings of these two opposing modes. It behoves a teacher or an examiner not to mistake a gross confusion between the two (like, for instance, the badly trained pupil who thinks he is working in the 'experiencing mode' but simply 'turns on' his bag of 'demonstrating' tricks) with a subtle dialectic that can mark the best work.

But the mode of acting behaviour is not to be confused with theatre *form*. The influence of the amateur theatre movement has for so long directed our attention to acting techniques as the basic tools of theatre that we have tended to overlook the more fundamental components of theatre: focus; tension; contrast and symbolisation. It is skills in the handling of these components as a means of discovering, sifting, enhancing, refining, sharpening and resonating contextual and thematic meanings that an examiner should be seeking to test. Traditional acting skills may or may not be part of the dramatic product, but the examiner is concerned with something wider and also deeper, to do with the participants' grasp of how the very clay of theatre works. It is so basic that the drama theatre dichotomy becomes irrelevant. All children in all kinds of drama are working with the same artistic form.

Summary

To summarise, in this paper I have assumed that a close look at the activity of drama will guide us on what to assess.

1 I have suggested that the product is always significant because it represents the participants' engagement with the objective world through the use of form.
2 The meaning(s) of the theme or topic must be of prime importance to both the participants and to their assessors. It is not unreasonable for an examiner to ask what the candidates now understand of the theme.

221

3 The way in which the participants handle the basic elements of theatre form in order to negotiate meaning, is also important for
assessment.
4 Whereas these basic elements belong to all kinds of dramatic activity,
a critical distinguishing feature is the *mode* of acting behaviour required. The mode will be a dialectic between two opposing orientations – 'experiencing' and 'representing'.
5 Overall I suppose this paper is saying we must not think that drama
is about acting techniques – like every other art it is about *meaning
in form*.

Assessment of practical drama. *Drama Control*, 1, Autumn 1981.
(Local Toronto magazine, address unknown.)

Drama in the curriculum

Before we can discuss drama and the curriculum we need to say what
drama is. I shall attempt to do this under three headings:

1 the nature of dramatic activity
2 levels of meaning
3 psychological and educational implications

I shall use these three sections to put forward an argument that although
drama is an art form and can consequently be justified in educational
terms along with other art forms, its potential for engaging the pupils
in a variety of learning processes requires us to view the subject in quite
a different light from the other arts.

The nature of dramatic activity

Here I shall use an illustration from a recent experience of practical
drama in the hope that it will provide an image compelling enough to
stay at the forefront of our minds throughout this discussion.

I was recently working with a class of fourteen year old coloured and black children in South Africa. Towards the end of the drama lesson, for which these politically aware pupils had chosen a topic painfully close to their everyday experience, I role-played a journalist interviewing, seventy years after the 'terrible incident', an old man of 84 who had been but a fourteen year old boy at the time, inviting him to recall what had occurred seventy years previously – in fact, a few minutes earlier in the lesson. The black boy adopted an old man's rambling mode of dredging up from his memory, but then I switched the angle of the topic. The dialogue went something like this:

JOURNALIST This is now the year 2050. You must have seen a lot of changes in South Africa in the past seventy years.

OLD MAN I have.

JOURNALIST Would you mind telling me, sir, what for you has been the greatest change?

OLD MAN We are equal now. (The old man looked the interviewer in the eye, not with resentment not hostility nor even triumph but with self-assurance, dignity and pride. Spontaneously the journalist and the old man shook hands.)

The basic medium of drama is exemplified in the action of that handshake. The attendance of the rest of the class and all the black teachers watching was riveted by that simple action. It was what Dorothy Heathcote calls 'a moment of awe', for it had so many implications for all who were present. It was indeed Drama: a simple action embodying significance.

Drama differs from most other arts in that it uses both time and space; and it is distinguished from dance by its high degree of concreteness, its partial resemblance to everyday actions in both detail and pace. Its power lies in the capacity of a single dimension of action to release a volume of meaning. The illustration I have given is from drama teaching – I could equally well have chosen a moment from our repertoire of theatre: Hamlet's jumping into the freshly dug hole that is to be Ophelia's grave evokes a web of imagery and meaning – but in fact when these significant moments do occur in the classroom they are often in essence indistinguishable from an equivalent moment in the theatre, for although critically different from each other drama and theatre draw on the same basic resources: children and actors are handling the same clay as it were, a point not always grasped by teachers who seek a complete separation between creative drama and performance drama. There is an important different of course. For the observers of that handshake I am sure it seemed like a moment of theatre they were sharing. But of course it wasn't really theatre, for it was not our intention to move that audience and in any case in theatre the spontaneous handshake would have been a planned handshake contrived to appear spontaneous.

Nevertheless, because of the intensity, the clarity of focus the basic elements of contrast in sound, light and movement and the symbolisation that are available to both kinds of activity, it can be said that drama and theatre are essentially the same dramatic art form. There is not a difference of status between them even though there is a difference of intention and technique. It is not reasonable to argue that whereas theatre can be both good art and good education drama can only be good education. Pupils in drama lessons may be trained in the use of an art form irrespective of any bias lessons may or may not have towards performance. All good drama and theatre seek the simple action to embody significance.

Having made this point about drama and theatre I shall, in order to avoid clumsiness of style, now continue to refer to them both as drama unless I particularly need to make a distinction.

Levels of meaning

As I have said, drama is the most concrete of the art forms. The meaning is created from the juxtaposition of two concrete events: the actual use of time and space by the participants and the simulated use of time and space in a fictitious context. Whereas the actor walks across the stage four times, in the fictitious context the prisoner is pacing his cell. Whereas the child is bestraddling a stick, in the fiction he is riding a horse.

The relationship between these two concrete events can be described in two significantly different ways. One way is to say that the relationship is representational, i.e. the actor stands for the prisoner; the bestraddling child stands for riding a horse. An implication of such a description is that there is some prior knowledge of prisoners or horses that becomes objectified by the use of the actor or the stick. I shall call this the contextual view of dramatic activity. Much teaching of mine in schools emphasises this view of dramatic action as accurate imitation of a physical reality. A more subtle, less extreme example is of the use of role-play that requires the child to imitate a stereotype attitude: an angry parent, a stern headmaster or a wicked step-mother.

A very different way of describing the relationship is to see it as a dialectic set up between the two concrete events, between the actor and prisoner, between the child and horse-riding. The meaning that emerges is the actor-in-the-prisoner-experience or the child-in-the-riding-experience. The meaning is unique to the interaction.

That both views can exist, at the same time, not only places drama at the opposite end of an artistic spectrum from music where there can rarely be a contextual aspect, it also places drama in a special relationship with the rest of the school curriculum, for most of our school curriculum is contextual, that is, it is concerned with the objectification of prior knowledge.

One of the paradoxes of drama is that in so far as it is contextual its meaning is dependent upon a point of reference outside itself and in so far as it is unique its meaning is within the experience of the participant. So what are some of the meanings implied by that handshake? At a level of representation the fourteen year old boy and teacher were imitating 'old man being interviewed by journalist'. One could say that thematically it was about the political situation in South Africa and one could judge the degree of authenticity in this respect that our representation captured. In other words one could make an objective comparison with the real world in terms of both the facts and the attitudes we portrayed.

But this was an intensely personal scene. I can only guess what it meant for the boy, a boy who in real life knew what it was like to be hit hard by the system, but for me the meaning had to do with being caught up in something I could not begin to understand, with the total respect I had for that boy's dignity and for the simultaneous, ambivalent closeness and distance of that handshake. I do not know what separate personal meanings the teachers watching attached to the action. (No doubt some personal meanings were quite irrelevant to the dramatic meanings. I was aware, for instance, that I had timed the interview to coincide with the time for finishing the lesson. I am sure that for the boy also there were thoughts of that extraneous kind.) Certainly much of the meaning was to do with our emotional responses within our fictitious roles. But earlier I described the occurrence of the handshake as a moment of awe, implying a meaning more special than whatever emerges from the participants' attempt to create a fictitious context combined with the emotional responses within the interaction. Moment of awe, although perhaps unnecessarily mystical, is an expression that does imply a poetic level of meaning, referring to something beyond itself, i.e. beyond the context and beyond the raw emotions felt.

In other words the action of the handshake was not only representative and evocative but also symbolic. Symbolisation implies a moving away from the particular, the specific context and individual emotional responses, to meanings more universal. This universal level of meaning if recognised at all by drama teachers, is differently perceived. Dorothy Heathcote tends to see it as what man has in common with man. B.J. Wagner echoes Jerome Bruner when she says, 'True gut-level drama has to do with what you at your deepest level want to know about what it is to be human.' Universals are to do with basic needs of protecting one's family, journeying home, facing death, recording for posterity, passing on wisdom, making tools, etc. On the other hand for writers such as Susanne Langer and Robert Witkin the deepest levels of meaning are even less specific. Langer refers to the projection of 'the felt tensions of life' into the art form. Witkin, concerned with relationships rather than content speaks of 'the structural and functional aspects of sensate experience that are universal and invariant'. They both find tensions of contrast, symmetry, ambivalence, balance, synthesis, attraction, opposition and rhythm to be basic to life and artistic form. The handshake expressed in the moment of the action some of these universals which go beyond the particular context.

There is an interesting difference in levels between what Dorothy Heathcote, the practitioner, and Robert Witkin, the theorist, perceive as universal. It may reflect their necessarily different perspective. Suffice it here to acknowledge that dramatic action can resonate meanings beyond the contextual and the personal. For the purpose of this paper I shall call this poetic significance.

I think then the handshake could be said to have had such significance. I have already drawn attention to the ambivalence in that it simultaneously drew me nearer to, and further from, my partner. Other tensions, some obvious, some subtle, strongly felt but unnameable, were also part of the experience.

I have used the illustration of the handshake to draw attention to what I see as three kinds of meaning that much drama expresses:

Contextual representation – referring to prior knowledge to do with facts or attitudes.
Personal engagement – emotional response within the drama to the themes and to doing the drama.
Universal implications – the felt tensions that are basic to all experience and to art in particular (Witkin) and/or tacit references to what is fundamental to man's humanity (Heathcote).

But I think it is necessary to draw attention to two peculiarities of the illustration. One is that the topic of the drama happened to be very close to the children's own lives. Their personal investment was enormous. The fiction therefore was only at one remove from real life. The second is that the part of the lesson I have concentrated on was a teacher-pupil rather than a pupil-pupil experience. Let me say I am not advocating the use of material as raw as this nor am I recommending that a teacher should always be at the centre of the drama. I chose this particular illustration because its very peculiarities allow me more easily to highlight a hierarchy of meanings: the tensions were more than usually close to the surface and I can authenticate some of the feelings because I, for once, was personally caught up in them. Please then, see this example as a point of reference about which to theorise, not as a practice to follow.

A further point needs to be made here. The illustration focusses on a moment in the lesson (perhaps the only moment) which could be claimed to have poetic significance. A great deal of the earlier dramatic action had been superficial and where there was significance the meaning was functional rather than symbolic.

Psychological and educational implications

The third level of meaning I indicated above was one of fundamental tensions within the dramatic form. Attempts have sometimes been made to find a way of describing the psychological process that puts an individual in touch with what is mystically called ineffable or unknowable and realistically called universal or invariant. 'Intuition', 'tacit understanding' and 'creative vision' are some of the labels used to identify a process that is not mediated by the normal categorisation and conceptualisation restrictions of cognitive thinking. In this connection Robert Witkin has built a huge conceptual framework in his *Intelligence of feeling* but I regret I cannot use it because I cannot understand it! That there is a knowing in my bones implying as that metaphor does a perception that is intuitive and fundamental, I have no doubt. I felt or sensed the action of the handshake carried a meaning that was ambivalent, but it would take a poet to encapsulate the complex meaning of that action in words. Such an act of faith, however, may be acceptable from one artist to another but what are the implications for educationalists? If this third level of meaning is critical to the drama experience how do we argue a case for its inclusion in our school curriculum if we are not able to identify it? How do we know what we are teaching? What do we put in our syllabuses?

A few schools share the act of faith and proceed to set up drama experiences (either creative or theatrical) that put the pupils in touch with the deepest levels of feeling. But these schools are rare. Many others play an avoidance game. There are many ways of making sure your students or pupils do not have a drama experience of any depth. Among them are included such popular activities as a continuous diet of dramatic trivia or training in performance techniques or learning about drama and theatre. Some children pass their CSE and O level courses without knowing what it is like to be touched deeply by a drama experience.

I now want to argue however, that such is the potential richness of the drama soil there can be considerable educational value even where there is little poetic significance. From now on I shall be referring to non-performance drama.

We need to go back to the other two levels of meaning which belong to the representational/personal/universal hierarchy. In the achievement of the first two of these, the representational and the personal, there appears to be a dialectic between two opposing psychological processes – the objectifying and the personalising of knowledge.

All drama, whether simple or most complex, is concerned with getting the balance right between accurate representation and personal investment of the participants. Sometimes, a teacher may work with a bias towards objectivity, for example getting a class of children as accurately as possible to portray a day in the life of a farmer in terms of a sequence of actions; alternatively he may want to break the stereotype assumptions of his class by making them face the probability that their heroes have flaws. Somewhere in between these two is simply giving the children the chance to personalise what they already understand intellectually say, for instance, having to put the arguments of the slave traders as if they were the slave traders – an effective and economical technique. But there is much more to it than this and the whole process of dramatisation can be analysed further in terms of its many-faceted educational potential.

I am inviting you at this point temporarily to leave aside notions of dramatic form and to examine role-play as a psychological process. (I am using role-play here to mean simply the action of entering a fictitious context.) I hope to establish that its use in education is powerful enough even when poetic significance is not achieved.

Role-play seems to have the following features:

1 While using time and place as its medium, thought predominates over action (as argued for play by Vygotsky).

2 Because it is a consciously contrived event, there is a special degree of awareness by the participant.
3 It combines cognitive and affective recall with cognitive and affective adjustment to the present situation.
4 The act of taking on a role is a movement from the general to the particular – the new situation is, in part, an instance of what is already understood as a general case. The significant phrase here for the educationalists is 'in part', for the major learning potential lies in the degree to which novelty may be injected into the present situation.
5 It is an approximation of any required event. That it is metaphorical in form (i.e. the juxtaposition of two often seemingly incompatible contexts – a child in the classroom playing Edward the Confessor on his throne) provides the cutting edge that sharpens awareness and resonates meaning.
6 It is a form of hypothesis – 'what would happen if . . .?'

From the above features role-play could be summed up as an animated thought process consciously engaged in. I maintain that its potential for learning (whether by ESN pupils, primary school children, sixth formers or executives in industry) has not been appreciated. The key to its power lies in the unusual degree of awareness it provokes and the connections it can make between what the participant knows (emotionally and intellectually) and the body of knowledge or skills to be acquired. This latter is the key to its use in school whether we are teaching children to read, i.e. using drama as a bridge between the children's experience and the printed word, or helping them to grasp principles, refine concepts, acquire language, hypothesise, perceive issues, think deductively and inductively, see implications, foresee consequences and recognise implicit values etc. etc.

I do not exaggerate the educational possibilities. Role-play happens to exercise skills that are basic to many learning processes. It is not a coincidence that the model of an objectifying, personalising dialectic as I have used it here to describe observable polarising tensions in dramatic action parallels significantly Piaget's model of a continual disequilibration between accommodation and assimilation in the learning processes. It could and should be regarded as a core experience in the curriculum – which brings us to the final section.

Drama and the curriculum

'Back to basics?' 'Core-curriculum?': Drama is basic; drama is central – although I don't think I shall live long enough to hear Paul Hirst say so, neither Paul Hirst, nor other educational philosophers, nor politicians, nor administrators, nor HMIs, nor head teachers, nor teachers, nor parents, nor pupils, nor caretakers and certainly not teachers of the other arts!

You may be assuming that in view of my argument that the functional use of drama has educational validity even if it does not achieve poetic significance, I shall further argue for drama as a method, a technique within the repertoire of all teachers. While recognising the value in other specialists using dramatic devices in the teaching of their own subjects, I see this only as a supplement not as a replacement of drama as a subject. There is still a strong case I believe for its regular use on the time-table in the hands of drama specialists. My reasons are as follows:

1 Whatever kind of approach to drama is favoured there are specific drama skills to be learnt.
2 Often an important drama experience is a process of slow maturing needing a length of time that another specialist using role-play has not available. (Perhaps for this reason alone drama should be time-tabled – but not in half-hour slots!)
3 Whereas a non-specialist may successfully employ role-play using small groups within his class, it usually takes the organising skills of a drama specialist to give the whole class a dramatic experience.
4 Most importantly, although I have been interested in arguing here that drama as personalising knowledge has considerable educational validity, I would not want to recommend any curriculum organisation that was exclusive. I support the view there may be many times when a teacher, drama or non-drama, has a perfectly valid but limited intention of using drama to help the pupils understand the facts, attitudes and implicit values within a particular context. Nevertheless I also recognise that the other-subject specialist is much less likely than the drama teacher to structure the dramatic experience in such a way that creates a potential for poetic significance.

In summary as far as drama and the curriculum is concerned, I am recommending a view that is catholic, eclectic and pragmatic. To the head teacher who wants advice I would say, promote the strengths of the staff you have, recognising there is educational potential in whatever direction they happen to lead, but if you have the chance to appoint the ideal drama teacher then you will have no difficulty in recognising him: he will be both process and performance oriented and at all times he will consciously harness either orientation towards meanings that are representational, personal and universal!

Drama in the curriculum. *Drama and Dance*, **1** (1), 1981. (Ken Byron, Knighton Fields Centre, Herrick Road, Leics., LE2 6DJ.)

Philosophical perspectives on drama and the curriculum

It was always been a headache deciding how, when and where to place drama on the school curriculum. The decisions seem to depend on locating its position at the intersection of three perspectives:

1 As assumption about education and knowledge.
2 An assumption about the status of the subject.
3 An assumption about the status of the teacher.

The headache has often been brought on either because one or more of these basic assumptions remains unclear or because they have seemed incompatible.

However I recently came across an example of straightforward coherence among the three perspectives. This was an instance of a teacher appointed to a senior high in the USA who was appointed to be responsible for the school productions. In this case, the assumption about education was that of the behavioural modification tradition; the assumption about the status of the knowledge was invested in the importance of performance skills in acting, stage-dancing and singing (the repertoire seemed to vary from rock musicals to the more 'classical' *Oklahoma*); and the status of the teacher was that of trainer and director. A parallel to be found in the UK, which matches the American example in straightforwardness but is even more circumscribed in its intentions, is the case where a teacher passes on to his pupils infor-

231

mation about the history of the theatre so that the pupil can regurgitate those facts in an examination. The assumptions about education here are that it is to do with the transmission of knowledge; that knowledge is whatever can be propositionally stated; and that the teacher's function is to impart such knowledge. Here we have, of course, a good old English tradition of education revered throughout the empire! Contrasted as the American and English perspectives appear to be, there are nevertheless similarities between the two. Neither of the teachers, for example, is interested in process. Both of them can claim considerable authority for the selection of what should be taught; and both of them can claim to measure the effectiveness of their teaching by testing what the pupil can reproduce, either in skill modification or in factual knowledge. Surely such examples must give curriculum planners an unambiguous sense of purpose and direction.

Their job would certainly be made easier if these two examples were representative of the drama scene. Speaking of the UK, it is true that a comparatively small number of children might be studying the history of theatre (and, regrettably, a much larger number of children study Shakespearian texts as if they too were propositional knowledge) but as far as performance is concerned, such training, although popular in schools since the sixteenth century, has usually been extra-curricular with little attention to training as such. Curiously, however, one aspect of performance training, that associated with 'elocution', as it used to be called, has hovered on the edge of our school system during this century. Although receding in importance during the past twenty years, nevertheless it still has 'colonial' pockets of influence, particularly among, for example, the 'English' whites of South Africa and, perhaps surprisingly, among a not insignificant number of teacher-trainers in Australia. I mention this as an example of an isolated activity persisting in the face of opposing philosophical currents, typifying the contradictions within the confused picture of drama education which the 1980's have inherited.

Two metaphors have been used to capture the examples I have given so far. The American example of training in performance skills, representing as it does the behaviourist trend in education, can be seen as the 'blank-slate' view of education with the teacher as the writer on the slate. The British transmission of knowledge view has been described as the 'empty pitcher' model; the teacher of course doing the filling with information. The latter metaphor, however, can only be applied to the most rigid and unimaginative examination devotees. Different metaphors have to be sought for the majority of drama teachers. In the UK a 'new' movement in drama teaching began just before the turn of the century with the classroom practice of a lively village school teacher, Mrs Harriet Findlay-Johnson, whose 'dramatic method' of making school subjects more exciting was admired and publicised by a board inspector, Mr E. Holmes,[1] who in his book, *What is and what might be*, wrote:

> In Utopia acting is a vital part of school life of every class, and every subject that admits of dramatic treatment is systematically drama-tised. (p. 174)

Mrs Findlay-Johnson was persuaded to publish her own credo in The Dramatic Method of Teaching at about the same time. From the private sector of the educational system another charismatic teacher in the Perse School was recommending the 'play-way' of education. This was Cald-well Cook,[2] who, as an English teacher, found a dramatic approach to help his pupils enjoy great literature. These two innovators who were so obviously interested in the process of learning were part of a trend that was fundamentally to challenge assumptions about the nature of education. The new metaphor, taken from the evolutionist's view of biological maturation was introduced by a German, F. Froebel, who saw a school as a 'kindergarten' and its pupils as 'flowering seeds' with all the potential for growth, given the right environment. Froebel was extending to education the Rousseauesque view of the child as good, with natural instincts which should be freely followed.

This view of education as a matter of helping pupils in their natural growth has had an enormous influence on the teaching of drama for it appears to reduce the teacher's status to that of 'gardener', patiently attending development, and it also reduces the subject's status as it is maturation, not content, that really counts. There are, however, dif-ferent ways of interpreting the seed metaphor, an indication of which appears even in these early pioneers of drama. Contrast the two follow-ing quotations, from Holmes and Cook, respectively:

> The teacher must therefore content himself with the child's expansive instincts, fair play and free play. (Holmes,[3] p. 163)

> The question of how to persuade a boy to feel responsibility for his own learning, and to realise that nothing can be taught him which he does not cause himself to learn, is perhaps the most difficult prob-lem which a teacher has to face. (Cook,[4] p. 73)

Whereas Holmes seems to advocate freedom of personal expression, Cook is emphasising the importance of responsibility for learning. Thus we have here in a nutshell the divergent views of the romantic school of such people as Montessori, A. S. Neill and, in drama, Peter Slade and to a lesser extent Brian Way; and of the progressive school of people like John Dewey and Jean Piaget and, in drama, Winifred Ward in America and Dorothy Heathcote in England, the former concerned to create a proper environment for natural growth, the latter stimulating engagement with the environment; the former emphasising freeplay; the latter stressing insight and problem-solving.

The flowering-seeds metaphor might seem as light-weight as the seed itself. And yet the history of drama in education during this century is a record of various pioneers attempting to adopt this romantic progressive view. The need to 'hold childhood in reverence' (Rousseau) has dominated their philosophy if not their practice. Indeed apparent incompatibility of philosophy and practice seems to be a not uncommon feature of our pioneers. The romantic in Cook caused him to entitle his book *The play way*,[5] but his pupils finished up as expert performers of Shakespeare: the romantic in Peter Slade[6] based his philosophy on child play (a markedly different concept from Caldwell Cook's 'playway'), yet he recommended the circumscribed practice of children re-enacting a story; the romantic in Brian Way[7] respected the 'individuality of the individual' and yet his book is full of Stanislavskian-type exercises for the teacher to impose on all his pupils at the same time; the romantic in Dorothy Heathcote respectfully believes that children can know more than she does and yet she does not hesitate to assess with devastating accuracy what their learning needs might be.

That there is this ambiguity, that our drama pioneers have often failed to iron out apparent contradictions, should as we shall see, not be interpreted as a weakness but as a strength (even though it causes distressing headaches in the meantime!) for the promotion of a unifocussed ideal in education in general seems to turn back on itself with no ready alternative within it that could be harnessed quite naturally for change. In America, for example, teachers are faced with accepting behaviourism or rejecting it with little room for ambiguity, or if one takes an example of another American movement which, as John Deverall[8] has pointed out, has critically affected education in Australia while skirting the UK: the trend of humanism, one can detect that teachers have either rejected it out of hand or have taken on board a distorted version. It is sad to read Abraham Maslow[9] in possibly his last published essay writing as follows:

The growing insistence of students that they be stimulated, inspired, entertained by the teacher may be taken as a symptom of the extreme child-centering of recent decades. (p. 63)

There has, incidentally, been a drama misinterpretation of the humanist movement which, at its most extreme has led to a self-indulgent spontaneity which eschews the disciplined hard work that Maslow and Carl Rogers[10] before him intended. When I visited Australia in 1978 the fear expressed by drama teachers that what I was going to offer was 'psychodrama' was but an understandable reaction to the over-introspective 'sensitivity' drama of the 1970's.

This need to reject a philosophy has led to 'positions' and 'camps' and 'labels'. (I was recently accused of failing to use the 'Gavin Bolton' method!) It is for this reason I think the standpoint of drama teachers in the 1980's is a healthier one: we are no longer so critical of apparent contradictions in the work of our pioneers; we seem more able to contain a dialectic of opposites in our philosophy; we are more inclined to see drama as multi-faceted; we can now, chameleon-like, adapt our subject to changing circumstances without denying its real nature. The rest of education may at this moment in time be rushing lemming-like 'back to basics'. Conceptually, for drama teachers this is no problem (although economically and politically their subject is, at least temporarily, threatened) for drama is basic, as I hope to demonstrate in the following discussion. Furthermore, whereas the dichotomy between traditional, subject-centred education and romantic/progressive child-centred education (or as it is being referred to in some quarters, between liberal and radical education) continues, drama manages to rise above this through its dialecticism.

I now propose to examined the truth of these claims in terms of the perspective I gave at the beginning: assumptions about education and knowledge; assumptions about the status of the subject; and assumptions about the status of the teacher.

Assumptions about education and knowledge

Richard Pring[11] succinctly describes the dilemma of education. He claims, quite rightly, I think, that education is to do with the development of the individual's mind. He goes on:

Central to the development of mind is the growth of knowledge, and central to this is the refinement and extension of the conceptual framework through which experience is organised. There is a difficulty however which needs to be resolved. The learner is an individual with a particular way of organising his experience, whilst the conceptual structures we seek to introduce him to are of others' making. (p. 23)

This dichotomy between 'knowing' as the organisation of personal experience and 'knowledge' as something independent of the knower, divides educationists into opposing factions which can be represented by the following quotations:

The traditional/liberal view

This is what makes 'initiation' an appropriate word to characterise an educational situation; for a learner is 'initiated' by another into something which he has to master, know or remember, (Peters,[12] p. 3)

What is clear, however, is that, if our training methods are not to remain the hit and miss business they are at the moment, the careful detailed analysis of the logical features of exactly what we wish to teach must be pursued. (Hirst,[13] p. 60)

The progressive/radical view

In teaching a child we are trying to help the child make sense of things for himself. (Curtis,[14] p. xx)

. . . in the meaning of knowledge, process and content are inextricable to the extent that process actually becomes an inherent part of the content. (Harris,[15] p. 177)

A principal difference between these two sets of quotations lies in their assumptions about reality. The first two place an emphasis on public knowledge of the objective world that has to be passed on to the next generation, the second two give credence to the learner's view of the objective world. The peculiar position of drama is that it can successfully contain both these in a perpetual balance. The activity of drama requires from the participants an 'as if' mental set. This particular representational act, while sometimes appearing to be an escape from reality (the very word 'make-believe' or 'pretence' conjures up something that is not true) in fact, by definition, must have something external to the participant as a point of reference. His actions will either bear a verisimilitude to the objective world in so far as he understands it or will be a deliberate distortion with no less a grasp on what is being distorted. If a child in symbolic play successfully repeats some typical actions of his mother, he is patently involved in imitation of the objective world. If he deliberately exaggerates his real perception of those typical actions they nevertheless still provide the baseline for his egocentric behaviour. Even where there appears to be no imitation of anything recognisable as his mother's overt behaviour, there will inevitably be a conscious adoption of something to do with his mother – perhaps her attitude or her situation. There will be some aspect, therefore, even where there is distortion that could be judged by an observer to be true or false.

The same applies to drama. However uniquely personal a child's investment in what he is creating may be there will always remain some criterion of appropriateness in terms of something other than itself. This is not to say that all drama, like a simulation game, corresponds as closely as possible with the environment for this would, in Richard Pring's words,[16] reduce art to 'a slightly bizarre way of giving an empirical account of the world' (p. 44). What I am saying is that a degree of objectivity is necessary to any kind of dramatic activity. Necessary but not sufficient, that is. For the significance of drama lies in its concern with a process of personal engagement with the objective world, not in merely mirroring it. In other words, as in the Kevin Harris quotation above, process does become an 'inherent part of the content'. Drama is simultaneously subjective and objective.

What is learnt as drama may only partially (and least importantly) be spelled out in propositional terms. 'American Indians' conduct on a "pow-wow"' may be a fact a child is able to articulate after his drama. But the experience may have resonated all kinds of 'intuitive', 'sensed' meanings not reducible to propositions. We are sometimes ready to rush to discuss our drama experiences in approximate 'knowledge that' forms, failing to recognise that the central experience of drama is what Arnaud Reid[17] calls 'knowing this'.

This implied relationship between the knower and the known will be further elaborated in the next section.

Assumptions about the status of the subject

a) Drama as knowledge

Although Arnaud Reid refers to the occurrent knowing of art as 'knowing this', when he uses the expression 'knowing that' he is referring to knowledge about art, not as I shall continue to use it here in connection with that aspect of the art content that has an objective reference. We have to distinguish, therefore, among three kinds of knowledge in connection with drama: knowing about the subject, which is what O- and A-level candidates would be familiar with, knowing how to do drama, which falls within our earlier tradition of training in stage-crafts, and knowing or understanding the substance of a particular drama. It is in the latter sense that teachers are justified in pointing out that drama is a kind of parasite, not having a subject-matter of its own.

But it is this particular usage that distinguishes current trends in drama teaching from earlier movements. I detect two principal sources for this particular emphasis: in the work of Dorothy Heathcote and in the practice of Theatre in Education teams. Both are concerned with using drama to teach something worth-while, and that 'something' could come from anywhere in the curriculum. There has been a fair amount of resistance to these kinds of aims from practising teachers and even the Schools Council[18] shied away from studying this emphasis in any depth, preferring to take refuge in the notion of drama for social skills or drama as dramatic statement. One of the problems for teachers is that it requires a skill in structuring at a more refined level of precision than previous trends have required. But there are other more fundamental reasons for teacher resistance which I hope to make clear as we look more closely at what is meant by teaching and learning in this context.

As already noted, at a superficial level drama can be concerned with the teaching and learning of facts. For example, Dorothy Heathcote recently taught a class of 9–10 year olds about a shoe factory, using the children in role as employees. They learnt a great many facts about leather and shoe-making processes. Much more important however was that the kind of personal engagement, referred to above, brought about an attitude in the children of respect for craftsmanship and the responsibility of craftsmanship. At another level, however (and this brings us to the crux of the matter), Dorothy was planning for cognitive development. She wanted these children over the few sessions of drama to learn about 'change', the need for change, what brings about change and the effects of change. Before we look at the implications here, let me use another example – from my own teaching this time. A few weeks ago I was working with a class of top juniors on the problems of 'safety precautions' in a zoo where wild animals have to be secured from the public and yet available for the public to enjoy. The children were in-role as architects, involved in elaborate designs of cages and compounds, detecting flaws in each others' designs and verbally sharing their findings. In the second lesson they were required in small groups to demonstrate by enactment how the most perfect safety precautions were not perfect enough. It was during the preparation of their demonstration that they stumbled on the significance of 'human error', a revelation that allowed the final discussions to take on a sobering aspect: to what extent can the safety of nuclear reactors be guaranteed as long as we have to rely on the human factor?

If we look at these two illustrations in terms of cognitive development the central concepts may be summarised as 'implications of change' and 'implications of safety'. No one could deny these are concepts of some consequence and of relevance to children of all ages. And yet given the educational 'establishment' view of the curriculum, these concepts would not normally be taught. By the 'establishment' view, of course, I am referring to Paul Hirst's reductionist's classification of the curriculum into seven subject 'disciplines'. Hirst is not only preoccupied with propositional knowledge but is determined to limit what is taught to the concepts that are fundamental to each major discipline. It is my opinion that such is the stranglehold that the reductionist/propositional theory has on our British school system that it is virtually impossible for some teachers to break out of it. They find it very difficult to identify the central concepts in a drama experience because all their thinking as pupils, students in teacher-training and as teachers, has been circumscribed by the notion of subjects, so that concepts have to be 'subject' concepts. 'Change' and 'safety' may be concepts that are critical to our common experience but they are not amenable to the categorical labelling of Hirst and other curriculum planners such as DES[19] and the Schools Council.[20]

It seems that the concepts we deal with in drama are more fundamental to living than subject classification will allow. It is in this sense that the popular claim that drama is about life can be justified, for there is a distinct danger that when Hirst and his disciples reduce the objective world to logical, propositional forms, what really needs to be learnt by our pupils gets left out.

Curiously, I have only come across one non-drama publication in which the authors (Neil Postman and Charles Weingartner[21]), in suggesting the kinds of concepts they consider could most usefully be learnt in school as part of an alternative, radical education, come very close to 'drama' concepts. Indeed, in reading their list I recognise some of the themes I have actually seen groups tackling in their drama work. I give a selection from their long list below:

How do you want to be similar to or different from adults you know when you become an adult?
How can you tell 'good guys' from 'bad guys'?
How can 'good' be distinguished from evil?
Where do symbols come from?
Where does knowledge come from?
What do you think are some of man's most important ideas?
How do you know when a good idea becomes a bad idea or a dead idea?
What is progress?
What is change?
What are the most obvious causes of change? What are the least apparent?
What's worth knowing? How do you decide?

These kind of questions cut across or go beyond subject divisions and yet they are basic to living. They seem to be ignored or dismissed by educationists.

Even Mary Warnock[22] whose balanced view of curriculum theory I often appreciate, while going so far as to acknowledge the radical challenge of Postman and Weingartner, seems to be dismissive without good reason of what they are trying to say. She writes:

> It is worthy of note, in passing, that the enquiry lessons quoted with approval by these authors almost all turn out to be on questions such as 'what counts as a rule?' 'Is there one and only one sense of "right" and "wrong"?' 'Can there be different versions of the truth?', and so on. (p. 67).

But although one might reasonably share her view that a whole curriculum made up of these kinds of enquiries would be ridiculous, one might nevertheless have expected that she would give them the serious consideration they deserve. She goes on:

> All these questions are, roughly speaking, philosophical. And there is no doubt at all that children of all ages, as well as grown ups, enjoy talking about them. But even the most extreme proponent of the co-operative or enquiry method of education, or the most self-interested professional philosopher, would hardly suggest that this is to be the whole of the curriculum. And even when philosophy is to be the subject, a teacher will probably be a better philosopher than his pupils and will certainly have more expertise. (p. 67)

In my view it is these very 'philosophical questions' that children come face to face with in their drama. Part of the subject's status lies in its potential for putting children in touch with very basic values of life.

To put the whole discussion so far on the status of the subject in summary form: it seems that when we emphasise the particular content of drama as critical for education we imply two conceptual levels of learning – the factual level relating to knowledge of the objective world and another more significant philosophical level often relating to one's responsibility towards the objective world (including oneself as part of that world). But this is only one side of the 'drama' coin.

b) Drama as aesthetic form

The reader may have detected that in the two lesson illustrations I chose, we had instances of good education but weak drama. It could be argued that if the former is guaranteed who cares about the latter? Well curriculum planners do! From the discussion so far it would appear they would have very little to plan. For it is quite clear that Dorothy and I were using drama as any primary school teachers, non-drama secondary subject-specialists and remedial secondary teachers could. All it requires is for any teacher to put his pupils in the 'as if' mental-set so that they can engage with any kind of subject-matter in this special way.

Merely to use the psychology of dramatic action in this functional way (valuable as it might be) is in my view to fall short of the art experience which I consider should be part of a child's total education. First we have to examine what I mean by 'art experience' in drama. Historically two contrasted claims have been made by teachers for drama as art – by those who trained children in the art of performance and by disciples of Peter Slade who claimed that child drama is 'an art form in its own right'.

Now although I have taken up considerable space in arguing for the importance of subject-matter, i.e. what a particular drama is about, it seems to me that a drama teacher must simultaneously be teaching the 'how' of drama and that there will inevitably be times when the 'how' will be more important than the content, whether this be at the simplest level tackled by Dorothy Heathcote in her 'shoe-factory' lesson where she had to spend a fair slice of time giving the children confidence to make the imaginative leap into making shoes that were not really there or at a more sophisticated level of introducing stage design to a CSE examination class. But I want to go further than this. Whereas I do not agree with Peter Slade that child drama has its own art form, it seems to me that children must be trained to become aesthetically aware, i.e. conscious of dramatic form. They are not likely to achieve this if their drama experience is confined to 'mantle of the expert' kind of role-play at its purely functional level described in the two illustrations. They must, over their school years, acquire the basic drama/theatre skills of selecting focus, injecting tension and creating meaningful symbols (I have written about this at length elsewhere, Bolton[23]). Given that these basic skills are acquired, the old drama–theatre dichotomy becomes redundant, not of course if the emphasis is still placed on the naturalistic Stanislavskian type of performance so long cherished by traditionalists who place the emphasis on performance techniques rather than on a fundamental understanding of the art form.

Notice I use the word 'acquired' rather than 'taught'. 'Consciousness of dramatic form' is something often sensed at a tacit level of comprehension. Although, as already remarked upon, neither of these illustrations was aesthetically strong, briefly, within each of them a move in the direction of drama as art took place – in two quite contrasted ways. At a critical point in Dorothy's series of lessons there suddenly occurred a confrontation between the employees of the factory and a stranger (teacher in role) who was actually seated at the boss's desk impatiently waiting for them to clock on at work. Here were all the elements of theatre; surprise, tension and teacher's selection of role as a 'time and motion' official, symbolising through officialdom and territory take-over the very theme of the whole series – facing 'change'. This was a classic example of a change of dramatic level achieved by the 'spectator' role in the children responding to the teacher's theatricality. In other words, the children were not themselves actively engaged in creating an art form – but the teacher was! This important 'half-way house' gives the children an aesthetic experience at a subconscious level before they are ready to carry the responsibility.

By contrast, in my lesson, the children were required to be theatrical in a way that young children can safely handle. Because it is protected by the task, to use Goffman's[24] term, it gives 'permission to stare'. They were in the crudest form of performance mode when they, in small groups, enacted how the most perfect safety precautions could go wrong: they were 'demonstrating' their solution – rather like a TV chef demonstrating baking a cake. Again they could be said to be 'acquiring' the skills of theatre for they were selecting for clarity of communication – not consciously to create theatre but to meet the requirements of the task.

It seems to me that a secondary specialist may sometimes be working in an art form with the participants (in a non-performance mode), only tacitly responding to its dynamic; at other times he may be encouraging them consciously to work for tension and symbolisation etc. Similarly, he may make decisions in respect of performance – of the degree to which the pupils should concentrate on form.

Assumptions about the status of the teacher

The concept of authority and the teacher has been given a great deal of attention by educationists in recent years. Whereas it has always been seen as a critical factor varying between the two extremes of the teacher-dominated traditional and behaviourist's classrooms to the pupil-centred romantic/progressive/humanist's 'healthy environment' classrooms, a recent interest in the nature of knowledge and the education process taken by sociologists of education, such as Michael Young[25] and Geoffrey Esland,[26] has led to a radical challenge of a teacher's authority. The new claim is that not only do most teachers improperly take it upon themselves to decide which public knowledge is important and how it should be taught, but they further use their power to control what is to count as knowledge. What should happen, according to these writers, is that the teacher should reduce his own authority by respecting that a pupil's perspective on knowledge is just as legitimate as his teacher's, for knowledge is socially constructed and whether it is true or false depends where you happen to be standing at the time.

As one would expect, big guns have been turned on this kind of argument; on this 'relativist' view. In untypically militant tones Mary Warnock[27] writes, 'For if creeping relativism is not rooted out, then it seems to me that educationalists might as well shut up shop.' (pp. 107–8). The implication of relativism for Mary Warnock is that if 'anything goes' then you cannot plan a curriculum. Which brings us close to the dilemma of the drama teacher who in recent years has often found himself asking his classes, 'What do you want to make a play about?' What could be more 'relative' than this? Few other subject-teachers invite their classes to make choices of this order, so does this put drama teachers in a radical camp where pupils are leading their teacher? Not entirely, for the invitation to choose is often not as open as it sounds, for the teacher knows there are really going to be what Geoff Gillham[28] describes as two plays: the play for the children and the play for the teacher. A clever teacher will blend these two so that the final drama experience meets both the pupil wants and the teacher's intentions. Teacher-status is then ambiguous. Although in my view such teacher manipulation is often justified (Dorothy Heathcote has coined the term 'benign manipulator') we must not be surprised if our critics charge us with dishonesty.

A further example of ambiguity (or dishonesty – depending on where you are standing) is often revealed in a drama teacher's attempt at being 'the one who doesn't know'. Mary Warnock[29] strikes home when she compares the traditional teacher with the enquiry (child-centred) teacher: 'The difference between this and "ordinary" teaching becomes very obscure: the only addition seems to be that the enquiry teacher, like a skilful negotiator, has to pretend that the other party had the idea himself.' (p. 66). It is interesting to compare Mary Warnock's and Kevin Harris's attitude to the model of Socrates as a good non-authoritarian teacher. In the *Meno* he is seen leading a slave to display his knowledge of geometry. Harris[30] respectfully quotes the well-known passage seeing it as an epitome of 'dialogical encounters, wherein teachers and learners together came to discover the real relationships that exist in the world they are exploring . . .' (p. 175) Mary Warnock[31] refers to the same passage in these terms: 'For nothing could possibly be more artificial, not to say bogus, than the famous passage in the *Meno* . . .' (p. 66) Artificial or not the 'Socratic method' is the approach which many drama teachers have adopted.

There is something about drama and the use of teacher-in-role in particular that does indeed make the teacher-pupil relationship more flexible. Teachers who perhaps in teaching, say, English would take a more traditional authoritarian stance, in switching to drama seem to relax their grip to a point where they might agree with Kevin Harris[32] that their responsibility lies '. . . in helping others in the common pursuit of knowledge' (p. 18). Dorothy Heathcote sees this loosening of the teacher's grip as a process of handing over power to the children. Again sceptics might perceive this as more apparent than real: they may feel that, paradoxically, in practice the greater the autonomy invested in the pupils, the greater is the power of influence retained by the teacher. Harris[33] is condemning the traditional situation when he writes as follows:

A person can learn x (that less dense liquids float on more dense liquids). He can also learn x in a power situation, where someone determines that he shall learn it and someone makes him learn it – even if in the most pleasant ways. In both situations he comes to know x; but in the second situation he comes to know y (that someone de-

termined that he learn x, and that someone made him learn x). Now
x and y, in this situation or any similar situation cannot be totally
disentangled, and so gaining knowledge of x is to some extent distorted, since part of the experiential situation of coming to know x
is knowing y as well. (p. 179)

But supposing a benevolent drama teacher subtly sets up a situation
which allows the pupil to reconsider some concept of significance to the
pupil's life (let us, too, call it x) will not his learning of x be just as
influenced by the teacher's structuring (y) as by the most traditional
teaching? Indeed is there not a chance that the teacher's influence will
be the greater because his teaching was covert? If this is the case the
status of the drama teacher is more powerful than it has ever been, even
when he was allowed to be the most dictatorial director of the school
play.

Summary

In this chapter I have attempted to show that the contribution of drama
to education depends on what general educational philosophy is in the
air, or what status is given to drama as knowledge and on the degree
and kind of authority a teacher can exploit.

Tracing the historical development of drama in education it becomes
clear that only in extreme instances could a coherent combination of
these three factors be found: most often there has been confusion or
even incompatibility. This, I maintained, should be seen as a strength,
for contradictions provide the means for growth and change. Indeed in
examining the above three perspectives in terms of current practice a
number of dichotomies have emerged.

In looking at present-day assumptions about education and knowledge, the opposing philosophical position of having respect for either
a body of knowledge or for the knower appears to be contained by
drama for, as we have seen, it can be both subjective and objective (a
view not held, incidentally, by the education and the arts philosophy
of Robert Witkin[34] and Malcolm Ross[35] who still follow 'an arts as personal expression' line).

The status of the subject itself is critically different from any previous
trend. It is no longer (as a matter of priority) concerned with techniques
or free expression or learning about theatre but is seen as a vehicle for
cognitive development giving significance to the learning of those kinds

of concepts which, while cutting across the traditional subject barriers, are nevertheless of central importance to living.

Concurrent with this usage of drama should occur the teaching (often indirect) of dramatic form – at a level more fundamental than acting techniques, a level that dissolves the rigid distinctions drawn in the past between drama and theatre by harnessing what they have in common.

But perhaps the greatest change is manifested in the status of the teacher who appears to be poised between opposing forces: he seems to offer choice with one hand while taking it away with the other; he seems to respect the perspective his pupils have of the world while tightly structuring for change; he seems to build up his own authority while giving power to his pupils. Somehow or other good drama teachers do find a logic within all these contradictions. It seems to me that the art of teaching requires this degree of flexibility and I would go so far as to say that in this respect teachers of drama may be ahead of their colleagues.

What hope do curriculum planners have of locating drama's position at an intersection of the three perspectives when the strands between them pull in so many different directions? I think there can be only one answer. They must plan for diversity and let the teachers in schools operate just as flexibly or inflexibly, broadly or narrowly and ambitiously or modestly as their personal security allows.

Philosophical perspectives on drama and the curriculum. In Nixon J (ed) *Drama and the whole curriculum*, 1982. Hutchinson (17–21 Conway Street, London, W1P 6JD).

Reference

1 Holmes E 1911 *What is and what might be*. Constable.
2 Cook H C 1917 *The play way*. Heinemann.
3 Holmes E op. cit.
4 Cook H C op. cit.
5 Cook H C ibid.
6 Slade P 1954 *Child drama*. University of London Press.
7 Way B 1967 *Development through drama*. Longman.
8 Deverall J 1979 Public medium, private process: drama, child-centred education and the growth model of human development. Unpublished MA (Ed), University of Durham.

9 Maslow A 1974 What is a taoistic teacher? In Rubin L J (ed) *Facts and feeling in the classroom*. Ward Lock Educational.

10 Rogers C 1961 *On becoming a person*. Constable.

11 Pring Richard 1967 *Knowledge and schooling*. Open Books.

12 Peters R S 1967 What is an educational process? In *The concept of Education*. Routledge and Kegan Paul, 1976 edition.

13 Hirst P 1967 Logical and psychological aspects of teaching. In *The concept of education*. Routledge and Kegan Paul.

14 Curtis B and Mays W (eds) 1978 *Phenomenology and Education: self consciousness and its development*. Methuen.

15 Harris K 1979 *Education and knowledge*. Routledge and Kegan Paul.

16 Pring R 1976 *Knowledge and schooling*. Open Books.

17 Reid A L 1980 Art: knowledge that and knowing this. *British Journal of Aesthetics* **20** (4) (Autumn).

18 Schools Council 1972 *Drama in schools*: report of conference of Schools' Council English Committee's Drama Sub-Committee.

19 DES 1981 *The school curriculum*. HMSO.

20 Schools Council 1981 *The practical curriculum* (March).

21 Postman N and Weingartner C 1971 *Teaching as a subversive activity*. Penguin.

22 Warnock, M 1977 *Schools of thought*. Faber.

23 Bolton, G 1979 *Towards a theory of drama in education*. Longman.

24 Goffman E 1974 *Frame analysis*. Penguin.

25 Young M F D (ed) 1971 *Knowledge and control*. Collier-Macmillan.

26 Esland G 1971 Teaching and learning as the organisation of knowledge. In Young M F D (ed) *Knowledge and control*. Collier-Macmillan.

27 Warnock M op. cit.

28 Gillham G 1974 Report on Condercum School Project by Live Theatre. Unpublished.

29 Warnock M op. cit.

30 Harris K op. cit.

31 Warnock M op. cit.

32 Harris K op. cit.

33 Harris K ibid.

34 Witkin R 1974 *The intelligence of feeling*. Heinemann.

35 Ross M 1978 *The creative arts*. Heinemann.

Drama and meaning

This article was written for a British Council course organised by Dorothy Heathcote in September 1982 for a group of 20 visitors from all over the world. Other papers written by Dorothy Heathcote, John Fines, Ray Verrier and Tom Stabler were collected into one volume by the British Council for distribution in 1983.

It has become quite fashionable among teachers in the UK in recent years to talk about drama education in terms of *Meaning*. Ever since the Schools Council Drama Project authors[1] gave us their sociological perspective on drama teaching and built their theoretical framework around the notion of 'negotiation of meaning', the significant content of a drama lesson which in the past might have been thought of as dramatic skills or life-skills or social skills or free-expression is now centred on the drama's meaning. 'They must focus on the meaning of the drama and then the subsidiary actions will come right and true,' (p. 29) says Dorothy Heathcote in *Exploring theatre and education* edited by Ken Robinson (Heinemann, 1980). One of the problems is that we lack a sophisticated language for describing the meaning of an experience either as a participant or as a teacher/observer. And it may be, as this paper will attempt to show, that whether or not the meanings are the same for both the participant and the teacher/observer depends on the kind of drama practised. A further attempt will be made to demonstrate that fundamental differences in philosophical positions can determine the *levels* of meaning available to both parties.

We have not entirely lacked a terminology for dicussing meaning in drama, for traditionally we have employed a literary categorisation distinguishing levels of meaning. The distinction is often drawn, for example, between *Plot* and *Theme*. By the former we mean a sequence of particular events; by the latter a more generalised level of meaning is intended, a higher order of abstraction of human behaviour of which the particular events are an instance. I would like to add a third level, that of *Context*, which refers to the chosen physical situation: place, period or idiom in which plot and themes evolve. Thus reducing Hamlet to its crudest terms, the *Plot* is a sequence of deaths; a *Theme* is Revenge; and the *Context* is the Royal Court of 17th-century Elsinore.

The levels of meaning of a novel could be set down in similar ways. The difference for drama, however, is that events take place in space and time through simulated *action*. Does this suggest then that the meanings can actually be *seen* in action? To what extent is it possible to claim that the various meanings can be observed? The question is relevant for the theatre critic and drama teacher alike, but as we are concerned here with drama teaching, let us confine our thinking to drama created by teacher and children. It is not difficult to transfer the literary categorisation to children's work. For instance, in a drama about unemployment, the Plot is, say, about a man being made redundant applying for another job; the Context is an 'interview situation'; and one of the Themes (or 'learning areas' using educational jargon) could be 'Self-esteem'. Are Plot, Context and Theme directly observable? The most obviously accessible of these seems to be the Context. Certain features of an interview situation would have to be overtly represented if the drama is to have any validity at all. And in so far as each action is seen to have coherence with its preceding and subsequent actions, the story-line of 'what is happening now and what will happen next' is certainly made explicit. So far, then, we can confirm that at least the levels of meaning, the Plot and the Context, are largely observable from the action. And although the angle is different, presumably in many instances of drama activity teacher/observer and participants could reasonably agree about those particular levels of meaning.

At this point we can note that there are at least two kinds of drama teaching where the priorities of the teacher are such that one or other of these two meanings entirely fulfils the teacher's educational requirement. The drama often referred to as *Simulation* (I am not using the word here as Dorothy Heathcote tends to use it) requires that the participants learn something about a particular situation in the world – for instance, how a large factory is organised; how to use a telephone; how decisions are made in Local Government; how law courts operate etc. When drama is used in this way to teach precisely about how something is done or should be done, it is eminently proper that the total concentration of the participants and the teacher should be on effective representation of the Context: when you are teaching young children about Road Safety you do not want them to finish up learning about something else! Less admirable, however, are the educational objectives of the teacher whose sole interest is in accurate representation of a Plot. This regrettable emphasis is still found among teachers of young children in particular. Story-line is given undue significance and treated as if it is the only meaning available. The children finish up 'knowing' the story but oblivious to any other level of meaning. Jerome S. Bruner, in *The relevance of education* (Penguin Educational, 1974) writes of children deprived of access to a 'deeper meaning'. He is not speaking of drama but the same point is being made. He is talking about how different children 'read' comic strips: *Pogo* and *Little Orphan Annie*. 'Either can be read in terms of "what-happened-that-day". And probably a fair number of children read the strips in just that way. But one can read each with a sense of its form, its social criticism, its way of depicting human response to difficulty, its underlying assumptions about the dynamics of human character.' (p. 104) Unwittingly, some teachers use drama to train children to stay with the obvious – that which can be made explicit through action.

And yet, left to themselves, those same children might well choose not to make explicit in their drama either the plot or the context. Shipwrecks without a sea or even without a ship are not uncommon, and to an observer the plot can remain curiously obscure! Thus it would have been more correct in the earlier paragraph to have qualified the assertion that at least two levels of meaning are 'largely observable', for sometimes plot and context can remain in the participants' minds and may not *necessarily* be depicted by the action. A word of caution is needed here however. By saying that something is occurring *'in the Mind' rather than in the Action* I am in danger of perpetuating a philosophical heresy I have no wish to support. I could be quite rightly charged with *Dualism*, that is separating mind and body, implying that the mind does one thing and the body something different. We need to look a little closely at this particular problem, for strange as it may seem, the philosophical position that one takes on this issue affects educationists and drama educationists in particular. The most extreme position is that adopted by the Behaviourist School who have avoided Dualism by affirming that what a man is or means is in his behaviour. His Mind is an irrelevancy. Teachers therefore are in the business of changing behaviour. In order to change it they have to observe it and measure it. Our fellow drama teachers, particularly in USA who are part of this 'behaviourist system' not surprisingly have adopted a kind of drama that allows the *total* meaning of the drama to be conveyed by the action. They train their students in *theatrical performance*, a mode the sole purpose of which is to make explicit meanings that are not normally communicable. What could be more explicit than the effort made by three young pupils on behalf of their teacher as described in the following extract from a report of the CEMREL Aesthetics Education Experimental Research Project:[2]

The teacher gave simple instructions to 'listen, watch arms, body etc.' The first three children were sad, happy and surprised in turn. The sad girl rubbed her eyes, commenting 'Oh, I'm so sad'; the happy boy exuberantly jumped up and down and commented 'Oh, I'm so happy. The sun is out.' Later, anger and fright entered the parade. (p. 318)

If we have reservations about the way the behaviourists avoid Dualism, we might also have doubts about the way our own Schools Council[3] seem to embrace it. There is more than a hint of a dualistic model operating in the following recommendations:

Children should become increasingly able to translate attitudes and ideas about various issues into dramatic statements which reflect their understanding. (p. 144)

In acting-out children are often given an idea and asked to go away and make something of it, perhaps to arrive at a dramatic statement which encapsulates their feelings and ideas about a particular topic or issue. (p. 32)

Acting-out then is the exploration and representation of meaning . . . (p. 16)

Problems . . . may also arise because some children have not clarified their ideas enough to devise a statement about them. (p. 13)

It seems to me from the above statements that we are unambiguously invited to think in terms of an idea in search of a container, as though the two could be conceived of quite separately. This should not distract however from the new emphasis that the authors were introducing: theirs was the first major publication to give priority to *Theme* as the principal content of a drama experience. The themes they recommended tend to be of social concern such as 'attitudes to minority groups' or 'the nature of responsibility'. But although the authors firmly espouse the importance of process rather than product, their dualism seems to trap them at times into confining the process to that of finding a theatrical expression for a point of view already held by the participants – searching for a product, no less.

There is an alternative view of process which is worth examining in detail. Drama can be used to *challenge* children's views and understanding, so that although the thematic meaning might still be the nature of responsibility, the drama can be so structured by the teacher that the children are confronted *existentially* by its implications – they experience, for instance, teacher-in-role failing in his responsibility or vice versa, so that the outcome is *felt*. But as far as meaning is concerned, it is here we begin to detect the need for making a distinction between 'teacher-meaning' and 'participant-meaning'.

Whereas it might remain legitimate for a teacher to label the thematic meaning as 'the nature of responsibility', when the drama has been of this experiential kind only in its most reductionist sense could the same label be applied to the participants' experience. That they share this thematic level of meaning is dictated by the structure, but what each child takes from the experience, cognitively and affectively, depends on characteristics uniquely his own. Equally important, in answer to the dualist question, the participant is not engaged with the theme or learning area in a compartmentalised way. Plot, Contextual and Thematic meanings converge not in the Action alone, not in the Mind alone, nor in a sequence of Mind and Action, but as an integrated whole. The meaning resides in the *person-entering-the-fiction*, and integration of Mind and Action.

Still less does the notion of theme seem applicable to the experience from the Participant's point of view if the definition of theme given by me on [the first page of this paper] is adhered to. I wrote that in using the term *theme*, 'a more generalised level of meaning is intended, a higher order of abstraction of human behaviour of which the particular events are an instance.' This is a pretty arid description of an aesthetic event! Arid or not, however, it remains appropriate if we wish to reduce the meaning of an experience to propositional statements. It seems to me that a teacher has little choice. The classification of Plot, Context and Theme is but part of the elaborate epistimological system we have for detaching ourselves from the particularity of experience and as such is necessary if the teacher is to offer himself and others a rationale for his planning. (I am not suggesting that Plot, Context and Theme are the only terminology available to him, but that if he does not use these words he will be obliged to use other conceptualisations.) But because dramatic activity is an art form, it is the very *particularity* of its meaning that counts. The participants do not experience 'responsibility' as an instance of a more general case, but as a unique event not translatable into terms other than itself.

This argument can be pushed further in terms of learning and meaning. Michael Polanyi in a number of texts has discussed different levels of awareness, distinguishing between what he terms subsidiary and focal awareness (see, for example, *Personal knowledge*, Routledge and Kegan Paul, 1958). This has critical implications for the drama teacher for it raises the question of which level of the dramatic activity should have the focus of the participant's attention and which level remains subsidiary (notice that the word 'subsidiary' does not here mean less important – indeed the opposite could apply – but at a lower level of consciousness). It may well be that if the participants enter the fiction with the learning area of 'responsibility' uppermost in their minds then both drama and learning could be unproductive. This point gains further support from some psychologists' acknowledgement that there is a passive, unconscious side to learning processes. In other words it is feasible if not probable that any refinement in understanding of 'responsibility' that occurs during or as a result of the drama experience could be described as *'caught* not taught'.[4]

All of which gives credence to the view popularised in recent years that in drama there is often a 'play for the teacher and a play for the pupils'. Whereas the teacher must continue to think and structure in terms of learning area and theme, it is also proper for the participants' focal attention to be directed towards creating a Plot and Context (not, of course, that they will necessarily use these terms in doing so). The teacher's skill, therefore, lies in an ability to set up the drama in a way that ensures a subsidiary awareness of the theme. A further responsibility of the teacher is to set up means for reflection – so that participants can tap for themselves and begin to share with others the meanings that have been implicitly understood.

In summary it appears that when the teacher looks for meaning in Action only, as, for example, when the story-line or performance modes are stressed, the observer and participant can be said to share the same meaning. Similarly, they can be said to share the same meaning-intention when both teacher and pupil have an abstract theme in mind like 'poverty in the third world' which is to be expressed in a dramatic product. On the other hand, when a teacher alone has a thematic intention which she wants the pupils to *experience* then the principal focus of attention of the participants should, paradoxically, be towards the more superficial goal of using action to meet the demands of Plot or Context etc. For this kind of drama, observer and participant do not share the same meanings, partly because the participant's experience is unique and partly because he is only subsidiarily aware of the very meanings to which the teacher is giving fullest attention. With this latter point in mind, it may be that Dorothy Heathcote's statement quoted in the first paragraph of this paper should be reversed to read: They must focus on the actions so that the meaning of the drama will come right and true.

Drama and meaning. Unpublished. (Paper read to British Council, Newcastle upon Tyne, September 1982)

References

1 McGregor L, Tate M, Robinson K 1977 *Learning through drama*, Schools Council Drama Teaching Project (10–16). Heinemann.
2 Smith L, Schumacher S 1977 Extended pilot trials of the Aesthetics Education Program: a qualitative description, analysis and evaluation. In Hamilton D *et al.* (eds) *Beyond the numbers game*. Macmillan, pp. 314–30.
3 McGregor *et al.* op. cit.
4 Fleming M 1982 A philosophical investigation into drama in education. PhD thesis, University of Durham.

Drama in education – a reappraisal

An examination of some of the 'myths' that have grown up around drama education

Elliott Eisner[1] some years ago wrote an article challenging the rationale behind many cherished views of art education, assumptions that made up for him a 'mythology' of art education. I shall try to do the same for drama education. There are two points that I need to make before I can start. Exposing a myth is not a denial in absolute terms. One does not argue that something is not valid, but rather that it is only partially valid or that its validity has been misunderstood, misrepresented, distorted or that circumstances have made it less valid. In other words a kernel of truth remains unchallenged. Another point to bear in mind is that just as the creation of a myth is an event in a particular time and a particular place arising out of particular needs, so the erosion of a myth is a particular historical/geographical/philosophical necessity.

Thus this brief study of myths in drama education will apply, and perhaps exclusively, to the English drama scene, both in the myths that were created in the early days of teaching drama to students and in the need in our present educational climate to reappraise our values in drama teaching. For America, past priorities and current challenges to the subject may be of such a different order that this chapter remains but of academic interest to American readers. I hope not. I have a hunch, however, that because of that unchanging kernel of truth within a myth, I am bound to be raising issues of universal importance to drama teachers even though my perspective is necessarily focused (if not blinkered!) by the development of the British educational system.

Myth No. 1: 'Drama is doing'

The sheer relief with which pupils and teachers alike find a salvation from strictures of traditional school studies in the contrasting activity-centred happenings of a drama session is evidence enough, one might have thought, that drama, if it is nothing else, is and indeed must be *'doing'*. Wide disagreement among practitioners as to content, purpose or method can be dispelled in seconds by the common understanding they all share that drama is 'doing'. Nevertheless, I shall argue that this is only partially so and that it is the neglect of the part that is *not* 'doing' that has distorted our understanding of the nature of drama and has caused us to underrate its potential for learning.

Of course the critical characteristic of drama is concrete action: it is this that distinguishes it from other arts, even from its sister arts of movement and dance, which, also action bound, nevertheless are spatially and temporarily more abstract. It is not, however, the concrete action alone that carries the meaning of the experience. Indeed I shall attempt to show that the meaning of a dramatic experience is not so much bound up with the functional, imitative meaning of the action, as with a tension that is set up between the particularity of the action and the generality of meanings implied by the action. The meaning of the experience is both dependent on and independent of the concrete action.

Action, even imitative action, is not in itself drama. A child miming the action of posting a letter is not in a dramatic mode if his sole intention is accurately to imitate such an action. He is merely adopting an imitative mode of behaviour, selecting an activity, the meaning of which can be denoted by the terms 'posting a letter' and recalling in

255

imitative actions precisely that function. There is but *one* dimension of meaning represented by the imitation: the denotative or functional one.

For the action to be considered dramatic greater significance of meaning must lie along other dimensions.* Such significance is determined by the combination of two contrasting sources: Whatever is uniquely personal and whatever is more universally relevant. Thus posting a letter as dramatic action must arouse affective memories in the participant to do with posting letters sufficiently strong for the action significantly to feed into appropriate meanings such as 'trust in a written message', 'irrevocability of a decision to post a letter', 'the anticipation of a letter's impact' and 'the impotence of not knowing the receiver's reaction'. It is these connotations that go beyond the functional meaning that the participant in drama must be concerned with. It is in this sense therefore that one can say the meaning of the dramatic experience is independent of the action. On the other hand the action of posting a letter is the vehicle through which such connotations are expressed. In that sense, therefore, the meaning is dependent on the concrete action. Thus the overall meaning is expressed in a relationship between the particular action and its more universal implications. Those teachers who are content to train their students in imitative skills are off target – imitating human actions and emotions is not drama. Likewise those teachers who, in their anxiety for students to achieve significantly thoughtful work, neglect the potential power of the concrete action do so at their peril – for the handling of abstract ideas, even in-role, without some spatial/temporal reference is not in itself drama either.

In England we have large numbers of the former teachers who see the training of students in skilful miming actions as sufficient drama training. It is to these teachers one has to exclaim 'drama is *not* doing!' whereas to the latter teachers, often found among teachers in the humanities who see the educational opportunities in holding discussions on some important issues in-role, one says 'this is really an abstract exchange of views which is fine as far as it goes, but drama *is* doing!' I hope my arguments have been sufficiently clear for the reader to appreciate that both forms of advice are misleading. Perhaps we should say 'drama is/is not doing'. Only with his sights ambivalently adjusted is a teacher likely to gauge correctly his priorities in teaching drama. We do not wish to limit our students to learning more precisely the

---

* Sadly, many Drama Education 'packages' seem to rely heavily on the one dimension of imitation, even to imitating *emotions*!

functional actions of life: it is the significance of the universal implication behind those actions that learning in drama is concerned with.
In attempting to challenge the myth of 'drama is doing' therefore, I am
not merely clarifying the nature of drama but, more importantly, showing that a teacher's priorities must inevitably become adjusted when its
nature is properly grasped.

Myth No. 2: 'Drama is an escape from reality'

Some play theorists see the make-believe play of young children as compensating for the 'slings and arrows of outrageous fortune,' as the
child's natural means of protecting himself from the cruel realities of
living. Because drama is undoubtedly linked with play (perhaps another
'myth' is that drama *is* play!) some practitioners see drama as an outlet
for their students, either in the sense of 'letting off steam' or as an opportunity to fantasise. The former describes a psychological disposition;
the latter is concerned with drama's content. I shall discuss these in turn
starting with the content.

a) The content of drama

To view make-believe activity as an escape from reality is, it seems to
me, to ignore a critical attribute of both play and drama: the child at
play, far from evading restrictions, actually imposes them. As the Rus-
sian psychologist, Vygotsky,[2] has pointed out play is about abiding by
the rules. The same applies to drama. However 'unreal' the make-
believe situation may be, the rules themselves objectively reflect the real
world, even if it is an inverse reflection: if, for example, the rule is, to
choose an extreme example, 'all parents have to be punished and sent
to bed early by their children' this merely (not merely – significantly
perhaps) reflects a very clear acknowledgement of reality, as does every
piece of apparent fantasy. But a feature of play is that a child may give
up playing or just change the rules when he feels so inclined. Drama,
on the other hand, requires students to agree on the rules, acknowledge
their parameters and keep to them, *even when it becomes uncomfortable*.

It so often happens that children choose a topic they do not fully
understand and when they begin to perceive its implications subtly start
to undermine the rules that are implicit in the situation. In other words,
instead of facing up to the rigour of thinking, decision making and coping with tension inherent within a topic, they prefer to slacken their

grip on 'the rules of the game'. Thus it is in this sense that drama can be an escape from reality, where an unspoken concensus between class and teacher allows a drifting into a 'rule-less' activity – immediately gratifying, eventually frustrating, educationally poverty stricken. I can think of many examples: of a class of nine year olds who in choosing to do their drama about hijacking sought 'fantasy' ways of solving the problem of being in the hijacker's power, by suddenly producing weapons (one boy tried claiming magic power!) they had clearly not had in their possession when the hijack first took place. At an adult level, I recall a woman who in playing a role of a singleminded determined person, under pressure from other people in the improvisation, 'succumbed' in a way that was quite illogical for the character she was playing.

On the other hand, I also recall as teacher of a class of 10–11 year olds *over*-insisting on keeping to historical facts. The situation was about Florence Nightingale and her nurses who were sent out by Queen Victoria to tend to the many wounded in the military hospital at Scutari, only to find on arrival that the doctors running the hospital were refusing to allow women on the wards [see p. 196]. 'Nursing is a man's job' they firmly declared. Now the boys and girls in this class representing the doctors and nurses respectively explored many of the facets of this confrontation during four or five drama sessions, the girls successively adapting their tactics along a wide range of ploys from demands to requests, from blackmail to persuasion. By the fifth day the doctors went into private conclave and eventually whispered to me that they were going to offer a compromise: the nurses were to be given a chance to work on the wards for just one day – to prove themselves! I am sure the reader will agree that this was a mature decision for young children to take. Unfortunately, in my enthusiasm for historical facts, I would not let them do this – for historically the doctors did not give in in that way.* Even as I write I shudder at the harm that some of us as teachers do! It is quite obvious that I as a teacher was allowing myself to be controlled by a very limited kind of reality – a particular sequence of events – whereas the more important reality was to do with how people adjust to an impasse.

What the boys wanted to carry out was *objectively valid*, in so far as they had examined the various factors in the situation and made a

---

* For those readers who are interested, the doctors at Scutari capitulated, not from choice, but because after a particularly severe battle, there were more wounded than the male orderlies and doctors could cope with.

reasoned judgement about them. This then is what is meant by the relationship of drama to reality – it is the perception, recognition and appraisal of events within the fictitious context. The context may be close to a known social context or an apparent fantasy, but it is the rules that govern it that must reflect the objective world for the activity to be worthy of the term drama and worthy of education.

b) *Disposition towards drama*

What people usually mean by 'letting off steam' is a psychological release from tension, so that participants are supposed to 'feel better' after a drama experience. This represents a pretty crude view of the mental state of drama participants, but there is a more subtle expectation of our students' mental state that was first conceived in England by the great pioneer of child drama, Peter Slade[3] and taken up staunchly by his disciples ever since. I refer to the quality of *absorption*.

It may puzzle the reader that I should include this admirable quality which most of us as teachers have at one time or another worked to promote in our students among the 'myths' of drama in education. I shall not argue that it is mythical in the sense that it doesn't exist (although some teachers working continually with recalcitrant classes may sometimes wonder!) but that we have been wrong to see it as a final achievement. Indeed I used to assume that if my students were absorbed then that was a necessary and sufficient concomitant of learning.

But I want to suggest that this may not be the case: that there is something about 'absorption' which hints at 'being lost' in an experience, thus escaping from reality. Now I know that the look of wonder on a child's face when he is so 'lost' can be something to be marvelled at, but I do not think it is moments such as these that we are working for in drama. We do not want children to 'lose' themselves but '*find*' themselves.

Certainly we want a high degree of involvement and commitment to the creative fiction, but if it is to be a worthwhile learning experience for the participant he must hold a dual perspective on the experience: an active identification with the fiction combined with heightened awareness of his own identification. So, far from escaping from life, the quality of life is momentarily intensified because he is 'knowing what he thinks as he thinks it'; 'seeing what he says as he says it'; 'evaluating what he does as he does it'. It is this reflection concurrent with identification that leads to learning through drama. Sometimes, of course, students are not capable of so reflecting. It is then that the teacher having attempted to discern what it is the student has experienced can perhaps, after the drama, help him to retrace the experience and reflect upon it or, alternatively, can attempt to create a frame of mind in the student that will bring about a more heightened awareness when he enters the next phase of the drama. With such sensitive handling by the teacher the student can begin to use fiction to understand himself in the real world.

Myth No. 3: 'Drama education is concerned with developing the uniqueness of the individual'

It is not insignificant I think that at the time Winifred Ward was establishing the term 'Creative dramatics' in America, here in England our Peter Slade was introducing the label 'Child drama'.

The latter terminology was intended to imply that within each child there is a potential for dramatic expression that is important because it is personal. The teacher's responsibility lay in nurturing a person's individuality. Such a philosophical view of the child and of drama as being 'within him' should be seen as part of a larger educational trend in Europe beginning with Rousseau, through Froebel and Pestalozzi and culminating in our own Plowden Report[4] in 1967 which gave a seemingly final official stamp of approval to 'Child-centred education'. It is perhaps true to say that whereas the 'humanist movement' in America has been a counter movement to the application of behaviourism to education, the 'child-centred' movement in England was seen as an alternative to the persistent image of children as passive recipients of an approved body of knowledge. It is not surprising when the child-centred movement was in the ascendancy in the 1950's and 60's that personalities in drama education should emerge to pioneer a view of drama that was also child-centred. The message of drama as personal development was welcomed hungrily not only in England but throughout the Western world for it bravely stood up to both the 'body of knowledge' and the 'behaviourist' explications of education. Drama teachers were grateful to Brian Way[5] in particular for articulating a philosophy that emphasised the *process* of dramatic experience rather than the *product*, that saw drama as a means of approach to self-knowledge and even (as taken further by devotees like Richard Courtney) as the very basis of all the learning and growth – *Developmental* drama was the Courtney label that spread through Canada.

In England our interpretation of Brian Way's philosophy tended to be manifested by our concern with the importance of individual creativity and free expression often paradoxically catered for in practice by exercise sequences for disciplined attributes like concentration or the puppet like response to a signal from teacher's tambour; with a growing hostility to the notion of children performing; with the assumption that there can be no sense of standards in drama work because each child is his own arbiter in this respect; and with the claim that 'Drama is Life' thus effectively reducing the activity to a meaningless catch-phrase.

But there is one aspect, our concern with promoting the uniqueness of the individual that perhaps more than the other manifestations goes in my view against the natural dramatic grain. There are some art forms, painting in particular, that are a vehicle for individual expression, but drama by its very nature is a group statement, commenting on, exploring, questioning or celebrating not individual differences, but what man has in common with man.

I have already mentioned different levels of meaning in dramatic action. In the example of posting a letter I suggested there are three broad levels of meaning – the functional (the imitative action of posting a letter) the universal (significant implications that posting a letter might have such as the irretrievability of the action) and the personal (whatever 'posting letter' memories a particular child may recall). Now each of these levels of meaning is important for the total meaning of the experience is made up of their interaction. But for the activity to be *drama* and not solitary play the concentration of effort must be at the middle level of meaning, that is it must have some significance related to the concrete action that all the participants can *share*. If the context or plot of the drama with six year olds is, for example, to do with 'catching a monster' the 'shared' or 'thematic' meaning might be 'We dare not make a mistake' or 'it is important to distinguish between "evidence" and "rumour" of the monster's existence' or 'Are we to be destroyers or preservers of Life? With ten year olds whose dramatic context is space travel the theme might well be 'is our training good enough for what we have to face?' or 'having to make a decision based on inadequate knowledge' or 'the responsibility we have to all those who will follow'. A group of sixteen year olds might be looking at 'family' contexts where the theme might be 'the dependence/independence ambivalence of the different generations', 'the treasure/burden ambivalence of rearing a child' or 'a family as a symbol of a past and a future'.

Of course each individual will bring all kinds of personal meanings to the above dramas, some more relevant than others. Indeed they could vary from traumatic for the six year old who is scared at the very thought of monsters or for the sixteen year old whose family is breaking up, to the neutral feelings of the six year old whose mind is really on his new birthday presents or to the positively destructive attitude of a sixteen year old who is hostile to drama. But if the experience is to operate as *drama*, individual differences must be channelled into the collective theme. Ultimately, however, it is what the individual draws from the collective meaning that matters, a process of 'finding himself in the meaning'. In that sense the importance of the uniqueness of the individual is not a myth, but like a member of an audience the individual has temporarily to hold his individuality in abeyance, sharing meanings he has in common with others in order that he may be personally enriched.

Myth No. 4: Drama is personal development

I do not wish to deny that drama, along with all aspects of education, can be an aid to personal development. Indeed I think I could argue the case that drama more than other subjects of the curriculum may accelerate the maturing process, especially for those children who for some reason or other have had natural progress arrested. Why then have I placed drama as personal development among my list of myths? The reason lies within our past reluctance to distinguish between immediate educational objectives and long-term maturation. Enthusiasm for the personal development of their students has often led to an act of super-arrogation on the part of drama teachers who claim that personal development is what they were actually *teaching*. One cannot *teach* concentration, trust, sensitivity, group awareness, patience, tolerance, respect, perception, judgement, social concern, coping with ambivalent feelings, responsibility etc., etc.; one can only hope that education will help to bring them about over a long term and as I have already suggested it could be argued that drama brings them about in a special way, but the achievement of these admirable qualities is *not intrinsic to drama*: it is an important *by-product* of the dramatic experience.

Certainly a teacher can effectively structure to create opportunities for continual practice of many of the above attributes but the drama must itself be *about* something. Sadly, it has so often been relegated to dramatic exercise in personal skills (just as in the old days poetry used to be abused in its usage as a mere vehicle for speech practice.)

Among the many immediate objectives a teacher may have for a particular drama lesson or series of lessons extending the students' understanding of the thematic content must be a top priority. Other objectives such as effective use of the art form and satisfaction from a sense of achievement follow closely. Now it seems to me that the students' regular opportunity for exploration of meanings within a theme through the effective use of the art form can cumulatively provide the very processes that will bring about trust, sensitivity, concentration and the rest. But the teacher's and students' immediate concern must be with *meaning*. In England we have trained a whole generation of drama teachers to whom this would be a novel suggestion – drama lessons for them have been but a series of varied dramatic exercises that purport to train the students in life-skills.

Myth No. 5: Drama is anti-theatre

The relationship between theatre and drama is a complex one the subtleties of which have been virtually ignored in the UK because of the historical situation which drove drama teachers into two opposite camps – those who saw school drama as the acquisition of theatre skills, training students as performers and those who believed in child-centred education, the 'progressiveness' of which was measured by the degree to which the students were *not* trained as performers. The latter claimed that the educational reward came from the dramatic process, not its product.

Although the position I take on this is that the greater potential educational value lies in students' *experiencing* drama rather than *performing* it, I nevertheless regret that polarisation into an either/or situation has occurred. It is not that I feel uncomfortable faced with alternative philosophies in education; I have no wish to martial everyone into the same camp. My regret stems from something much more fundamental: that teachers have not been given a sufficient conceptual basis from which to make a reasoned choice between the two.

I propose to examine what I see as essential differences and similarities between drama and theatre in respect of *mode* and *structure* (other aspects, for instance, that theatre is normally linked with a *place* and that for many people theatre is a *job* I shall not discuss here).

Mode

By mode I am referring to the quality of the behaviour of any participant who is consciously engaged in some form of make-believe activity.

If we were to watch a child in a garden being a policeman, we would say he is 'playing'; if we watched an actor on stage being a policeman, we would say he is 'performing'. We might agree that although both are 'pretending' there is a difference in *quality* or *mode* of action. It will be useful here to attempt to determine at least some of the characteristics of these two behaviours. You will notice I have called them 'playing' and 'performing', apparently avoiding the term 'acting'. At the risk of offending those readers who have a very clearly defined notion of acting as something only an actor does, I intend to use the term as all-embracing, applying it to both the child's and the man's behaviour. This allows me to think in terms of *continuum* of acting behaviour rather than two separate categories:

Dramatic Playing $\longleftarrow$ Acting $\longrightarrow$ Performing

I have changed the terminology at the left end of the continuum to '*dramatic* playing' rather than just playing – this is to distinguish it from much child play that does not involve make-believe or pretence – such as ball playing. I am now in a position to argue that the *mode* changes according to which end of the continuum the acting behaviour orientates.

Let us look at the extreme left end first. It is not easy to find the words adequately to describe a child absorbed in dramatic playing: 'being' or 'experiencing' might well convey the right qualities. It seems to be both active and passive in the sense that the child is responsible for his own playing and yet is at the same time submitting to the effect of his own contriving. Thus he could say 'I am making it happen, so that it can happen to me' and he could add 'and it is happening to me *now*'. Thus the experiential mode of dramatic playing can be distinguished by (1) both a deliberate devising and a spontaneous responding, (2) a sense of 'nowness' and (3) ME in the experience. If we take our child playing a policeman the three features are demonstrated as follows: (1) In order to give himself a 'policeman' experience he must contrive to recall and imitate 'policeman-like' activities, at least, as we have discussed earlier, in so far as they are relevant to the *personal* meaning he is exploring. (2) He must achieve a sense of 'policeman' things happening to him as he plays, for example visualising that traffic is *now* whirling round him under his control and (3) the experience, while ostensibly about 'policeman', is really about him in a 'policeman' context.

I have discussed earlier the 'heightened awareness' that increases the chances of a child's reflecting upon and learning from the experience.

A feature of this awareness that is relevant here is that whereas a child can say 'It is happening to me now' he also knows it is fiction. This paradox that it is happening and yet not happening ('psychical distancing', a term employed by Bullough[6] in relation to audience attitude in particular, might be appropriate here) provides us with a fourth essential characteristic of the *mode* of a child's dramatic playing.

Now if we move to the extreme right of our continuum, it becomes clear that all four features, contriving responding, sense of 'nowness', sense of 'me-ness' and psychical distancing, although essentially present for the actor are significantly reduced or over-shadowed by a new set of intentions to do with interpretation, character portrayal, repeatability, projection, communicability and empathy with an audience. Heightened awareness, not to mention entertainment, must ultimately be enjoyed by the *audience*.

Child drama, creative drama, creative dramatics, educational drama, whatever we care to call non-performance drama in schools seems logically to be placed towards the left rather than the right of the continuum for the ultimate responsibility, intention and skills of the actor must lie in his ability to give someone else an experience. In other words the fundamental difference in the *mode* required lies not just in the skills employed but is a matter of *mental set*. This difference seems to be so decisive that one might wonder whether indeed the notion of a continuum should be scrapped and replaced by distinct categories, thus validating the anti-theatre attitude among drama educationalists, a view that in practice one sees painfully reinforced by those many occasions in schools where young children are directed into a totally inappropriate mental set of taking responsibility for entertaining adults. The harm in my view lies not just in demands made on the children by the particular occasion itself, but in the subsequent attitude of those children who, feeling inadequate, are put off drama by the experience or those who, finding a flair in themselves for entertaining, continue to view drama as an opportunity for furthering facile techniques, which teachers, also unfortunately deceiving themselves, persist in encouraging.

Nevertheless, inspite of evidence of some appalling examples of children thrust into harmful theatre experiences, in spite of the distinction that logically can be sustained of alternative mental sets, I now propose to argue that there are enough occasions in children's play, student's creative drama and theatrical performance when the acting mode in terms of the participant's intention of mental set is ambiguous and not purely one thing or another to justify the image of a continuum rather than separate categories.

265

There are a number of instances when child play, dramatic activity and performance seem to shift their position along the mode continuum. I propose to list some examples of these.

Child play

Sometimes a child playing on his own, absorbed in make-believe – let us take our 'policeman' example – will say to his mother when she enters, 'Look Mummy, I am a policeman'. Now this implies not only a shift in intention (he was up to that point doing the actions for himself only) but a possible change in meaning. For whatever *subjective* meanings the 'policeman' action expressed may now be held in abeyance for the sake of communication. Just as language has a private and public function, so *action* has both connotative and denotative functions. Although to a hidden observer the child may be repeating the same 'policeman' actions, it might well be only the public functional meaning that the child is now interested in sharing with his mother. This does not of course become a theatrical performance, for the actor's responsibility is to make sure the audience identify with all levels of meaning.* But the point I want to make is that using fictitious action for the sake of communication to someone else can start early on in child behaviour. To put it another way, a change of some kind in the quality or mode is well within the capacity of a child, even a young one.

Dramatic activity

We rightly claim that students in 'experiencing' drama are not concerned with communicating to an audience. And yet this does seem to ignore three features:

1 That they often as they participate adapt the quality of the mode in order to communicate a variety of levels to each other.
2 That the use of constant intervention by teacher, in inviting them to reflect on what they have just done or are about to do, also invites them to see their work very much as a series of products to be evaluated rather than a process to be left undisturbed.
3 Inspite of the concentration on 'experiencing', when the quality of

---

* It is relevant to refer here to the form of drama, popular particularly in our secondary schools, where students are required to improvise in their groups 'making up' a play to show the others at the end of the session. In such circumstances the teachers, unwittingly, may be inviting the students merely to prepare the *denotative* meanings for the sake of easy communication.

work is aesthetically satisfying to the participant, the many layers of meaning communicate themselves to an observer *even when there is no intention so to communicate.*

I think the above three points sufficiently illustrate that within the process of experiencing with its overall orientation towards the left of the continuum there appear to be contrary pulls in the other direction. Similarly, when we now look at 'performance' we can detect a less rigid position.

Performance

The obvious examples of a different orientation:

1 Those times in rehearsal when an actor is drawing on his own resources to find meaning are very close to what a child goes through in a drama experience.

2 Those performances where spontaneity of interaction among the performers themselves is deliberately kept alive so that fresh meanings can emerge for the actors. In other words the actors are operating at a double level of both communicating pre-conceived meanings and at the same time generating (actually experiencing as in drama) new meanings.

I hope I have established that in terms of quality or mode of acting the form of behaviour that one might expect of a child at play, a student in drama and an actor in theatre has at times sufficient in common at least to blur the edges of distinctions between them. Let us now examine the drama/theatre dichotomy in terms of form.

Form

It is when we examine drama and theatre form that we find not just similarity but a considerable overlap, enough to justify the argument that structurally drama and theatre are indistinguishable. The basic elements of both are focus, tension, contrast and symbolisation. It seems to me that just as a playwright working for theatre is concerned with using these elements to convey his meaning, so a teacher working in creative drama is concerned with helping students to explore meaning through the use of these same elements.* So in a curious way when even

* For a detailed discussion of theatrical elements see: Bolton G M 1979 *Towards a theory of drama in education.* Longman.

young children are working in creative dramatics they are working in a theatre form and the teacher's function can be seen as an extension of a playwright, sharpening and deepening that form.

Let me now summarise this long section on the relations between drama and theatre. I have claimed that one of the myths about drama is that it is anti-theatre. Even as I write this I am aware this is a dangerous thing to say for people will assume I want a return to the old 'train children to perform' days, so let me first spell out what I do *not* mean:

I do *not* want drama to be seen as training in acting techniques.
I do *not* want to encourage large-scale spectacular productions of the kind that require the teacher/director to be brilliantly inventive and the performers to be conforming automatons (unfortunately such presentations can be so impressively polished and slick and the loud prolonged applause can convince parents, education officials, teachers – and, of course, the treasurer – that they must be of educational value).

But, on the other hand, I am convinced there are firmer connections between drama and theatre than we have in the past acknowledged, subtle connections which, if more understood, would allow us to *harness* the notion of 'showing' drama instead of either despising it or using it superficially. Different kinds of performing, varying in the degree to which they are formal/informal, audience oriented/audience ignored, finished product/lasting a few seconds, a script interpretation/a group's dramatic statement, a collage of scripted excerpts/a whole play. Whichever of these dimensions is selected the potential pivotal relationship between 'experiencing' and 'showing' which we have tended to ignore can occasionally sharpen the work at the dramatic playing end of the continuum and always enrich any move towards the other end.

Final comment

In this chapter I have outlined what might be called the 'mythology' of drama education. The 'myths' I have selected are 'Drama is doing', 'Drama is an escape from reality', 'Drama is concerned with the uniqueness of the individual', 'Drama is for personal development', 'Drama is anti-theatre'. Having argued against all these I perhaps need to remind readers what I said at the beginning, that in important ways they *are* viable: drama in a narrow sense *is* doing; drama for some children can be used as an escape from a reality that is painful to them; drama